harry
THE RIDE OF MY LIFE

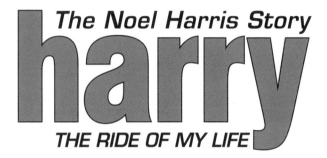

The Noel Harris Story

harry

THE RIDE OF MY LIFE

with Wally O'Hearn

Hodder Moa

National Library of New Zealand Cataloguing-in-Publication Data

Harris, Noel, 1955-

Harry : the ride of my life / Noel Harris with Wally O'Hearn.

ISBN 978-1-86971-257-0

1. Harris, Noel, 1955- 2. Jockeys—New Zealand—Biography.

3. Horse racing. I. O'Hearn, Wally. II. Title.

798.40092—dc

A Hodder Moa Book

Published in 2012 by Hachette New Zealand Ltd

4 Whetu Place, Mairangi Bay

Auckland, New Zealand

www.hachette.co.nz

Designed and produced by Hachette New Zealand Ltd

Printed by Everbest Printing Co. Ltd., China

Cover photos: Race Images

To all the wonderful people who have made my memorable career possible and to the loved ones I have lost, most of all, my mum.

Contents

Foreword

by John Wheeler

Harry, Handbreak, NG or just plain Noel. He has always been entitled to be a little bit different, distinctive, special and sometimes outlandish as it is a genetic throwback to his grandparents. His granddad Silas, better known as Jack Harris, was an English sailor who jumped ship in New Plymouth and met up with Noel's nana, Jessie, to begin the creation of the Harris dynasty.

This family has roots that are deeply etched in the fabric of Taranaki history. Noel's father, Jock, was a champion jockey and Jock's family were all outstanding sportsmen and sportswomen. They were brought up in the New Plymouth suburb of Moturoa (often referred to as Tiger Town, an area around the port of that vibrant city). Silas and Jess lived in Harbour Street for all of their married life.

Because I always admired Noel's father Jock, first as a jockey then as a trainer, I became an avid admirer of Noel and his brothers and sisters who were all accomplished riders and, of course continuing the dynasty, Noel's son Troy.

Though Harry was born in Palmerston North and served his apprenticeship under the guidance of his father in Woodville, he has always had many of the attributes of a true 'Naki man — with a strong personality, humble but quick-witted, naturally gifted, extremely generous and giving, and humorous — although he can sometimes become a nuisance when he has had a taste too many.

Noel is a courageous man as he has proved in his riding. He is well over 50 years old, but is never overawed by the youth coming through the riding ranks. You always know Noel is different when you see how short he rides and how low in the saddle he gets when driving to the line, typically from the rear down the outside, to get up in the last couple of hops. That's Harry's trademark. However, he is just as devastating on a leader in a race, usually rating them to perfection. This is an aspect of his riding that most people don't consider as, in general, he is asked to ride horses that race from the rear.

Noel has ridden many of my top horses over the years, and one he had a particular affinity with was Poetic Prince, whom he rode in 12 of his 16 wins, including the 1988 Cox Plate. In that same four-year-old year Poetic Prince went on also to win the Tancred Stakes and the Queen Elizabeth Stakes in Sydney, with Noel as rider each time. Those three are the biggest weight-for-age races on the Australian racing calendar.

There are a few funny stories about our time in Sydney with Poetic Prince around Tancred time. Read on and you'll hear Noel's version of the one about getting a bit rowdy and him nearly losing his finger. I can't stop laughing as I recall watching him being ushered to the lift and him remonstrating and saying he would win the $1 million Tancred Stakes on Saturday, come back and buy the hotel on Monday, sack all the staff and run the hotel according to his rules from then on.

Another story that unfolded at Rosehill that week before the Tancred was on the Monday preceding the great race. Noel has his version inside, but it's worth hearing it from me, too. Noel and I had a big lunch with many of our close Sydney mates at a local restaurant. The lunch got out of hand, which did seem to happen quite regularly when Harry and I were in charge, and we got home late after a big day and had no alarm clock for the next morning's trackwork. Harry said, 'Never fear when Noel is near.' I thought this was great so I went to bed, assured that Harry would wake me up at 4.30 am.

Alas, we never woke till half past seven (and the track closes at

8 am). We rushed off. I arrived at the track leading the Prince, with Harry in the saddle, still in his slippers, at about 8.15 am — the course was closed. The course curator at the time, John Jeffs (a great bloke), opened the track to let the horse gallop, which was a huge relief. Sadly, our prearranged galloping partner had already worked so we had to exercise Poetic Prince on his own. The local trainers were perplexed by the curator's very charitable decision to reopen the track. It had probably never happened before and probably never since.

A close friend of mine, Dr Geoff Chapman, a champion Sydney trainer and personality and former Wallaby loose forward, actually acquired a Sydney Turf Club letterhead. He sent a letter to me stating that we had overstepped the mark and as far as the Turf Club were concerned we could 'F' off back to the Shaky Isles; it was signed by the chairman of the time.

I smelt a rat so I went to Kerry Jordan, a fellow Kiwi and prominent trainer in Sydney who looked after McGinty in his youth for Colin Jillings while in Japan. Kerry is a close friend of the Doc, and I told him that I had talked to the CEO at the Sydney Turf Club and they were disappointed that one of their trainers should send out an STC letterhead and fraudulently sign the letter as if it was from the chief. I told Kerry that the STC had got the police in as they took this very seriously. Kerry informed the Doc, the Doc took the bait, putting an apology on the noticeboard at the track. This was a great result (New Zealand 1, Australia nil).

Harry hates a beer and a long lunch. Another such day started with a meeting on a Friday morning at Queensland's racing headquarters at Eagle Farm to discuss the possibility of cancelling the races the next day, as there had been torrential rain for 48 hours. An early decision was made and they were cancelled, which we were in favour of as our runner in the Grand Prix the next day was Flying Luskin, who was never happy on a wet track. At the completion of the meeting Noel said, 'What shall we do?' My reply, which he had already anticipated, was, 'Let's have lunch at the Breaky Creek Hotel.'

I rang a few Queensland mates and told them the races were off and hastily organised a lunch. We all had a famous Breakfast Creek steak washed down with copious quantities of the local brew XXXX. Harry drank his favoured brew VB (Victorian Bitter) at the rate of three stubbies an hour. At 3.30 pm I had to go and feed my horses (no afternoon walk as it was still bucketing down). On my arrival at my apartment to get changed for work I came across Grant Cooksley (who had flown over from New Zealand to ride the next day). When I told him that the races were off he thought it was a good idea to head to 'the Creek' to have a quiet one with Harry. After returning to my apartment after putting my horses to bed for the night, Bruce Compton (BS) had just arrived from New South Wales not knowing the races had been cancelled, so I dropped him off at the Breaky Creek to rinse his tonsils with Noel and Cookie.

A couple of hours later Cookie arrived back at my place smashed and looking for a bed. An hour later BS was home smashed and looking for a bed, but no sign of Harry. At three stubbies an hour I thought Noel would be ready to come home so I went down to the local to pick him up. After another hour and three VBs I got him home by 11 pm. He came in and found a slab of VBs in my fridge so proceeded to eliminate them. Noel has an amazing ability to be incoherent after his first few stubbies and still be the same 10 hours later. What a day — and what a leviathan performance by Harry. At weight-for-age he would have devastated the infamous Aussie cricketer David Boon.

Noel is probably the only New Zealand jockey that the Aussie riders always ask after when I am in Australia — such is his impact and their regard for him, particularly in the eastern states. He is definitely the most respected of all Kiwi riders in the eyes of his Aussie colleagues and also the Aussie punters and racing public.

Even the stewards know he is a straight shooter. I remember one day Harry thought he had timed his run to perfection in the Werribee

Cup, just getting up to win in the last hop, thus getting The Bandette a start in the Melbourne Cup. Unfortunately, the judge saw the result differently, calling The Bandette in second. Noel requested a viewing of the photo finish before correct weight was announced. I overheard one of the senior stewards say, 'Noel would definitely be genuine, but I hope he isn't right.'

The judge was correct, but they certainly took into consideration Noel's experience when viewing the photo. As an aside, The Bandette was allowed a start by the VRC in the Melbourne Cup that year. Unfortunately, he finished in eleventh placing.

Harry has been so colourful, literally and figuratively. His absurd hair styles at times and his impish style of dress have always made him stand out. One of Noel's greatest attributes is that he has always been welcoming to new apprentices in the jockeys' room. He offers advice readily and is always ready to help newcomers. If I had a new apprentice at the races I would always tell them to ask Noel if they had any problems or issues. He is just one of those blokes and that is why we all love and admire him.

Murray Baker, one of New Zealand's top trainers, has always had the utmost respect and admiration for Noel's riding. This partnership has been extremely successful over the years. Murray says, 'When the end comes for Noel they should donate his body to medical science to see how it all works.'

There is no one quite like Harry. He smokes so heavily he should have a chimney stuck in his head, he drinks like a fish and eats like a sparrow, and yet he defies medical science. He is a spectacular rider.

Good on you, Noel, and congratulations on your book. It's a special read.

John Wheeler
New Plymouth, March 2012

Foreword

by Tony Lee

Form is temporary, class is permanent. From a baby-faced apprentice riding in the Melbourne Cup to the present time, Noel Harris is as competitive as ever, his longevity amazing.

Racing tests every facet of your being. Friendships strain and relationships waver. Jockeys are judged and must ride the highs with the lows. Harry has experienced it all and remains highly respected.

I have met many racing people in my travels and when Harry's name comes up, they all know of him. They all admire his skill as a jockey and his rare gift of empathy with the horse, an understanding that is the difference between winning and losing.

Out of the jockeys' room Harry ambles, always relaxed, but once legged up, you will see the concentration. It's game on and Harry is in the zone, stirrup irons up high, reins in hand, then out comes that special ability to become one with the horse, that rare gift that sets the greats apart. Trainers know Harry will understand the horse and work with it.

And if the horse isn't up to the task, one of Harry's best qualities shines through. He will never bag a horse after a bad performance. He will always offer some hope to connections. He cares.

When I came into racing, Harry was already a legend. I got to know him professionally and personally. He rode my first winner, Uncomplicated, at Hawera, and that thrill is still with me today. I've seen him record several milestones and, as a commentator, I've called many of them, too.

Harry has enjoyed life and loves racing. Racing loves Harry, too, and so it should. He's a person of depth and substance, a person who has tasted racing at the coalface, the game that has every emotion experienced within a short timeframe. He's ridden the best, for the best, against the best, and they all rate him.

Harry and his lovely wife Kylie are a great couple. Kylie is a soul mate who allows Harry to be Harry, reins him in when required, but is always there with obvious love. Awesome!

Nga mihi nui.

Tony Lee
Wellington, March 2012

Acknowledgements

As you read my life story, you will appreciate I've crossed paths with so many people in my life. I have tried to include as many as I can in this book, but obviously there are even more not mentioned. To those people, you are not forgotten and I thank you for your input into my full and entertaining life.

When I do finally ride off into the sunset, it will be with a smile, thinking not only of my family and friends, but also of all the racing folk who are so dedicated to the sport and the lovely animal which makes it all possible. Without horses, I don't know where I would be. And without top horses I wouldn't have achieved the success and recognition that has come my way.

I have a small tattoo of four aces on my back. In poker, it's regarded as hard to beat, but it is beatable. And that's how I look at my life as a jockey. On horseback, I do my best to be hard to beat, but I've got to accept it when I'm beaten by a better one on the day. That's life and I can honestly say I've had the ride of my life. I wish to thank everyone who has made this book possible, including the photographers for the images which help me relive special moments.

A special thanks for the encouragement and support of my wife, Kylie, and thanks to Wally for the long days of sitting and listening to all my stories. I'd been on to Wally for more than 20 years to one day write my book. I could think of nobody better than such a close friend to put my life stories into print. I hope you all enjoy it.

Kia kaha my friends.

1

Car chase

'These pricks are on to us!' That was the response which had me shaking in my seat. It was like something you see in the crime movies, and it was about to happen to me.

I was staying in Singapore with Keith Watson, an Australian jockey from Perth. It was 4.30 in the morning and we were leaving his place on our way to trackwork. Just as we went through the front gate of the property we spotted a car on the side of the road, just a lane before you reach the main arterial road. Next minute, Keith had planted his boot and I asked what was wrong. And, as he replied, I knew what pricks he was talking about.

From a virtual standstill we just took off, reaching around 100 kilometres an hour within 10 seconds. They roared up from behind and got on the outside of us. There were storm drains on both sides, but somehow they squeezed past us, and once ahead they slammed on the brakes, spun their car across in front of us and forced us to pull over. It all happened so fast. I'd seen it hundreds of times in the movies, but now I was part of it. And it was no movie! I was bogging myself, and by the look on Keith's face and the way he was driving I knew he was scared, too.

If we tried to go around their car we would've ended up in the storm drains. There was no option but to stop. Keith slammed the car into reverse and the next minute six guys jumped out with battens and ran towards us. I said to Keith, 'Fuck, why don't we see what they want?' It was a dumb thing to say, but it just came out. I knew that as soon as I said it. All he said was, 'Fuck you, we're out of here!' He planted the boot and nearly ran over one guy, who sprinted to the side of the road and dived into the ditch.

I just sat there shit scared, and we didn't speak again. We reached the track. It was only a 10-minute drive and I was as white as a ghost — a white Maori!

I was still shaking when I spotted Bruce Compton, another Kiwi jockey also riding on the Singapore–Malaysia circuit. He was as white as I was. He told me he'd been approached earlier that morning by the same guys. They'd gone to see him in his hotel first. Luckily, he'd come away from it without being hurt. I don't know how he did it, but he was lucky.

After that weekend we read in the paper that a punter had been robbed of $45,000 at gunpoint, by a group in the same car that chased us. Apparently, they robbed someone after the races on the Sunday. I don't know if they were going to rob us, but they sure were going to threaten us. They meant business and they weren't just going to tap us with the battens, that's for sure.

That was in my second year up in Singapore and Malaysia. I knew there was a lot of corruption and there had been a lot of threats and even shootings, but until then I hadn't been involved. Suddenly, here I was in the middle of it. It was a real wake-up call, and it really shook me up.

It took a while to get over the incident, but in the end I decided to stay on. But it put me off staying with Keith Watson. I went back to living in the hotel after that and keeping to myself. I think the robbers were probably more after Keith — he was one of those guys who lived on the edge.

Here I was a little Maori boy from Woodville thinking: *what the hell have I got myself into?* I'd not only left New Zealand as the top apprentice, I'd finished up at the top of the Jockeys' Premiership, equal with David Peake. I had set records for an apprentice and I was excited about the future. But, suddenly, here I was scared for my life. That's not the way it was supposed to be.

There was a lot of that going on over there in those days — threats and violence. It was all down to the punters and their gangs. The situation was so corrupt. But all I wanted to do was ride winners and make money.

I remember Aussie riders George Podmore and Chris Gwilliam being given police protection after threats were made on their lives. They'd received live bullets in the mail. The envelopes had been sealed, just like the ones they say the triads send out. George and Chris had police escorting them from their homes to the racecourse and back. The rumour was they had refused to pass tips to bookmakers.

George and Chris were just some of the ones I knew who were affected. There were more who came out worse off, much worse, but I'll get into that later on. Thankfully, the Singapore–Malaysia circuit has come a long way since those days back in the 1970s. I've been back since and I've seen the difference, especially in Singapore. It has cleaned up its act and is far more professional now. Some of our best trainers, Laurie Laxon, Bruce Marsh, Mark Walker and Stephen Gray, are settled over there and flying. And before them Paddy Busuttin had luck there. It's a completely different ball game from when I was first in Singapore–Malaysia.

When I think back, it was a risk going over when I did, but at the time I was young and adventurous. I didn't think too much about it; I just wanted to give it a go. I had been going to ride in Mauritius. My oldest brother, Johnny, had a stint riding there and I was ready to accept a contract. Then Graeme Rogerson, one of our top trainers, came along and asked me whether I'd be interested in going to Singapore. He arranged for me to ride for the champion trainer Ivan Allan. That appeared to be a better option than Mauritius, more lucrative, so I went.

I was 22 at the time, and it was a real eye-opener. I'd never experienced anything like it.

You could say Ivan ran Singapore racing and Teh Choon Beng ran the scene in Malaysia. They were the kingpins. In Singapore Ivan could do virtually whatever he liked because his friend Runme Shaw — who along with his brother Run Run Shaw introduced the film industry into Singapore — was the virtual head of racing, as chairman of the Bukit Timah Turf Club. After I'd left, I heard they had a bit of an investigation into racing in Singapore. They asked Ron Hutchinson, one of the jockeys, to come back and give evidence, and a few trainers got grilled. Later on, the Bukit Timah Turf Club became the Singapore Turf Club and Ivan went to Hong Kong.

I ended up staying in Singapore and Malaysia for three seasons and won the Jockeys' Premiership the last season. I made some good friends and I've got a lot of memories, some good and some bad. It was an experience, that's for sure — corruption, suicide, death threats and death. I've seen it all in my time in racing and most of it centres around my stay there. I've also been very fortunate to have enjoyed the other side of it all — the success and plenty of good times. You take the good with the bad in racing and in life in general; I always feel the good outweighs the bad. And, really, that sums up my time in racing.

All I've ever wanted to do was ride in races. That's all I've known and you could say it was bred into me. My father, Jock, had been a good jockey, on the flat and over fences, and he went on to be a top trainer. My brothers and sisters have all ridden as jockeys and my son, Troy, has gone on to be a jockey, too. It's in the blood. We were born into racing and that's all we knew when we were growing up.

Jock came from New Plymouth and as soon as he was allowed to leave school he was off to be a jockey. His father, Jack Harris, got him in with George New, who trained at Awapuni. George New more or less said, 'Yeah, he might get big in time, but we'll give him a go.' He had taught a lot of top riders, the likes of Bill Broughton, Vic Dye, Stewart and Bubs Waddell, George Tattersall and Jim Hely. When New retired Jock headed back to Taranaki and completed his apprenticeship with Bill Fowler, at Stratford.

Jock rode his first winner, Blank Cheque, at Hastings in 1947 and went on to win almost 400 races. He won some of our biggest races — the New Zealand Derby, New Zealand Oaks, Manawatu Sires' Produce Stakes, Great Northern Derby, Auckland Cup and Easter Handicap — and when he switched to jumps riding he also did well. I know he won a Wellington Steeples on Aligarh and my youngest brother Peter came out and won it, too, 26 years later on The Assassin. When I started off riding all the trainers who used to put Jock on told me what a top rider he was. But he always struggled with his weight.

I've heard a lot of stories from Jock over the years, and one that sticks in my mind is to do with him battling with weight. After being suspended at Trentham he and Billy Aitken went up to Whangarei for some deep-sea fishing. They ate snapper and boiled potatoes, drank beer and played cards for over a week. When he got home his weight was over 11 stone, about 70 kilos, but nine days later he was back riding at just under eight stone eight pounds, about 54.5 kilos. He'd lost 15.5 kilos, over two and a half stone, in just over a week. He would even sit in the dung heap with sweaters on, as well as running every day. I'm lucky I've never had to lose that much. I don't think there'd be many who could do it. But in those days Jock had to do it to keep going.

When Jock retired he worked at an auction mart and as a builder's labourer and even had a go with the trotters. He worked in Cambridge for Peter Skousgaard, but that lasted only a few months. Apparently, Fred Smith, a top driver in those days, told him there was no money as a trotting driver with so many owner-trainers driving so he went back to Palmerston North and started training gallopers. Maybe my life would have turned out differently if he hadn't gone back to the gallopers. But I can't see myself whipping around the tracks in a sulky.

I tried that once, but I'd rather be on a horse's back.

Jock only had a few horses in work when he started off, and he got his first winner at an Ashhurst meeting in 1961 with a horse called Goa. My first memories of him training were when we shifted to Woodville. That's where it all happened for him and he had a lot of top horses through the stable. Later on, my oldest brother Johnny went into partnership with him and my other older brother Dessie had a stint in partnership with him, too. Jock then shifted back to Palmerston North and he retired in 1988 because of health problems. He's called Palmy home for years, but Woodville was where his training career took off, and that's where my brothers, sisters and I all got our start in racing. There were a lot of good trainers in Woodville at that time.

In those early days we'd spent most of the time around the stables, but we got away from home at times, and that's when I met some of Jock's family. I remember going up to Taranaki to stay with my grandmother, Jessie Harris, during the school holidays and I met my great-grandfather, Daniel Keenan. I had only a few trips and met a couple of cousins, but we were never really close.

As for my grandfather, Jock's father Jack Harris, the story goes that he took off over to Australia and he was over there for 35 years. When my brother Dessie and I started riding and going to Aussie we had letters from him, then we got to meet him at the races in Sydney one day. At the time Jock didn't know whether Granddad was alive or not. We got his address and we gave it to Jock and he started writing to him, and before long Granddad was back in New Zealand. He came to live here for the last 12 years of his life — I think he lived until he was 92. Jock was able to spend some time with him, and we all got to know him a bit better. To think nobody had seen him or heard from him for 35 years!

Jock was one of seven, three sisters — Billie, Hinga and Wiki — and three brothers — Donald, Noel and Desmond, who was known as Dodo. And there's Wiki's son, Grant, who was like an adopted brother.

Dodo was a jockey, too. He was killed in a race at Marton on New Year's Day, 1952. Dad was riding at Hastings that day. Apparently, Dodo came off and hit the running rail or the post and was killed instantly.

As for Mum, Daphne, I don't know much about her side of the family. I only recently found out my grandfather's name was Francis Henry. I knew Maude was my grandmother. I also knew Mum's sisters, more so Aunty Noeline, who used to come and stay. Mum's sisters would come and have Christmas Day with us, but it was never the same after Mum died. When I was growing up nothing much was said about Mum's side of the family. It was all about the Harris family and racing.

2

Growing up in Woodville

The Harris terrors. People used to call us all sorts of names like that when we were young. We got into a fair bit of mischief, but nothing bad, just normal kid's stuff. We were growing up and having fun and everything was about adventures.

I was born in Palmerston North, on 14 January 1955. The first I remember of my early years was when we shifted from Awapuni to Woodville when I was about five or six. Jock bought Charlie McCullough's stables when Charlie retired. It had been hard times for Jock and Mum. I remember Mum telling me that when they got married they lived in a garage in Palmy. When Jock got established with his riding, they shifted into a few houses before buying the stables and house in Upper McLean Street, opposite the Woodville racecourse. It was half rundown, but they fixed it up and built staff quarters and extended the stables.

Coming from a city, Palmerston North, to the country was great. There was plenty to do, like building tree huts, riding ponies and playing all sorts of games. It was such a brilliant way to grow up. I wouldn't change it for the world. We'd go to a movie and come home and re-enact it. All kids do that right? But my oldest brother Johnny always took it a bit further. If it had been a movie about the Romans or something gladiatorial, he'd tie all the kids up and he'd get the stock whip out, re-enacting what he'd seen. I didn't like him seeing those types of movies — stuff that!

I remember another time with Johnny. We had an old oak tree at the front of the stables and there was an old steel cage you'd put calves in. Johnny got a rope, tied it to the cage and put Lance Robinson in it, locked it up and hung it from the tree. He then started swinging it and washed down Lance with a hose. Johnny was coming up as an apprentice about that time and Lance was only a kid, a couple of years younger than me. Lance later became apprenticed to Jock. He's ridden more than 500 winners and he's still going as a jockey down south. Jock got calls from Lance's father, Moss Robinson, over what Johnny had done. He was furious, but Johnny thought it was a great joke.

It seemed half of Woodville were kids and they'd come home to play at the Harris's. There was always something to do on the weekends. There were some little misdemeanours, yeah. We used to go around the back of the hotel and nick the old lemonade and Coke bottles and sell them at the dairy. We'd raid the old apple orchards and plum trees and stuff like that. We'd get told off here and there. They were minor things that kids do. It was all part of growing up and having fun.

On the Sunday after the races at Woodville we knew where we could break into the stands. It was something we learnt off the older ones. There'd be half a dozen of us kids, and we'd get over there and we were into the grog. They used to have the old tap beer and the bowsers. We also drank the dregs from the empties, so we'd all be a mess by the time we got home.

If one got into trouble, we all got into trouble. We certainly got into heaps of strife for the racecourse drinking. The old man kicked our butts. But it was like a challenge for us. When you were told as a kid not to do it, you would go and do it. We were little turds.

We got quite a few rark-ups from Jock. He was tough, but he taught us respect. He wasn't shy with a boot. I was on the receiving end quite a few times and that's why I often say my arse is shaped like Italy. It was the old man's boot.

In the old days Jock was a hard taskmaster. He hated people being idle, and when you did something wrong he made you think about your actions. It was a good thing in a way and a bit scary in another way. We had to call everyone Mister or Missis and even to this day you still call the older trainers Mister. That's lost with the younger generation; a lot of that respect has gone.

Another thing we did after the races at Woodville was to get a chaff sack and away we'd go collecting tote tickets off the ground. In those days everybody did it, and it was amazing how many winning tickets you found. We made a bit of money out of it, but my Aunty Noeline did best. She used to have a bit more patience. We'd go through just so many and get sick of it, but my aunt kept going and she got some good collects.

One of the good old Woodville trainers, Ian Bradbury, used to breed fox terriers and they were top stable dogs. Our dog, Brad, was named after him, and used to go mad on water when you used to throw out the buckets of water. You'd knock the rats off the rafters and he'd grab them, too.

Our first dog was Poochie, a sausage dog. When we came to Woodville he got paralysed in his back legs, so we made a little cart for him to be mobile, but it was just a matter of time before he had to be put down. Jock used to buy the big ice cream cartons, and we've got movies of Poochie inside the carton licking it out. I can remember Jock out with the movie camera. He took a lot of movies and we'd have a night going through them all.

There were times when the old man would stop at the pub and have a few drinks, while we'd go down the park or rugby club. When he came out of the pub we'd ask if we could get in the boot for the ride home, so he'd open the boot and we'd all pile in and he'd drive us around town. He'd open the boot up and all these kids would come flying out. It'd be pretty frowned on today, but in those days you did things like that. It was an adventure, a secret hiding place.

Johnny and Dessie and I were all pretty close. There was a lot of rivalry between us, then my younger brother Peter came along and he joined in. We four brothers just wanted to beat each other at everything. My sister Karen was next on the scene and a few years down the track, Jenny was born. Johnny didn't really grow up with them, especially Jenny. He'd left home as an adult by then.

Everything was a competition between us boys. We'd make our own bows and arrows — we couldn't afford the good stuff. We were pretty good at making them in the end. Then one day we went upmarket and purchased one of the new modern fibreglass sets. Bill Smith, the neighbour, had ducks and chooks, and Dessie decided to give it a go with the new bow and arrow. He ended up shooting one of the roosters.

No sooner had we savoured the success of our new acquisition than we heard Bill Smith's truck come up the start of the driveway. Dessie panicked. He rushed over and grabbed the rooster and threw it in the incinerator by the stables. He poured petrol on it and set it alight. Burn the evidence mate. Suddenly, it flew out of the incinerator. It wasn't dead, just stunned. Talk about chasing a chook without a head. This thing was all over the place. It went flying into the outside wash-house still on fire. Panic stations. Dessie dived in after it and knocked it on the head to put it out of its misery.

It wasn't until years later that Bill Smith heard the story.

Sometimes at night we'd take candles and head to the back paddocks, backing on to Bill Smith's farm, about 150 acres. Next minute you'd get the cattle wandering along to investigate, making a hell of a noise and scaring the bejesus out of us.

We also used to go possum hunting or eeling, and later on Dessie and Peter got right into pig hunting. We'd always keep ourselves busy. I was a Cub and enjoyed that, but when I got into Scouts and had to work through all the badges I quit. Sitting the tests for the badges became too hard.

The headmaster at school and the track manager used to worry a bit about us Harris boys. We'd be riding the horses to the track, these big, powerful animals and us just little kids. There was no fear in us. We were very bold with animals.

I remember Johnny had a pony called Rebel. He was quite spooky, but once you got on him he was fine. We used to take him around the paddocks and on different farms, but not to the actual Pony Club. We weren't into Pony Club; we'd just go down there to check on the girls. Johnny used to sit there with his slug gun firing at the girls going into the Pony Club. He hit some of them on the butt, which earned him a bit of strife.

Johnny was a bit of a rebel. Jock used to roll his own cigarettes and one day Johnny put a fire cracker in one of Dad's rollies. When Jock went to light it up, he spotted the cracker so he grabbed Johnny and put the cigarette in his mouth and lit it. The burn blistered Johnny's mouth — the trick had truly backfired on him.

Jock and Johnny saw red when they were together. They didn't really get on. There was a bit of a clash and in the end Johnny transferred from Jock to serve the rest of his apprenticeship with Wally McEwan in Hawera.

Johnny, as a big brother, looked after me. He was my idol and somebody to look up to, especially with his riding. I used to keep a scrapbook on him and listen to all of his rides on the radio. It was always good to see him when he came back from Hawera to visit. I'd go to the races so I could catch up with him.

I was always obsessed with horses. I remember my school teacher, Mrs Patterson — who was quite a hard old thing — became sick of me writing about horses, so she thought she'd steer me away from the topic. She told us to do a story on flowers. I started off talking about flowers and turned it around and said how horses eat flowers. So I got back to horses again. She couldn't change me.

My favourite was a horse called Loch Nagar. I must have been about 10 or 11 and Rex Cochrane, a top trainer from down south, was a friend of Jock's and he sent the horse up to us, thinking that she had potential for the northern races. She was a good sprinter who ended up winning 14 races. When she arrived I fell in love with her. I decided she was going to be my pet horse. I came home from school and the first thing I'd do was check her out. I was fascinated by her. I brushed her every day, and I would stand on a bucket to get up to strop her. One day she kicked the bucket from underneath me, but that didn't change how I felt about her.

I didn't mind school. I liked the sport part of it, but I hated the homework. I was a middle-of-the-road student. I went to primary school in Woodville, then to Tararua College. We had to catch the bus there, 10 miles from Woodville. We'd be up at 4.30 am to go to the track, and then catch the bus about 7.30. We'd get home about 4.30 pm and still have to go out and pick the horses' hooves and do the stable work. It was quite a long day at that age. But you couldn't be seen to be idle, as we all knew being idle was Jock's pet hate.

Half the time we wouldn't do our homework, and we got into trouble for that. I just thought I wasn't going to be an Einstein and all I wanted to be was a jockey. Actually, Jock said I didn't have to go to college for the last few months, but the college rang up and asked where I was. Jock said I was sick. I had to go back to school and sign out. Jock said I was going to be no good at anything else but being a jockey. Even Johnny, who was probably bright enough to be a vet, got permission to leave a little earlier because Jock explained to the principal that Johnny could earn so much money at a young age in racing. As it turned out, weight got the better of him as a jockey.

I loved my gymnastics at school and I was on the school team. I suppose that's where I've got my pole dancing habit from, my old gymnastics days. I'm known to do a bit of pole dancing when I've had a few too many drinks. Pity you couldn't make money out of pole dancing then, eh? I was fit and I enjoyed gymnastics and Dessie used to enjoy it, too. He's got all the gold badges.

I was quite good at running and I loved playing rugby. Every Friday I'd clean the old rugby boots and have them all polished up for the next day, even though sometimes I was on the reserve bench. School rugby was good, and we used to play teams from the likes of Dannevirke and Pahiatua. We were in the midgets. Dessie was captain of the A team and I was captain of the B team. Nine out of 10 times we'd have to meet each other in the final, but Dessie's team was always the better. I was just so small. I keep saying if I was bigger I could have gone on to better things as a rugby player! I played wing and Dessie was halfback. Sometimes when Dessie was in our team we needed to play with two balls, one for the team and one for him. He thought he was Mark Donaldson, the halfback for Manawatu. He'd just take over.

We also had social rugby games with the stable staff.

There were some fun times at school, but in the end Jock said, 'What's most important to you? Do you want to be a jockey?' If I had to wait another year it wouldn't have worried me, but Dad said I was better off out of school and doing stable work. With Johnny and Dessie's track record in mind, I thought I could be just as good as them, so it wasn't hard to convince me.

Mum was resigned to the fact that we were all going to be jockeys, except for the girls. Female riders were frowned upon at that stage, but when my sisters Karen and Jenny were old enough, female jockeys had been given the go-ahead so they became jockeys, too. Mum went along with Jock's thoughts and it was Jock's choice that we were going to be jockeys. There were never really any doubts that I would follow behind Dad, Johnny and Dessie. I always wanted to be as good as them and I didn't want to let the family down.

Can you pick me out in this Woodville school patrol photo? I'm standing proudly with my sign in the second row on the left.

Taking in a day's racing with Johnny (left), Jock and Des (far right) as I anxiously waited for my chance on the track.

The thrill of my first win. Returning to scale on Phar Lace at Foxton, 16 May 1970.

Proud of my whip trophy after my first win, but someone had nicked it before the day was over.

Heading off to the start on Patrida, while trainer Stuart McColl looks on. I so wanted to win a race for Mr McColl.

Studying the form with the master, Bill Skelton. I'm proud to be in the 2000 win club with Bill, one of New Zealand's greatest jockeys.

My first ride on the freak sprinter New Moon at Woodville on 5 December 1970. It was so easy and she set a track record.

Proud to be an apprentice jockey standing between my brothers Johnny
(left) and Dessie.

So that's where I got my liking for a drink! Being presented with a bottle of vodka as an apprentice prize.

I've got my first Group One win all sewn up as I cruise to the finish on Egmont Park in the George Adams Handicap at Trentham on 16 February 1972. I had a lot of luck on him.

Returning to scale on Sharif, one of the most versatile horses Jock trained.

A trifecta for the Harris brothers. I won the Resolution Handicap at Trentham on 21 September 1975 on Gideon and Peter (right) was second on Clef and Dessie third on Arctic Rest.

The ride everyone always talks about . . . finishing second on Glengowan in Gala Supreme's 1973 Melbourne Cup. I'm on the outside with Daneson in the centre and Gala Supreme on the rails.

Leaning over the rail with Roy Higgins as we wait for the start of the 1974 Waikato International Stakes at Te Rapa. We had no luck. I rode Count Kereru and Brian Andrews won the race on Battle Heights.

Above: Peg's Pride looks to be flying across the line as we beat Swell Time and Corroboree in the 1973 Wellington Derby.

Right: The late Bill Sanders, one of the truly great trainers, and a man who had a huge influence on me.

3

Jockey on the horizon

Well, the day finally came. It was my first big step to becoming a jockey. I had done the work around the stables and ridden horses in pacework, but it was time to have my first gallop. I still remember it clearly. I think I had to reach the three furlongs peg — 600 metres — and I got to the line and my eyes were watering — I thought I was going so fast. Next minute the old man's yelling out, 'Go again, go again. You went too slow.' So I had to go around again and he was yelling, 'Let him go, let him go.' I had this fear the horses were going too fast. Your first gallop is like *Wow, how fast can this horse go?*

I was about 13 at the time and I couldn't wait to be a jockey. Johnny and Dessie were doing their apprenticeships and it seemed forever before I started mine. Jock just kept saying to me to be patient, and he said the same when I was riding horses in work. That's where my patience in riding a race came from. It was Jock's advice and it made me who I am. He'd give me useful guidance now and then.

Like other kids, I started off getting led around by someone else and trotting the horses. I think I was about 10 when I'd be leading two over to the track. It was your job to take them for a pick, give them a roll and hose them down. At that time there were a lot of young kids around my age always wanting to work in the stables to make a bit of pocket money.

In saying that, you weren't getting paid a lot, so you actually had to love horses to do it. I had schoolmates who would come and fill in their weekends working for us. Jock seemed to be approached by a lot of kids who came from broken families; he would always give them an opportunity to come and work in the stable.

In those days Mike Donoghue was working for Jock. He wasn't a bad rider on the flat, but he was getting heavy, so he wanted a go over fences as a jumps jockey. Jock taught him the ropes and Mike ended up one of the top jumps jockeys. He was good for Dessie and me because he was that bit older than us. He taught me a lot about stable work and about different horses.

As far as being an apprentice jockey, I wanted Jock to put me on a horse so I could ride it to the track, but he thought I was too young and not ready. Another trainer, Stuart McColl, used to say, 'Come around and help me out and I'll put you on a horse.' So after school I used to go to his place and he used to lead me to the track. I had it fixed in my mind that I was going to be apprenticed to him. That was probably when I was about 12. Mr McColl got me going and I was very keen. I thought if Dad's not going to put me on I'll be apprenticed to Mr McColl, so Dad started calling me Noel McColl.

I rode my first few trials for Mr McColl, and I did get to ride Patrida for him quite a few times on race day. Patrida was a good sprinter-miler. He won an Easter Handicap at Ellerslie and a couple in Brisbane, and he ended up winning 19 races. He had a lot of pace and was quite easy to ride. Mr McColl always wanted to give me my first winner, but it wasn't to be. I ran second on Patrida in an open six furlongs at Hastings. That was my first and only placing until I rode my first winner in my twenty-first ride.

I've got a lot of fond memories of Stuart McColl and the days of going to his place after school. It's funny how it turned out. He was chopping his team back by the time I was ready to get my licence, so I ended up apprenticed to Jock. But Mr McColl is the one who really got me started.

It seemed I had to wait a long time for my first race-day ride. Jock wasn't in any hurry. He wanted to make sure I was ready, and when I did finally have my first ride it was for Jock on Donate at the Napier Park meeting, on 28 February 1970. I'll never forget the day. I must have packed my riding bag about 100 times. When we got to Hastings someone wanted a photo of Johnny, Dessie and me, and I was probably the proudest jockey on course. Now I look back at that photo. The silks and boots were all hand-me-downs, the silks look like bloomers, the riding boots were probably about three sizes too big and they were curling up at the front, but I felt as ready for the part as John Wayne in one of his westerns. I was kitted out and ready to go.

Donate didn't have a lot of form, but just to have a ride was a buzz. I was nervous all week, just wondering how she would go. I remember passing one horse and I was so rapt, but the next minute that horse passed me. I think I ended up running last, but I was still buzzing when I got back into the jockeys' room.

I had to wait almost three months after my first ride to get my first winner. Other apprentices riding at the time, like Arnold Taiaroa and Trevor Chambers, were racking up their first winners in their first half-dozen rides. Their trainers were putting them on the best sprinters. But Jock was putting me on jumpers and stayers in open sprints, horses that couldn't win. I was thinking, *Why, why won't you put me on a fast horse?* But when I was back at the tail of the field I could see what the whole field was doing, which jockey was doing what. He wanted me to get more experience on the older horses, and I think he was worried about success too early and it doing more damage than good. I've looked at a lot of jockeys who have started off with a hiss and a roar as apprentices and they've gone nowhere. They've been put on the better horses and been up in front or on the pace and out of trouble. Sure they've won, but they haven't learnt a lot. When you're on a jumper or stayer in a sprint and sitting back watching 10 horses and 10 different jockeys you see a lot happening and that's part of learning. A lot of top jockeys have taken a year or two to break in. I was just excited to have a ride in a race, but I always wondered when that first win was going to come.

Finally, in my twenty-first ride I got that first win. It was on Phar Lace — no not Phar Lap — at Foxton. Jock trained him and he was a form horse. He was always travelling like a winner, and I don't think I even pulled the stick on him. He won by about a length and a half and cruised to the line. I just kept him balanced and was only steering him. I think Jock put me on because Phar Lace was quiet and easy to ride. Nowadays the kids get thrown in the deep end. I remember one apprentice's first ride being in a two-mile race. That was unheard of in my time.

Phar Lace became a bit of a favourite around the stables. But that first win was both my happiest and saddest day. As a trophy I received a plaited whip, an antique one from an old jockey, and I was very proud of it. I had my photo taken with it, but within five minutes of winning the trophy I'd lost it. I never did find out who took it.

After that win on Phar Lace I had to wait a month before my next win; during that period I didn't even get a placing. But then after my second winner, Richard The First at Hastings, within five rides I rode three winners and a second and one of those was Phar Lace again, in my first open handicap win. After winning one race, at the presentation I was given a bottle of vodka as a prize. Here I was a kid and the trophy was a bottle of spirits! You could imagine what would happen if they did that now.

I rode four winners from 54 rides that first season, then things started to take off for me the next season and I won 25 races. In December that year I had my first ride on New Moon and won at Woodville. Jock trained her and she was a freak, a flying machine that you'd die to ride. I was going to ride her again, but I slept in one morning and the old man warned me: 'If you sleep in and you can't ride trackwork you won't be riding her.' So I lost the ride on New Moon. Dessie ended up riding her and she was unbeaten in six or seven runs then was just beaten by

Ajasco in the Railway Handicap at Ellerslie. She later went to America and won a Grade Three race at Santa Anita. Trainers used to get angry if you slept in, and often someone would go and throw a bucket of water over you.

One day I brought a colt in from his paddock and I tied him to the fence to pick his hooves out. I didn't realise New Moon was in the next paddock. She came up and they sniffed and — bingo — he kicked me in the chin and put my bottom teeth through my tongue. I had to go and get stitches in my tongue. It was a good wake-up call. I learnt my lesson the hard way and that wasn't going to happen again.

Like other young riders, as I started to get more experience and ride more winners I got some better rides. In my third season (1971–72) I ended up the leading apprentice with 55 wins. I was following a family tradition because Johnny had been the leading apprentice for three consecutive seasons in the late 1960s and Dessie was the leading apprentice the year before me. When my younger brother Peter started riding he didn't have the same luck, but later when he started riding over fences he was the leading jumps jockey one season (1976–77).

At the beginning of that season as the top apprentice I had my first rides at Ellerslie without any luck. But when I returned for the Easter meeting I rode a couple of winners and was third in the Easter Handicap on Nausori. Over the years since then I've had a lot of luck at Ellerslie, especially in the big races. And that season I got my first win for Jock on Sharif at Feilding. He was a great old horse. That day I also rode three winners on the card for the first time. As well as Sharif, I won on Blue Nile and Ballycastle, who later went on to be a top jumper. Grant Cooksley won a Waikato and Great Northern Steeples at Ellerslie on him.

Actually, when I look back, that November was a good month for me because a couple of weeks after the treble I got to ride Glengowan for the first time and won an apprentices' hack race at Woodville. After that he became my horse. The following February I won the Rangitikei Cup on him and a couple of months later we won the Hawke's Bay Cup, too. Eighteen months after that I was off to the Melbourne Cup with Glengowan, but more on that later.

Brian 'Deak' Deacon gave me my first feature win. It was on Egmont Park in the 1972 George Adams Handicap at Trentham. The race name has changed over the years, but it has always been recognised as one of the best Group One 1600-metre races in the country. Winning Group One races is as good as it gets. I've won plenty of Group Two, Group Three and Listed races over the years, but the pinnacle is to get the Group Ones. Some jockeys go a lifetime without a Group One win, but I've been lucky. I've had my share and probably their share, too.

Egmont Park was by Copenhagen II and I think he was the only Copenhagen who liked a wet track. Deak had a lot of good apprentices then and it was hard to get a lot of rides from him, but I rode the odd one for the stable. He was a top trainer of horses and apprentices. Jimmy Walker, Maurice Campbell, Gary Stewart and Greg Childs all did their apprenticeships with him and Garry Phillips finished his time off there.

During those apprentice days we'd play a lot of pool when we had time off. Pool was the in thing to do. We all met down the pool room at the RSA and I'd get the key off the old guy. We started playing pool for our wages. It got quite scary, actually, with the amount of money that was changing hands. I don't think a lot of the bosses of the apprentices and stablehands knew what we were up to, money-wise. Many times I went home broke. I wasn't very good to start with, but when you begin losing all the time you learn to get better or else. When I was losing I started borrowing off my brother Dessie and then he'd want to charge me interest.

Another thing I got exposed to at a young age was sex. I was probably about 10 or 11 when I was helping out around the stables. You'd hear some noise going on in the background, and being an inquisitive little fella I'd go for a look and — hello. There were the stablehands with girls in the horse boxes or sometimes in the straw shed, and it would be, 'Wow, what's going on here?' It was quite a common thing around the stables. Not so much girls working in the stables, but stablehands getting the girls to meet them there. You'd walk around the box and find the biggest gap in the wall to peek through. These days it's left to the schools to give the sex lessons, but I think by the time I was 15 I'd seen enough that I probably could have written a book on it myself.

Sex education isn't the only area where times have changed. When I was young all the apprentices, even the good ones, used to go to the races and home again on the float. These days most apprentices have got their own cars and, if not, they travel in cars with other jockeys. Back in my younger days on the long trips home we'd be sitting down the back compartment of the float with half a dozen beers we'd sneaked in. We were pissed by the time we got home and we'd sneak to our rooms and hope the boss didn't see us.

I remember one float driver, Turoa Haronga, a guy from Feilding. He'd often come and pick up the horses from our place. It was my first trip away, to Hamilton, and we got to around the Taupo–Tokoroa road. He used to get me to roll his cigarettes and next minute he said, 'Come on Noel, you can take over. I just want to shut my eyes for a couple of minutes.' He let me drive. I was 14 at the time and here I was driving this float with about seven or eight horses on the back. I don't think I'd driven a car yet, let alone a float, and I had to steer. We were going up a hill and it was getting slower and slower and slower and I had to yell and scream, 'Turoa, what's the go mate? We're losing power' and he was yelling back, 'Pull the red button, pull the red button up,' and it kicked back into gear. It was unbelievable. He was a real laidback Maori, a lovely guy.

Later in my apprenticeship I got my first car, a Mazda RX3. One day when Jock went to put a saddle in the back seat I turned around and said, 'What's the boot for?' I wish I'd never said that because I still feel his boot going up my arse. I had a lot of pride in that first car. Brent Thomson, Garry Phillips — we all had Mazdas. It was a prestige car for the jockeys at the time.

We used to have a certain amount of time to get to the races and you'd go as fast as you could. And straight after the races you'd be flying back to the local pub to see where the parties were. We apprentices would have races to the race meetings through the Manawatu Gorge. We'd have time trials and it was quite scary because the gorge was quite windy and dangerous. It was tarseal, but had shocking corners. We'd race from the boundary in Woodville to the gasworks in Palmerston North. At the time we didn't think about how fast we were going; we were at an age like the boy racers of today. Thinking back, we're lucky we didn't have an horrific accident.

There have been jockeys killed in car accidents, but when you think of all the mileage we all do there have been very few. I remember Mike Donoghue was going up to Hastings and he took a mate with him. He came around a corner just out of Woodville and went off the road and his mate was killed. That was very sad and something Mike has had to live with. It shook us all up. Sadly, Mike was actually killed in a farming accident a few years ago.

Mark Heaney was also killed in a car accident and down south so was Des Tucker. It's amazing a lot more jockeys didn't get killed with the speed most of us were driving. When you're young there's no fear.

4

Robbed of outright premiership title

The 1972–73 season is one I will always remember, both for winning the Jockeys' Premiership and for not winning it outright. It all started to come together for me that season. I ended my four-year apprenticeship in February, but signed on for an extra year. I wound up dead-heating with David Peake on 91 wins in the Jockeys' Premiership, but when I think back I should have beaten him.

I copped a three-week suspension at the Wellington Cup meeting. I'd won the Trentham Stakes on Glengowan, and later I was put out when I ran third on Nordic Star in the George Adams. It was just my fourth suspension after 1200-odd rides and it cost me probably 13 winners and the premiership. I should never have been put out. Phil Reid was the stipe — the stipendiary steward — and I'm still annoyed with him. He even had the audacity to thank my brother Dessie for giving such truthful evidence. The biggest shock was the film cut-off. We'd got to the point just before the turn, about the 600, and the cameras changed over. They'd gone from the horses being in one position to another and there was no film of any interference; they didn't have proper film coverage of it. All they were basing it on was other jockeys' evidence — all hearsay. It's like convicting without any evidence. Me being an apprentice, I had to cop it and I've copped it for so many years and it still makes me wild.

I've had other suspensions over the years and taken them on the chin. There are even times I've wanted to get suspended. I needed an out to just get away. Perhaps it was winter and there was nothing to look forward to, but you never got a month's suspension then. No, you always got it in the summertime, when you can lose out on much more money. You're self-employed and the stipes and judicial committees can take away your livelihood. Sometimes you get so frustrated. I often felt like saying, 'You haven't ridden a horse but you feel you can judge me?'

That suspension at Wellington robbed me of the premiership outright. The way I look at it I lost 13 potential winners, but whether or not I won on them all, I only needed one to beat Peakey.

Probably the other biggest disappointment for me was that Alan Bright, a Central Districts (CD) guy, was helping David Peake with his mounts. Alan was reporting for the Manawatu *Evening Standard* as well as doing radio race commentaries. Peakey was always going to be my main rival for the premiership in the sense that he'd won so many premierships and he had the contacts and the good rides. Halfway through the season I had ridden a decent number of winners and that's when it became a goal to win the premiership. Unlike Peakey, though, I didn't have any help. There were no actual jockeys' agents in those days, not like now when even a lot of apprentice jockeys have agents.

I heard from my brother Johnny, as well as Earl Harrison and other riders, that David Peake thought apprentices were worthless. And there were little things I picked up as an early apprentice. Johnny told me one day that David Peake blew up at him. When Johnny was an apprentice down in the CD he was the kingpin. I think it might've been at Te Rapa, David Peake had a go at him when pulling up, and Johnny just turned around and said, 'Don't talk to me like a dog on a chain.' That always stuck in my mind. And it hit home for me one day. Max Skelton was the leading South Island rider, I was the leading CD rider and David Peake was the leading North Island rider, and someone just wanted a photo of us all together, but David Peake said, 'Nah, I won't have a photo with him' — meaning me. I've never forgotten that day. After that I had a goal, not just to ride a lot of winners, but to beat him.

Going into the last day of the season I was on 90 wins, two in front of David Peake. It was neck and neck, and I had some fantastic rides. I had come up to ride at Ellerslie and the same day David had gone to ride at Waipa. He had some beautiful rides, too. It turned into a nightmare, because throughout the day people would come up and tell me, 'Peaky's just ridden a winner, Peaky's just ridden a winner.' I had six rides and I'd finished second on Jandell, unplaced on Sauron, won on Pukepapa Lad for Baggy Hillis, and finished second on Regal Sal and fifth on Mikasa. By that stage Peaky had ridden three winners and we were equal.

Earl Harrison was to ride Nelsonian in the last race and he knew it would be a top ride, but he wanted to help me win the premiership so he gave the ride to me. In those days you didn't have declared riders and you could do that, but it wouldn't happen now. I ran second on Nelsonian. I'll never forget Earl for what he did. When I look back, he didn't have to do it. He was a battling jockey and there was a riding fee and it was money, and that's what we're in the game for. These times most jockeys wouldn't consider giving up a ride to another jockey. To me, though, if it means more to someone to have the ride then so be it. Let them have it. But what Earl did that time was special. Someone who stands down for you is a true jockey mate.

After I rode Nelsonian, David Peake still had one more ride to go at Waipa — Mia Bella, the favourite who looked unbeatable. I had to sit around for half an hour wondering if he was going to win on that horse, too, and beat me in the premiership. In those days there was no TV coverage; it was all via radio. Syd Tonks, the commentator at Ellerslie and a real gentleman, invited me up to the commentator's box to listen to Mia Bella's race. There was only Syd and me there, and when Mia Bella got beaten Syd turned to me and on air he asked, 'Noel Harris, what have you go to say to David Peake?' I just said, 'David, if you're listening, congratulations.' Short and sweet. If he'd won on Mia Bella it would've been unjust. After all that, I was happy to accept a dead heat on the day. But, thinking more about it later, I still feel angry about that suspension.

I never did have any actual run-ins with Peaky on the track. We just never got on. I was polite and said hello or whatever and, probably nine times out of 10, there'd be no reaction from him. I was so young then and there was a lot I wanted to say, but now it's probably best left alone. Looking back, I was an apprentice and he was an experienced jockey and we'd been brought up differently. To me, to be a good winner in life you've got to be a good loser. Today, David and I get on and we can talk about it. I can joke about those times and he'll laugh about it. But back in the day, it was different. He was very competitive and he didn't like apprentices.

We ended up sharing the premiership and the trophy that went with it. I got a silver jug without the tray and David got the tray. You'd think they'd have made two trophies; at least I'd then have had a complete one to show for my premiership win. It probably doesn't matter to David because he'd already won the premiership the previous season, and he won four more after that. But I look in my trophy cabinet and there is a lone jug — half a premiership win.

I hadn't set out to win the premiership — it's just the way it happened. Every year you try to better yourself, and as it worked out halfway through the season I was going well. I'd ridden 56 winners the previous season and had got on some good horses, like Curly Wave, who gave me my second feature win, in the Wakefield Challenge Stakes at Trentham. I started the new season off with a double on my first day, and a couple of months later I got my 100th win on Kia Maia at Waverley. Then I won four in a row two months on the trot. I was travelling more and more outside the Central Districts and even went up to the old

Kensington Park track at Whangarei and won the Whangarei Cup on Happy William for Ray Verner.

I had my first ride in the Auckland Cup and though I finished unplaced on Ben Adhem, I came out and ran second for Jock on Sharif in the Railway Handicap. Bob Skelton beat me on Lilt. I ran second on Glengowan later in the month in the Wellington Cup, and guess who beat me by a half-head — David Peake, on Merv Ritchie's horse, Rustler. But I came out and won the Telegraph Handicap on Sharif, then a couple of days later I won the Wellington Derby on Peg's Pride for another good old trainer, Joe Bromby. Sure I copped the suspension on the last day of the carnival, but that Wellington Cup meeting was still a good one for me as I won three of the big ones — the Telegraph, the Derby and the Trentham Stakes, on Glengowan.

That season I also got to ride another really good horse, Fury's Order, a big chestnut with a powerful finish. He was trained by Wally McEwan and Charlie Gestro. I won a two-year-old six-furlong race on him at Awapuni then won three more on him that season. Dessie picked up the ride on Fury's Order the following season when I went to Aussie, and he won the Wellington Guineas, 2000 Guineas and New Zealand Derby on him.

Fury's Order was a good horse for quite a few jockeys. Jimmy Walker won the Hawke's Bay Cup and New Zealand Cup on him and Brent Thomson rode him when he beat Kiwi Can and Analight in an all-New Zealand finish in the 1975 Cox Plate. And I remember riding against him in the International Invitation Stakes at Te Rapa in 1974. Bob Skelton rode him that time and he finished third to Brian Andrews on Battle Heights and Kevin Langby on Peg's Pride, while I rode my old mate Count Kereru. Lester Piggott and Larry Olsen were also among the invited riders at the meeting, and it was a big day for the club and for me, too. I was riding against not just the best in New Zealand but some of the best in the world.

I'd also ridden in an invitation series at Ellerslie a few months earlier.

That was the IATA International Stakes, and I finished fifth on Kiwi Can. It was the year Jesus Guce, from the Philippines, won the race on Sharda for Clem Bowry. The finishing photo got a lot of mileage because Jesus was so excited he was up in the irons waving to the crowd even before he went past the post. Jockeys didn't do that in those days, not to the extent he did, although it has become more common now. I've even done it myself a few times, but not before the finish. And over in Aussie it's quite common, especially with Glen Boss. He's yahooing and dancing in the saddle when he comes back to scale.

5

The Melbourne Cup

'You know something mate. Us blacks are going to win this Carnival.'
I can still remember Darby McCarthy's words. I'd gone over to
ride Glengowan in the Melbourne Cup that year and here I was an
18-year-old kid sitting in the jockeys' room at Caulfield at the start of
the carnival listening to everything they had to say. There was Darby
McCarthy, an Aboriginal and a great jockey, Frankie Reys, of Filipino
and Aboriginal descent, and Herbie Rauhihi, a Maori and a top jockey
who I always looked up to. Darby just turned around to Herbie and
made that comment. It was beautiful. Lo and behold Herbie came
out and did well on Just Topic. He had won on her in Sydney and she
won the 1000 Guineas and the lead-up to the VRC Oaks. Frankie Reys
won the Melbourne Cup and ended up beating me on Glengowan and
Darby had a good carnival, too. That comment was typical of Darby
and it summed up the situation beautifully.

Here I was in the big smoke. I'd grown up hearing all about the
Melbourne Cup and suddenly as an 18 year old I was getting to ride
in it. Our trip to Melbourne had been planned from the previous
season after I finished second on Glengowan in the Wellington Cup.
Glengowan's owner, Doug Debreceny, had a few horses with Jock,
but nothing anywhere near as good as him. He was a big, lop-eared
chestnut and he used to sweat up quite a bit. He was by Arragon and
that was typical of the breed. They were quite a nervy sort of horse, but

he was beautiful to ride, all power. He'd actually been with Noel Eales to start with, then Jock had him.

My brother Dessie rode Glengowan early on, then I got on him in the welters and intermediates, and the season before we went over to Aussie he'd run third in the Avondale Cup and Waikato Cup. Dessie beat me in the Waikato Cup on Fort Hagen. And when he won the Trentham Stakes he beat Clem Bowry's two good horses, Black Rod and Topsy.

I won the Group One Caulfield Stakes first up on him in Melbourne and we beat Roy Higgins on All Shot, one of the best weight-for-age horses in Aussie. Roy had done his homework and knew all about Glengowan. He thought he had us beaten and he actually hit him over the nose with his stick a couple of times up the straight — we were that close together. But Glengowan refused to give in and he came back and beat him.

Back in the jockeys' room Roy just said to me, 'Over here we look after each other.' The stewards called me into the inquiry room and asked if Glengowan had been hit by Roy. I told a little white lie and said no. Mind you, if Roy had beaten me it would have been a different story. Roy got warned about his riding on All Shot and moving in and causing interference to us. As for me, by sticking up for Roy I was accepted over there. I was one of the boys. It's a bit like honour among thieves.

I got a lot of praise from the media for my ride in the Caulfield Stakes, but how things changed after the Cup. That Caulfield Stakes win put Glengowan into early favouritism for the Melbourne Cup and had champion trainer Tommy Smith interested in him. Luckily for me, Doug Debreceny turned down the $100,000 offer. He'd gone to Australia to run in the Melbourne Cup and he wasn't going to sell him.

After the Caulfield Stakes win I ran fourth on him behind Taj Rossi in the Cox Plate then we finished second to Australasia in the Mackinnon Stakes. He came from last and in another stride he would have won the

Mackinnon. Everyone was saying it was a winning Melbourne Cup trial and the bookies brought him into outright favourite. If you'd read the write-ups in the papers you'd say we'd already won the Cup. One of the Sunday papers had the intro 'G-L-E-N-G-O-W-A-N. The nine-letter inscription can be ordered now for the $3000 gold Melbourne Cup.' Another newspaper intro read, 'How are they going to beat Glengowan in the big one on Tuesday?' There was the talk he could become the first favourite to win the Cup since Galilee in 1966.

There was so much attention on him. The media even wanted to have a donkey in the same paddock as him because he had the loppy ears. They wanted a photo of the two together, comparing the ears, but the last thing you want is a donkey knocking his ears off. There was a lot of press attention and at the time you try to take it in your stride. But closer to race day I was starting to feel the pressure. And when I got to Flemington and saw the big crowd — more than 103,000, which was the best for 23 years — it really dawned on me. This was it: my chance to win the Melbourne Cup.

Probably being over there earlier to ride for Gary Lee was a big help. That broke me into it nicely. It wasn't as if it was my first ride in Australia when it came to the Melbourne Cup carnival. I'd got used to riding over there, but the nerve-racking part was in the jockeys' room before the Cup. That last hour in there you could almost have heard a pin drop. I'd never experienced such silence in my life. It would probably relate to the sound in a hospital at night. I was very anxious to get out there. Jockeys say they're just going to get out there and ride it like any other race, but the Melbourne Cup is no ordinary race. It's legendary. The race that stops two nations. Just making the move out to mount my horse was a bit of a relief.

On my way through the birdcage I was thinking about the race, hoping Glengowan settled in his preliminary and didn't drop me or do anything to embarrass me. He went down to the start nicely, no worries there. And once I got around to the barrier there was the excitement of knowing it was about to happen. I heard the gates close behind me and I couldn't wait for that click of the starter's button to let the field go.

I wanted him to jump clean and get into a good position. I didn't want to be caught wide or get too far back. As it turned out I got a lovely trip, just past midfield, with one of the favourites, Dayana, ridden by Roy Higgins, tracking us. He was always relaxed. I knew then he'd get the distance. Coming to the home turn we were in with a big show and I started to get a bit excited. As we straightened he started to mount his run and I knew by the feeling he was giving me he was going to finish it off strongly and beat the ones up in front. Daneson was down on the fence and I knew I had him beaten, but then Glengowan started to roll in. He'd done it before.

I could hear Gala Supreme coming through between us and with only 49 kilos on his back I knew he'd be hard to hold out. About 100 metres out I still thought we might get it, but I had to stop riding for about two strides to straighten Glengowan. That was the difference between winning and running second. I kept coming at him, coming at him, but when Gala Supreme kicked I knew he'd held me out. There was only a long head in it. Sometimes you can get to a horse and think you're not going to beat it, but in one stride it can falter and you can get up. I kept trying, hoping that would happen, but it didn't. Gala Supreme just kept kicking.

When I went past the post I knew he'd beaten me. It was only by a long head and we'd tried hard. Glengowan had given everything he had. If only he hadn't rolled in. Coming back, the first thing I thought about was Jock. I felt sorry for him. I knew it was his only chance to win a Melbourne Cup and I'd have loved to have done it for him. I'd have other chances. As time has gone on I've had a dozen or so rides in it and I haven't been able to win it, but that's how it goes. At least I've had my chances. Jock had one chance and he came so close.

The press had a field-day, blaming my inexperience for getting Glengowan beaten. One of the headlines in the next morning's paper read: 'Harris' error made the Melbourne Cup a present for Gala Supreme'. I copped it big time in the media. They were all saying I shouldn't have stopped riding to straighten him. I should have kept going and worried about it later. He'd done it at home before. He used to run in and he didn't actually win races by big margins. He'd just do enough to get there. But as far as they were concerned it was a case of a boy on a man's errand. They said if Roy Higgins had ridden Glengowan he would have won. But when they asked Roy he made the comment that he had followed me on Dayana and he said if he'd ridden Glengowan he would have done nothing different. That made me feel a bit better, hearing it from a top jockey like Roy.

I still remember one of the comments I heard on the radio when I was going back to Mornington after the race. The guy said, 'Noel Harris, if you're listening you could have been going home with a sheila on both arms, but instead you're going home with a horse in a float.' That was the difference between winning and running second in the Melbourne Cup. The Aussies love a winner. Second is not good.

I've kept the newspaper clippings, even though I felt the criticism was unjust. I know Glengowan would have kept boring in if I hadn't stopped to straighten him. I wouldn't have had a licence for a long time if I'd kept going. I still get reminded of it when I go to Aussie. 'You're the boy who got beaten on Glengowan,' they say, and I just answer yes. When anyone mentions Glengowan they remember the Melbourne Cup. Most years the runner-up is forgotten, but not Glengowan. I'm remembered more for that Melbourne Cup than any of my big wins over there. It keeps coming up in the papers every time I have a Melbourne Cup ride. I've never been able to get away from it.

Glengowan came back to New Zealand and I won on him at Woodville, beating Auckland Cup winner Kia Maia, and after finishing unplaced in Battle Heights' Wellington Cup we finished second to him in the Trentham Stakes and third at Hastings to Guest Star, who won the Wellington Cup a couple of years later. Glengowan later pulled up sore at the track one morning and was retired. He was such a good horse to me — so many memories.

After Glengowan, I was fourth on Lord Metric in the Melbourne Cup for Merv Ritchie. I was also fourth on Kiwi the year At Talaq won it. That year I thought I was going to at last win the Cup, but in the last 100 metres Kiwi pulled up short as if he'd broken his shoulder. When I pulled him up I jumped off and I wish I hadn't. My legs were like jelly. I got a ride back in the ambulance and by the time he got back he was all right. He must've pinched a nerve. He'd won the Melbourne Cup three years earlier when he flew home from last for Jimmy Cassidy, and the way he was travelling for me in that 1986 Melbourne Cup I was sure he was going to win it a second time. He was really winding up.

I was Kiwi's regular rider for most of his last couple of seasons and I rode him in two Melbourne Cups. He finished down the track the first time, two starts after I'd won the Taranaki Stakes on him, and the year he ran fourth he'd won his lead-up, the Watkins Handicap at Trentham. I won three on him. He was a great old horse to ride. And I loved riding for his trainer and owner Snow Lupton and his wife, Anne. They were lovely people and every year they'd send me a Christmas card. They also had Westgate, who was a good horse, but obviously not in Kiwi's class. I won nine on Westgate and he won six in a row one year.

The year Kiwi won the Cup I was seventh on Fountaincourt. He was a good horse and his trainer, Cyril Pfefferle, was a great guy. Fountaincourt won an Auckland Cup when Phillip Smith rode him and I won the Werribee Cup on him before I rode him in the Melbourne Cup. He then came out in the next start and beat McGinty in the Queen Elizabeth in Melbourne, before McGinty went to Japan. I was second on him in the Sandown Cup after that. I don't think people appreciate how good Fountaincourt was; he never got the recognition he deserved.

The closest I've been to winning a Melbourne Cup since Glengowan was when I was third in the 1992 Cup on Castletown. That was to

Subzero, ridden by my old mate Greg Hall, and Veandercross. I went back over the following year to ride Castletown again, but things didn't work out and he finished down the track.

I've ridden The Bandette, Hail, Princess Coup and Capecover in the Melbourne Cup since then, but have never got close to the money. And it's getting a lot harder these days with all the European stayers coming over. Even the Aussies are squealing that they're being squeezed out.

But I can say I've ridden two Melbourne Cup winners. Yeah, Beldale Ball and Tawriffic. I won on Beldale Ball at Moonee Valley and you'd have classed him as a highweighter if he'd been in New Zealand. He ended up having about 49.5 kilos in the 1980 Melbourne Cup and Johnny Letts rode him. I still can't believe he came out and had that sprint at the finish in the Cup. And it was much the same when I rode Tawriffic up in Brisbane in the winter. He felt like a highweighter, too. Then Shane Dye won on him later that year in the Melbourne Cup. I've never seen a horse improve so much.

Despite the Melbourne Cup criticism over my ride on Glengowan, that 1973 Melbourne campaign was a great experience for me. I'd just dead-heated with David Peake in the premiership and started the new season off riding for Gary Lee in Melbourne. I spent three and a half months over there and rode six winners. I got my two biggest wins at that stage of my career with the Caulfield Stakes win on Glengowan and the Feehan Stakes on Audaciter, for Gary. Audaciter also ran second in the Heatherlie Stakes to Gala Supreme and that turned out to be top form after the Melbourne Cup. Audaciter was a good horse, winning 21 races.

I'd ridden for Gary when he was training at Riccarton and I'd won the Waimate Cup on Audaciter the previous season. Actually, it was Jock who got me going down to ride for Gary Lee, telling me he was a top trainer, but soon after that Gary decided he was going to shift camp to Aussie. He set up at Mornington and he helped me when I got over there. I won the Pakenham Cup on Red Boy, as well as winning on Audaciter for him. It worked in well for me with Glengowan going over.

I'll never forget what Gary did to me one day. You've got to get up early to go to the track in the morning, but Gary didn't have any success with me so one morning he threw a tarantula on my bed. Fuck mate, if you do that to me I'm gone. From that day on every morning when he touched my bedroom door, I was up dressed and gone. We laugh about it now, but at the time it was frightening seeing one on my bed. You ever seen a Maori turn white?

6

Back to Wiki Waki Pa

After copping so much flak in the Aussie media over my ride on Glengowan in the Melbourne Cup, it was good to get back to New Zealand — back among friends and family and back riding winners. I knew I'd done my best in the Cup and I just wanted to get on with life.

I'd bought an old house on the corner of the racecourse at Woodville, an old weatherboard home that was over 50 years old. I think Johnny had bought it off Jock and I bought it off him. I set up camp there and Baggy Hillis, a long-time friend of the family, came down and, being the comic he is, he decided to name the house Wiki Waki Pa. I said, 'Hang on mate. You know with the Maori, you've got to be careful what you name things.' So he got the name checked out. There's no such name so he was going to get it blessed. He put a couple of tiki on a sign which he placed on the corner of the road, and the name just stuck. It was *Where's the party tonight?* and everybody would say, *The Wiki Waki Pa.* Baggy had been a top jumps jockey and was training at the time. He used to stay when he brought a team down and I'd give him the key.

I'd met Baggy when he used to stay with Jock. He'd come down to the Woodville races and Jock, being a jumps jockey himself, got on well with him. Baggy used to bring steak and DB beer in the big bottles and stock up the fridge. Next door Jock would have potatoes growing and Jock told Baggy to help himself so Baggy enlisted Jock's staff to dig them out. He ended up going home with a trailer full of spuds. Jock didn't mind him taking the spuds, but it was using his staff and his time. But that's Baggy. He'll never change.

There are so many funny stories related to Baggy over the years. I remember he went to a party at Palmerston North on a Saturday night and, being a great drinker, he'd drink beer all day then Bacardi and Coke at night. At this party there was a large aquarium, like a birdcage on a stand. Old Baggy's starting to jive and he goes jelly in the legs, hits the aquarium and it's sloshed all over him. He got drenched. Next thing he's trying to get the goldfish and snails off the floor and put them back in the aquarium and apologising at the same time. We were never invited there again. But that's not the end of the story.

We came back to Wiki Waki Pa and Baggy was using my room. On the Monday I poked my head into the room and said, 'Geez, something's smelling around here Bags. It's just not good mate,' and he said, 'Yeah I've smelt it since yesterday. It's shocking, isn't it? It needs fumigating.' I told him I was off to the drycleaners and he said to take a pile of clothes he had in the corner. I grabbed them and gave them a shake and the next minute shells and a couple of dead goldfish dropped out of the cuffs!

Another time Baggy and I and Ron Gurney, a local racing journalist, went over to the Woodville racecourse for drinks. We were leaving full of piss and went down past the kitchen on the way out. Bags spotted the catering utensils, the coffee and food, and he said, 'We need this stuff at your place Harry, sugar, tea, you need some knives and forks, tea towels . . .' He had shorts on and he loaded himself up. We went past the horse stalls and we weren't far from home and next minute we were having running races and Gurney was tackling him and we were having a ball. There were knives and forks and coffee going everywhere. I think Baggy had grabbed enough to last a year.

The next morning Baggy had to go and work his horses and the racecourse caretaker approached him. 'Mr Hillis, we don't stand stealing. We want all those utensils back.' They got it all back apart from the coffee and tea spilt and Baggy got a reprimand. It's just Baggy's nature, and it was so funny at the time. In those days it was harmless fun. In the morning he'd be pouring a big bottle of DB in the pan and cooking it with the steak. Drunken steak, eggs and chips he'd call it. Everybody knows Baggy for the comic he is.

One day in Palmerston North when Gus Clutterbuck, Baggy and I were staying together, we'd all had a big night out and I told Baggy we'd work his horses. I said to Gus, 'We'll work them quickly. I'll ride one and lead two and you do the same.' We got them in the middle, into the bull ring, started off and next minute I lost the two I was leading then Gus lost his two and we were chasing around trying to retrieve them. We finally caught them and we got back to the motel and said to Baggy, 'You won't have to gallop those horses tomorrow. They've done enough galloping today.' It didn't upset Baggy. As it turned out, one of them won and another ran second. It was nothing for Baggy to line up one horse twice in the same day. He did it on several occasions. In those days you were allowed.

I've ridden a lot of winners for Baggy — the likes of the Woodville Cup and Marton Cup — and over the years he's had some good horses, like Princess Cecily. She was part-owned by Ali Cunningham and years later I won the New Zealand Derby for Ali on Hail, who was trained by Bruce Marsh. Baggy was just one of those great guys to ride for, a real character of racing. Nothing fazed him and when he got beaten it never worried him. I grew up with the Hillis family, with Wayne and Paul riding. And I've ridden winners for Wayne since he's been training.

When I had Wiki Waki Pa John 'Kiwi' Kiernan was my flatmate. He was a blacksmith with Bill Pratt and we had some great times. He taught me a lot. He used to travel with Syd Brown's horses overseas, horses like Daryl's Joy, Triton and Weenell. He was very knowledgeable, up with the play, and if there had been jockeys' agents at that time he would've been a great one. He's a great talker and he knew his form.

You wouldn't get a better blacksmith than Kiwi and he's gone on to do well as a trainer. He learnt off Syd Brown, a top trainer here who broke into Sydney when it was very tough. Syd had a lot of great horses. Kiwi has trained a couple of Group One winners — No Mean City and the Adelaide Cup winner Pillage 'N Plunder. When we were young we had our big ideas of where we wanted to be, and it's good to see him making it as a trainer.

There are so many funny stories from those early days. Mind you, some of them mightn't be funny now. Like all young guys, we used to drink a lot. It's become a problem in today's society, more so with drugs, but back then people used to get pissed, wake up with a hangover and get on with life. It was all about living for the day and not worrying about tomorrow. I did some silly things when I was drunk.

One morning I woke up in the ditch outside my place and my car was parked in the middle of the road. Fortunately, in Woodville in those days there was bugger all traffic. I'd come home from the pub and for some reason just stopped the car on the road. As I got out I must've fallen over in the drain and gone to sleep there. Luckily, it wasn't full of water. Early the next morning Ian Bradbury, one of the local trainers, was going past on his way to the track and he spotted me. He went to the door, yelling out to Kiwi that I was in the drain. Kiwi stumbled to the door and said, 'Oh, is that all. He'll be all right.' And he went straight back to bed. He knew what I was like. Alcohol, everybody used to do it.

I remember when colour televisions arrived to replace the old black and white ones. I got a colour TV and, wow, it was the go. We'd been out one night, had a good time, got home and I was looking at this TV and I thought, *It's meant to be colour, isn't it?* so I rang my brother Dessie and said, 'Colour TV, what's the go? It's black and white.' I didn't realise it was a black and white movie on. Perhaps my perception was affected by the alcohol.

Before Wiki Waki Pa I shifted to Palmerston North and flatted with Gus Clutterbuck for a while and we had a lot of laughs. Gus and I go way back, as apprentices together. He was apprenticed to Jim Selwood in Palmerston North, a great horseman. Gus used to get on his horse and he'd be singing at the barrier. He'd settle the horses right down. He had a stutter and he'd be singing while stuttering. Next minute he'd be commentating races while riding work. He'd keep you entertained, that's for sure.

Later on when Gus went out training he did well. I won the New Zealand Cup on Wake Forest for him and that was his first big win. Then I won a few on Lady Agnes. One of them was the Adrian Knox Stakes in Sydney and that was Gus' first Australian winner. I always remember Gus the morning of the races when Lady Agnes went to Australia. He asked a trainer at the place where we were staying if he could do his tie up for him. The Aussie trainer thought he was joking, but Gus was stuttering away, 'I'm s-s-s serious.' Here's this Aussie trainer thinking a Kiwi is taking the piss out of him.

Gus' father, Lionel, was also a jockey and Gus was like us Harris boys. He used to sneak into the birdcage through the iron bars and was just full on for horses. But he was accident prone. I remember about 20-odd falls he had. He's broken just about every bone in his body except his neck. I think he broke his pelvis twice. That was Gus. Injuries galore, but he kept bouncing back.

We had a lot of fun times flatting. We were like students: it was all about women and our fridge full of beer — and ice blocks for when we were wasting. That's all we needed. We were living like there was no tomorrow. 'She'll be right mate. We'll make money next week.' It's just that attitude when you're 18 or 19: not a care in the world.

But we got into a bit of trouble with the chief stipe George Tattersall. We thought we were the kingpins, busy thinking about women, wine and beer, and we weren't turning up to the track in the mornings. Mr Tattersall just came straight to us and said, 'You keep this up and you won't have a licence. You'll get blacklisted.' It was a bit of a wake-up call. If you stepped out of line there were a lot of top riders to take over. But it was something most jockeys did when they came out of their time in that era. They would fall off the rails thinking they were bigger than Texas. It was a way of working life out.

Over the years I've been known for not riding trackwork. It probably started in Palmy when Murray Baker was training in Woodville and I was riding most of his team. I never had to ride work. As far as Murray was concerned I rode at the trials and races for him. I've never been what you call a constantly good track-work rider. But when I went to Aussie I rode trackwork, and as I said to a lot of trainers when I shifted up to Matamata, 'If you want me, ring me and I'll be there.' I've gone down to ride work for everyone who has rung me. I can get away with it whereas a lot of jockeys can't. If they don't turn up at the track, they don't get the rides. Everyone seems to have me on about it, but it worked for me. In this day and age, if I was just starting out, it would be different. I'd have to be at the track every morning.

Riding regular trackwork does help your fitness. But I feel race riding keeps you fitter. From the time you jump out of the barrier to when you hit the winning post, those short bursts, going hell for leather, that's what really cleans you out. It's like a horse having a gallop. You can pace work him for a whole month, but you give him a gallop and that will clean his wind quicker than all that paceworking.

When my son Troy started off as an apprentice I encouraged him to ride trackwork. He was apprenticed to Mark Walker and he wouldn't allow him to miss trackwork. Good on him. Mark was good to Troy. In a stable like that you don't mess around because you don't get the rides.

7

Record-breaking apprentice

I ended my apprenticeship with 207 wins. It was a New Zealand record for the most wins as an apprentice and the stake-money won. I'd beaten the record previously held by my brother Johnny, but it was a record that didn't last long. Brent Thomson came out and broke it soon after, and the record has been smashed more than a few times since then. Michael Walker and James McDonald have set new records in recent seasons.

My first win as a fully fledged jockey came on one of the great gallopers, Grey Way, the 'Washdyke Wonder'. It was my fifteenth ride as a professional jockey and I won the Railway Handicap at Trentham on him in 1974. Earlier in the day, I'd been second on Count Kereru in the North Island Challenge Stakes and third on Chelsea Tower in the President's Handicap. I'd won the Jackson Stakes at Wanganui a month beforehand on Count Kereru. He was a good old horse trained at Woodville by Kay Bowman, a lovely old lady. I think I rode my 201st winner on Count Kereru.

I didn't ride Grey Way a lot, but I can say I contributed to a couple of his 51 wins. I rode him 10 times and was never out of the money on him in New Zealand. And I am the only jockey to have won a race on him in Australia. Pat Corboy, his trainer, took him over to Melbourne in the spring of 1974 as a four year old and I won first up on him in the

Chirnside Stakes. He didn't like wet tracks and his owner Peter South tried to scratch him, but the Aussie wet tracks can be different from ours. I remember it absolutely bucketed down on the morning of the races. I think he paid about $11 that day. He had a few more runs over there, but the soft tracks eventually got to him.

When he got back to New Zealand he went to Avondale and I ran second on him in the Pegasus Stakes, and later that season I was third on him in the Telegraph Handicap, third in the George Adams at Trentham, third in the North Island Challenge Stakes and my last ride on him was when he ran third over 1600 at Trentham. He really was a great horse and one of the things I remember most about him was the way he worked. Over in Aussie I rode him in trackwork and I'd go to trot him and he'd start ambling because he'd been used to working behind the trotters. It's strange to have a galloper doing that. For a start I thought he was sore and not hitting out properly, but it was just his idiosyncrasy.

Dad had his stint in a trotting stable and I suppose when I rode Grey Way in it work was the closest I've been to trotting. Although, when I think back, one day Gary Lee had a trotter down in Christchurch. He put a saddle on it and I had to work it around the chute at Riccarton. Jesus! I've never been so uncomfortable in my life.

Over the next two seasons I rode 102 winners, and one of the highlights was at the Trentham September meeting in 1975 when I won on Gideon. It wasn't a big race, but it was special because it was a Harris trifecta. Peter ran second on Clef and Dessie was third on Arctic Rest. There were plenty of times we boys, Johnny included, had picked up quinellas, but from memory I think that's the only time we got a trifecta. That was the same year I won the Wellington Derby on Kenann for trainer Colin Cooksley (Grant Cooksley's father), and a year later I won my first 1000 Guineas at Riccarton on Porsha, who was trained by Bill and Graeme Sanders. Jock had sent me up to Bill Sanders for a week as an apprentice and I had started riding more and more for the Sanders stable from then on. They were beautiful days.

Bill Sanders was a legend; I will always remember him. He was a chemist by trade and he could actually speak fluent Maori. He always used to say the horses are professional racehorses, in this world to race. Feed them big and race them hard. He was the only guy I knew who would never spell a horse, and they'd go out of form and run back into form. He would gallop horses three furlongs (600 metres) the morning of the races. I remember riding Fort Street in the Wanganui Cup. The morning of the races I trotted her three times in the bull ring, paceworked a round and when I got to the winning post did three-quarter pace then sprinted her up the last 600 metres.

One morning at the Sanders' as an apprentice it was pissing down and I was sitting in the stall waiting to work a horse. Bill Sanders said, 'What are you doing son?' I said, 'Mr Sanders, it's raining.' He replied, 'Skin's waterproof son. Get out there.' Another time we were at Wanganui, arrived at the track and I went to help saddle up the horse when he said, 'Nah, you're a jockey. Sit down here.' He gave me a packet of Rothmans cigarettes and said, 'Son when I want you, I'll whistle you.' I got the whistle and I went to hop on one of the horses and he said, 'Son, where's your whip?' I replied, 'I haven't got one,' and he said, 'Son, that's like going shooting without a gun. Go and get a whip.'

Bill Sanders always took a team to Wanganui meetings and any horse that got a nick had an antiseptic purple powder put on them. In the end you could always tell his stalls — it was unbelievable the amount of purple around them.

Once when I was staying up in Te Awamutu I went out cutting grass with Kevin Cullen, a top jockey who I looked up to, and I cut my finger. The next day I had to ride trackwork and I had my finger bandaged. Bill Sanders said, 'What's the go?' and I told him what had happened. He said, 'You're a jockey, not a stablehand.' Then he turned and ripped into Kevin, saying that I shouldn't have been out cutting grass. Kevin said, 'Well, what am I?' He was the Sanders' number one rider, not a stablehand either.

I loved riding for Bill Sanders. If the horse got beaten, he'd say, 'Don't worry about it. We'll make another horse.' He was such a lovely guy and it was no fluke that he and his son, Graeme, won so many premierships. In fact, I quite expected Jock to let me finish my apprenticeship with Bill Sanders, but it didn't happen. I know they talked about it.

Back in the early 1970s I had a big day riding at Tauherenikau and the next day I had to ride for Bill at Wanganui. It was a long drive and the next morning I got up at 4 am and rode eight or nine horses in work. I went back to the motel to have a couple of hours' sleep and slept in. I was to ride Baby Bear for Bill in the first race, but I arrived on track as she was going past the winning post in first place. The first comment I got was, 'Harry, were you hibernating?'

I was devastated and I was fined $50 for being negligent, or whatever they called it. If Bill Sanders had come along half an hour earlier he'd have ripped the shit out of them and I'd probably never have been charged. I make a habit of not letting people down. But I lost that winning ride and now Baby Bear is in my mind forever.

I rode a lot of top horses for Bill Sanders. I went over to Melbourne to ride Shaitan for him, but Shaitan got run into the fence in the Hotham Handicap, was sore afterwards, and had to be scratched from the Melbourne Cup. Mayo Mellay and March Legend were two other top horses of his. I won the Wanganui and Waikato Guineas on Mayo Mellay and I think he ended up with a hairline fracture of the pelvis. March Legend was racing in the same year as Balmerino and he was always running second to him. The only chance I had of beating him was in the Wellington Guineas, but he shied at a bit of paper on the track and Balmerino got up and beat us by a nose. He should have won that day. Later on they found out he had bone chips in both knees. When Bill finished with him he was trained by the owner, Don Nash, and he came back and won the Lion Brown Sprint at Te Rapa.

Another of the Sanders' horses I'll always remember riding is Special Son. He used to get back last and had a brilliant burst. He was owned by a lovely lady, Claudia Ellis, and she named it after her son, John, who was 14 when he died. I won a race at Wanganui on Special Son and that meant a lot to me.

A few months later I went over to Melbourne with Graeme Sanders, who took over Quick Answer for the stable. Quick Answer ran second to Bellota in the Coongy Handicap. On that trip we were staying at the Newmarket Hotel in Flemington and next door was a car-sales yard. We got to know the man there, John Whittle, and Graeme bought a dunger of a car from him, a rent-a-bomb. The next morning we hopped into the car, turned on the ignition and — nothing. So we went to Plan B. We were on a bit of a hill so we decided to get out and push. We had three goes without any luck so we got a taxi to the track.

After we finished trackwork we had breakfast and waited for John to open up. Then we confronted him. 'You bloody Aussie, you tried to put one over us. You sold us a dud car.' He went around the front, lifted the bonnet and there was no battery. Someone had flogged it overnight. 'You dumb Kiwis, didn't you check?' he replied, laughing away. John befriended us and a lot of the Kiwi racing people, and we'd often play cards. That story has been told quite a few times.

When I started riding for Bill Sanders, there was a guy named 'Big Paul' Harris — no relation to me — who was his foreman. Big Paul was huge, about six foot six or seven and he was a gentle giant who lived for his racing. He died when he was only 32, but he packed a lot into his life. He was a great friend and we had a lot of fun times together. He looked after me and most of the jockeys. He used to run around and get my rides, and when he'd ring up for me to ride one of the Sanders horses I knew it could win. He would have been a great manager these days.

I remember one night Chris McNab, Big Paul and I were at the pie cart and we were pissed to the eyeballs. As we left the pie cart we pushed open the mesh door. Paul and I exited, then as McNab did so he let the door go and it hit a guy behind him in the head. He went to grab Chris when Big Paul grabbed him, smacked him straight in the nose and said, 'That's the way the door swings bro.' And in the pub if we got harassed Big Paul would go over and sort it out. When he died it left a big hole in our lives.

Over the years the Sanders' stable had quite a few apprentices. One of them was Clifford Brierley, who rode a lot of winners, but you could say he wasn't terribly intellectual. Graeme Sanders tells the story that one morning Clifford was at the table with the newspaper and Graeme asked what he was reading. Clifford replied, 'I'm reading the fields.' So Graeme asked him to read them out to him and he was going on about the weights, stumbling through the names. Then he said to Graeme, 'This field is pretty good. Look at the horses in it. They're all good ones.' Turns out he was reading out the Free Handicaps, which are the ratings put out at the end of the each season weighting all the best horses in order. Everybody got a good laugh over that, but Clifford took it on the chin. Like I said, throw him on a horse and he knew how to ride winners, but he was never going to be a rocket scientist.

Another funny time I had at the Sanders' stable was with Tommy Fallon, who was working for Bill. There was a little Maori kid who had just started off working at the stables. It was about 5 am and Bill had a black horse called Tom's Mate. He was paddock-trained so Tommy went out to the paddock with the kid to go and grab the horse to take him to the track. It was pitch-black and Tommy went in one direction and the kid in the other. Tommy yelled out to the horse, 'Where are you, you black bastard?' and the little apprentice yelled back, 'I'm over here Tom.' That story got a lot of mileage. Bloody hilarious.

I loved my time riding for Bill and Graeme Sanders and have ridden for Graeme since then, too. I won the 1980 Wellington Derby at Trentham on Lovelace Watkins for Graeme. Those first few seasons out of my apprenticeship was a time I was enjoying life and its experiences and virtually taking each day as it came. But in the end I was looking for a change. That opportunity came when I got a contract to ride for Ivan Allan in Singapore–Malaysia.

8

Singapore awakening

'Jesus Christ, you look like a gangster, not a jockey.' That was the first reaction I got when I stepped off the plane in Singapore to be greeted by Ivan Allan's right-hand man, Jimmy Mulchand. Gangster. That was a word I heard a lot of as time passed during my three-season stay riding for Ivan Allan. But this was the only time it was directed at me.

I'd stepped off the plane dressed in my 1970s gear. I had six-inch platform heels, flared jeans, jean jacket and long hair. I thought I was cool, but Jimmy just thought I looked like a gangster. We went into the immigration section to get the green card and I looked at a poster on the wall which read: 'People with long hair will be served last.' You were classed as a hippy. Monday morning, Jimmy took me into his department store and I ended up with six pairs of sports trousers and about 10 silk shirts, and he said, 'Now you look like a jockey.'

I shortened my hair a bit. I'd had trouble with my long hair in New Zealand beforehand. It was down to shoulder length and Phil Reid, the stipendiary steward down our way, told me I had to get it cut. Jockeys had to be cleanly shaven, but a lot of jockeys refused to get it cut. Jock asked how long it could be and he was told one inch above the collar. Jock replied, 'Well, how would Michael Jackson go with his afro?' I copped a bit of flak over it when I started riding in Aussie, too. But it was the fashion at the time and a lot of jockeys had long hair.

Anyway, Jimmy Mulchand had me dressed up and looking the part.

He was one of Ivan Allan's owners and he ended up being like a father to me over there. He used to look after me as well as Lester Piggott, picking him up and running him around, taking him here and there, and telling Lester and me the dos and don'ts. Lester was a champion jockey, a legend, and he was used to being looked after, but it was different for me. I'd have been lost without Jimmy.

I'd heard a lot about Ivan Allan before I arrived. I knew he was the kingpin, and he virtually ran racing in Singapore. He was the top trainer and to ride for him was a big break for me. It was a real eye-opener and I had to learn quickly.

When I got up there, suddenly the racing scene was so big. To get into Singapore you practically had to be at or near the top of the premiership in your country. I was riding against the likes of Lester Piggott, George Podmore and Ron Hutchinson — all top international riders. It was interesting, especially with the English riders coming over to ride in their off-season. There was a real international flavour and I learnt plenty.

One of the first things Ivan Allan got me to do was to ride shorter. As young apprentices we used to put the stirrup leathers up a couple of holes to ride a bit shorter when the boss wasn't looking, but he wasn't happy and we'd have to put them down again. But when I got to Singapore Ivan insisted that I ride short. He told me their horses didn't like being bashed with the whip. He explained how the horses imported from England and Ireland were thinner skinned and couldn't take the whip like Australian and New Zealand horses. I was to ride short and just tap them every third or fourth stride.

When I came back to New Zealand many of the trainers thought it was a gimmick, but it had become natural for me. If I put my links down even a little bit it doesn't feel comfortable. It's just the way I ride and it suits me. I prefer to push forward and use my balance, and it is important to find the balance that suits you and the horse. That's something Jock drummed into me as a kid. To make me understand the meaning of balance he said it was just the same as carrying a sack of spuds. If you let it slip down your back it's hard work. Keep it up by your shoulders and it's easy.

Every time I rode for Ivan Allan if he didn't go to the races he'd always write out instructions on how to ride a horse. They'd be presented to the stewards, so if I didn't ride them the way he wanted I was in trouble. In Singapore, Ivan could do virtually whatever he liked because movie tycoon Runme Shaw was the virtual head as chairman of Bukit Timah Turf Club.

One of the big things in Singapore and Malaysia was jockeys having their punters, usually owners who would cover you on tickets on the horses you were riding. They'd also put it to you as to whether you wanted to punt on other horses or not. In contrast, in New Zealand, you can bet on your own mount if the owner gives you permission, but it's illegal to bet against your mount. Over there at that time everybody just knew that if you were a jockey and you had friends around you, you were usually tipping to them and they were punting for you. An owner would put, say, 100 tickets on the horse you were riding for him, and who was to say you were going to put more money on it or get someone else to put more money on? It got scary in the sense of who some jockeys dealt with.

In Singapore–Malaysia they trained them to win and then sometimes decided not to win. They'd just say: 'Cannot win. Owners don't want to try.' It sometimes got to the stage where a jockey got into the birdcage, hopped on the horse thinking he could win and then was told he couldn't. In one instance two senior riders and an apprentice were all riding different horses for Ivan Allan. When one of the senior riders hopped on his horse Ivan said to him, 'You're not trying.' Then just before he went out of the birdcage he came back and said, 'Change of mind. You're on. Tell the other two to get lost.' He got around to the barrier and told them, and apparently they both went white as ghosts, because in the meantime they'd signalled to their own punters what has supposed to happen. But they did get lost.

Ivan Allan always said, 'The day my jockey tells me my horse can win I'll give up training. I know all the jockeys' signals.' And there were all sorts of signals. The rider might go around to the start and if he was not trying he might trot around near the inside fence. If he was on — trying — he trotted around by the outside fence; and if he trotted up the middle he was an each-way bet. Another signal was leaving the chin strap tied up or undone when the rider jumped on. It was a signal of trying or not trying and the same went with leaving the feet out of the irons in the birdcage. The rider walked once around the birdcage with his feet out, meaning he was on or off.

It reached absurd lengths when the owners would say, 'If I put a white towel up or a red towel and you're around the barrier you look up to the hotel room and you'll know whether to try or not.' Apparently they used to use umbrellas in the same way, too.

Ivan didn't know my signals, or at least I thought he didn't. My signal was to my punters letting them know my best rides. When Ivan put me on a horse he thought would win he'd cover me with tickets and I'd also get my punters to back me. In the end he told me that he knew my signals, but it was mostly scare tactics.

I had a code for Jimmy Mulchand to let him know my best rides. He would ring me and my code was GOD SAVE HIM. Ten letters, 10 races. If I wanted race one, number three I would say G D (one, three). And after a time we would reverse it. Eventually, it got to the stage where you were in your hotel room on race morning talking on the phone and next minute you heard a click. It would be punters outside on the lines clicking in. They'd climb telephone poles to click into your line. They'd do what they could to get tips.

I had a couple of punters who would put 100 or 200 tickets on — one ticket was a $5 unit, so that would be $500 or $1000 on a horse for me. One weekend I rode five winners in a day. I followed that weekend up soon after with another four winners and I got about AUS$40,000 from the two weekends. That was in 1979 and it was huge money back then. It's still not a bad couple of weekends' work now.

But with tipping there is always the element of danger. I've already told you about the terrifying car chase I had with Keith Watson, but that was only one of many gangster-type incidents which were part and parcel of racing in Singapore and Malaysia at the time — angry punters wanting revenge.

9

Bashings and threats

Digging your own grave, kneecapping. Sounds like *Underbelly* or a Mafia movie, but that's what was happening during my first stint in Singapore–Malaysia. It wasn't just pretend. They wanted to get the message through and they meant business.

A lot of jockeys copped threats. I don't know what they were promising punters, but if it didn't come through they were in trouble. There was one local chap we nicknamed Radar, who didn't ride many winners, perhaps one or two a year. He came home on a couple of horses that were outsiders and he must've said beforehand, 'Horse no good, cannot win.' They took him down to the cemetery and told him to dig his own grave.

He told me the story and I said, 'What's the go? You're still here,' and he replied, 'Well, I dropped the spade and just said I'm a humble man and so they just dusted me up.' They gave him a hiding. It was more a fright, a don't-mess-with-us sort of thing.

And then there was another local jockey, who was going to the track and he got hit around the shins with an iron bar while he was in the carpark. It split his jodhpurs and when he walked into the jockeys' cafeteria you could see the meat hanging out. It was dealings he had had, but they hadn't gone right. It was scary, but he got off lightly.

They were tipping or not tipping and when things went wrong they got targeted. I had my scare when I was with Keith Watson and we'd been chased. Luckily, that was the only time it happened. I kept my nose clean. I did get some threatening calls, but I was always told not to worry about the crank ones; it's the ones that come and see you. I am a great believer that if you don't mix with shit you never get shit. I was safe in that way, but a lot of the jocks came out and asked for big tickets and played people out. Next minute they were back on the plane and out of there. I was going day to day, just doing my job. Most average jockeys don't get past three months or six months, but I ended up staying three years.

There were so many things happening over there. I remember Tunku Khalid, the starter in Malaysia. It was a 2000-metre race at Kuala Lumpur. We were all lined up and off we went and Tunku turned around and there was the favourite, a grey horse with red colours, standing behind the barriers. He screamed, 'What are you doing here?' He thought it was the clerk of the course's horse and had forgotten to load it up. They ended up fining him.

Another time one of the overseas jockeys on the hot favourite drew next to me and he had one foot in the iron and one on the side of the stalls, and just as they jumped he screamed out. There was no way they were to beat this horse and it jumped out with no jockey on. They fined Tunku Khalid again. I felt sorry for him because it wasn't his fault. It was the jockey who actually didn't want to win, so he let the horse out loose.

At one meeting in Penang, the staff working around the barrier were pushing for better pay so they went on a go-slow. It would take them half an hour to shift the barriers from the 1200 to the 1400, and they were doing their go-slow all day. By the last race the club decided to tape start it. When the starter took the tape away I was facing the wrong way. I ended up being beaten a short margin by a horse who wasn't supposed to win.

Brian Dean, another Aussie jockey who is now training in Singapore, was riding in Malaysia at the time. He was in the last race and was around at the barrier as I was leaving the course. On the way out to the jockeys' carpark you had to go past the 1400 metres start. As we were driving past I beeped the horn and Brian on his horse waved to us. It was purely saying goodbye to a mate. Lo and behold, they held him back after the race for about an hour and accused him of tipping out and signalling. He was totally innocent.

Bruce Compton also went over from New Zealand to ride on the Singapore–Malaysia circuit when I was there. You'd do two weeks in Ipoh, two weeks in Kuala Lumpur then two weeks in Singapore at Bukit Timah and just keep moving around. The cleaner racing was in Singapore.

Bruce rode for Teh Choon Beng, who was the big gun in Malaysia, and Teh, being a rival of Ivan Allan, didn't like his jockeys mixing. I thought that was a bit on the head so Bruce and I made a pact that we'd talk to each other's boss. I told Ivan that Bruce was a good mate of mine and we'd been friends for a long time. In the end they accepted it and I was the first Ivan Allan jockey to be invited to Teh Choon Beng's house. They were scared that two jockeys from different stables being good friends would be working in together. Ever since then I've been good friends with Teh and I've ridden quite a lot for him at different times. I didn't ride for him when I was with Ivan, but when I broke off on my own in the last season over there I got rides from him.

Bruce and I would get together in Singapore after riding trackwork and we'd find a trishaw, a bike-type rickshaw that you ride instead of pull. They had all the stereos underneath for music, and Bruce and I would visit our owners, such as Jimmy Mulchand. You could drink alcohol in the shops and by the end of the day we were paralytic, falling out of the bikes. Once when Big Paul Harris and Ron Gurney were over from New Zealand we went to Bugis Street and paid the trishaw riders to sit in the back while we cycled. We'd be full of alcohol and we'd race each other back to the hotel. It was all good fun.

At times all the owners and jockeys would get together and book out a motel room. Some of the owners would play mah-jong; others would play cards all day. I remember playing stud poker and at the end of the day I owed S$15,000, which was probably about NZ$7500. I'm not really a gambler and that was big money for me. Ivan paid my debt and it took me a month to pay him back. Ivan played, too. It was like a knockout tournament and you'd get down to the last two players. I still remember three kings got up and beat me when I had been holding three tens. It cured me of playing cards for money. If I play for money now, it's only one or two dollars.

The whole scene was a real eye-opener. They'd order lunch, along with some girls. It was amazing coming from a place like Woodville or Palmy and being thrown right into the deep end with the big boys. Once I jumped into a taxi and the driver asked: 'Do you want girl?' And off he went halfway up Orchard Road, another couple of detours around the back of a sleazy hotel and there was a big white van. He opened the back door and there were 12 Asian girls. 'What one you want? Take your pick,' he said. I couldn't believe it. The taxi driver would get a commission.

When I was in Malaysia, Francis Daniel, the public relations officer for the Regent Hotel, used to look after me. His boss owned a lot of horses. Francis was like my minder, a great guy to be with. In saying that, over there at that time if you were seen with a jockey you had mana, like pop-star status. Francis was an Indian, as black as the ace of spades, and he could speak seven different dialects. He was brought up by a Chinaman. We'd be on a plane flying from one meeting to another and all the Chinese would be talking about me, and Francis would be interpreting every word they were saying. They thought an Indian couldn't speak Chinese. Francis had a police siren in his car and we'd be going to lunch somewhere and he'd put the siren on and everyone in front would pull over. He never got picked up by the police; he had too many connections.

We used to race every Saturday and Sunday so on the other days after riding trackwork there wasn't much to do but go out to lunch or for a drink somewhere. I remember going to the track one morning after I'd had a big night on the piss. Ivan could probably smell me. He hated smoking and drinking. Dead set against it. He said, 'Hop on this horse. It's one of our hardest pullers. Go half-pace around the course proper on it.' I was worried because I knew how hard it pulled and especially in the heat it was going to be tough, but I wasn't going to be beaten. I half-paced it around and I hopped off and my heart nearly jumped out of my body. I had a sweat jacket on and I broke out in a cold sweat and I said, 'Ivan, you win. I've got to go home. I'm sick as.' It taught me a lesson and he knew he'd won.

When we were riding in Malaysia the owners would take several of us jockeys out for lunch and dinners. Once in Penang we were mucking around and playing a bit of soccer and we all went back to a pub, which had a German boot, a bit like a yard glass and as big as my leg. There was an honours board up and so I, being a Kiwi and a beer drinker, had a go at it. I broke the record. All the local jocks were betting among each other on whether I'd do it. One of them then came up and said to me, 'In five minutes you not spew, I win $3000.' I held on until five minutes was up and 30 seconds later I was out in the toilet throwing up.

I did have one very scary moment during one of the party sessions with the other jockeys. It was Christmas and everybody was having a good time. There was an Irish or English jockey and a couple of times he'd say something and I'd say, 'That's not right.' He just snapped and smashed a glass and went straight for my throat. It never pierced the skin, but it was scary how someone can turn nasty so quickly. His wife made him apologise and he did the next day. That kind of thing had never happened around me before.

10

Singapore premiership and Ivan Allan

It might sound like all fun and crazy times in Singapore, but I was up there to do my job and Ivan Allan knew what was needed. Ivan said, 'Go in quick,' and he put me on the right horses from the start. I was riding exclusively for him for the first six months, then he let me ride outside a bit. He was a good judge of a horse and he was quite ruthless. It was all about him, and he knew if he got me going well he'd win plenty.

My first season up there I rode 36 winners. It mightn't sound a high number, but it was a good start, especially riding against some of the best jockeys in the world, and the race meetings were only two days a week. It was just a matter of getting a nice number of winners up.

Once established, things really picked up and I finished the second season with 42 winners. That put me second equal with George Podmore behind Ron Hutchinson on the Jockeys' Premiership. That year I got on to a really good horse, Star Prince. I think Larry Olsen had been riding him, but he got put out and I picked up the ride. He was a bit like Glengowan, but a sprinting version, a big chestnut horse, with semi-lopped ears and strong. I was lucky and privileged to get on him. He was so good he won five in a row I think. He was taken back to England to race and stopped off in America and was sold.

Garnet Bougoure officially trained Star Prince for Malcolm 'Butch' Thwaites. Butch was an amateur rider who had been put out for life at the time. He couldn't officially train or anything so he had his horses under Garnet's name and spread around with some other trainers. I won the Sultan's Gold Vase, one of the big sprints, on Star Prince, and the previous start I won the Gold Vase Trial by six lengths in course record time. Garnet had won the Sultan's Gold Vase twice when he was a jockey.

Garnet had been up there for years and he had an interesting background. He'd been a good jockey in Australia and rode in India, France and Singapore–Malaysia, then in the 1950s he went to Europe and linked up with top trainers Vincent O'Brien and Paddy Prendergast. He became one of the leading jockeys in England and Ireland. He was the only Australian to win the Jockeys' Premiership in Ireland.

He won a lot of big races over there, including the Irish Derby a couple of times as well as the English Oaks. He continued riding for a while when he came back to Singapore, then started up training. He was a lovely old guy and a good trainer, too. He finally went back to Australia after he gave up training in 1995, and he was 85 when he died there in 2008.

A couple of months after my wins on Star Prince I won the Singapore Gold Cup on Saas Fee for Ivan Allan. Margaret Bull had trained the horse in New Zealand and when we won the Gold Cup he was just too classy for the field. He kicked away and won by four lengths. The following year Lester Piggott won the Singapore Derby on him. Another good one I got on was Butterfly Boy. I won the Lion City Cup on him, and at good odds, too. He was an Irish-bred horse and a real favourite over there. When I went back up to Penang 30-odd years later three or four people yelled out 'Butterfly Boy' when they saw me. They still remember him. He was a really good sprinter.

In the last of my three seasons in Singapore–Malaysia I won the Jockeys' Premiership with 55 wins. It was special for me because not many New Zealand jockeys can say they've won a premiership in two different countries. I was neck and neck with George Podmore for a long time and in the end I beat him by five. George could ride a lot lighter than me so obviously he got a lot more rides. Nevertheless, I did five winners in one day at Ipoh in October and four the next weekend. That got me thinking that I did have a good chance of winning the premiership.

I had broken off with Ivan after two and a half years and gone freelance. Ivan was using a few other jockeys and I was going for the premiership and thought it might just open up the way to getting more rides. The press played on it and said that now I was freelancing, I was riding more winners. They were intimating that Ivan Allan had controlled me. That day I rode five winners at Ipoh, two of them were for Garnet Bougoure and the others for three different trainers.

Though I wasn't riding full-time for Ivan, he was still giving me some rides. He'd given me a big opportunity in Singapore–Malaysia and I was grateful to him for that. But Ivan wasn't everyone's cup of tea. He was arrogant and looked after number one. He was either a great friend or a terrible enemy. And he was known for being quite unforgiving and entirely ruthless with officials.

About three years after I'd left Singapore and was back riding in New Zealand Ivan was shot, but he cheated death. It was March 1983. A guy on a motorbike shot him in the back five or six times. Typical Ivan, he bounced back to again be the number one trainer in Singapore then he shifted to Hong Kong and was a top trainer there, too. I think he still had a bullet left in him that they couldn't remove.

Ivan was 68 when he died in November 2009 from diabetes and kidney problems. An obituary written by Murray Bell in the *South China Morning Post* summed Ivan up perfectly. He described him as a man of 'sky-high intellect who lived the life of a jet-setting, racehorse-owning playboy' and as 'a consummate genius when it came to horses . . . a genius who managed to bamboozle racing officialdom for years, making millions of dollars along the way'. As Bell wrote: 'His ability to judge the fitness and readiness of a racehorse was matched by an extraordinary capacity to execute clever betting stings. In his early days on the Malayan Racing Association circuit he described the business as being "so easy, it was like picking money up off the ground".'

The story goes that when Ivan took Fairy King Prawn to win the Yasuda Kinen in Japan in 2000 he left a friend in charge of the betting and the winnings of nearly US$1 million were taken off the course all packed in sushi boxes.

Lester Piggott won the English St Leger for Ivan, and Ivan raced horses in New Zealand from Alan Jones' stable. He had Jolly Jake, who won the 1984 New Zealand Derby, and My Tristram's Belle, the filly on which I won the 1986 VRC Oaks. I also went over and rode Teddy Doon in the Western Australian Derby in Perth for Ivan. Graeme Rogerson was training him at the time.

Alan Jones and Ivan Allan must have got plenty of money from the Oaks win. Tristram's Belle had been ridden by Alan's New Zealand stable riders, Linda Ballantyne and Cathy Treymane, but Alan had purposely not taken them to Melbourne as he wanted to avoid media attention. Female riders were common in New Zealand, but they would certainly have attracted publicity in Melbourne. Alan kept Tristram's Belle out of the spotlight by waiting until the night before the Oaks to offer the ride to Brent Thomson, but he already had another filly, and that's when I got the call. I was over in Melbourne to ride Kiwi in the Cup and I was happy to pick up the ride in the Oaks . . . and even happier when I got one over Brent.

Ivan had trained as a lawyer, but he loved his racing more, especially the punt. I read that when he recovered consciousness after being shot the first thing he asked was, 'Which horses are we backing this afternoon?'

Bell's obituary of Ivan also summed up his private life, which had become exposed to the world mainly because of a bitter dispute with

Canadian actress Glory Clibbery. She was resisting eviction from a £1.7 million property owned by him.

> On the basis of a 15-year relationship, Clibbery claimed she was already married to Allan. Allan claimed she was only a prostitute and the court ultimately ruled in his favour. The trainer told the British High Court (Family Division) that 'the truth of the matter is that the applicant has been one of my mistresses. I have, and have always had, several mistresses in different parts of the world'.

There's one thing I can never forgive Ivan for — what he did to Jimmy Mulchand. Jimmy, who owned a department store with two brothers, was told by Ivan that certain horses were going to win but a lot of these horses weren't winning. Jimmy would ask me, 'What happened to this horse?' I would say, 'Well, it mustn't have been trying; it wasn't on.' This was what Ivan was doing to Jimmy and they were meant to be good mates. Jimmy must have been borrowing money off the company. I told Jimmy I would let him know my best rides and things went well for the rest of the time I was there.

But a couple of months later when I came home I got a phone call from Jimmy asking me to come back. I could just tell by the tone in his voice that things weren't right. Ours was like a father–son relationship. He had looked after me so well in Singapore and would have done anything for me. I didn't think too much about the call at the time, even though in the back of my mind I wondered if he might be in trouble with his betting. It wasn't long after that I got a phone call from my brother Dessie saying that Jimmy had hung himself. I couldn't believe it. I didn't think he'd take it to that extreme. You think you know someone and then he does that. He must have felt he'd lost face.

I blame Ivan. He knew Jimmy was gullible and that whatever he told him he'd believe. I tried to get that through to Jimmy. 'Ivan's not sincere with you.' I thought Ivan was meant to be a friend . . . but to do that to a friend? It's something you'd only do to your worst enemy. It was all because of Ivan Allan's greed. He tipped them out to Jimmy, and Ivan would then back another horse to get good odds. I can understand why Ivan got shot. There are plenty more people, too, who wanted to shoot him.

11

Singapore friends

Lester Piggott is a legend, one of the best jockeys in the world, and the best I've ever ridden against. He could do things in a race that other jockeys would never dream of doing. During my time in Singapore I got to know him quite well. Like me, he was over there riding for Ivan Allan, and a few times we got together for a night out. Lester has a speech impediment, is partially deaf and very hard to understand. I can be hard to understand at times too, especially when I've had a few drinks! Lester loves his cigars and red wine and we'd be trying to hold a conversation. He was mumbling, I was mumbling, and we couldn't understand each other. But we had a good time just nodding and laughing.

Ivan used to get Lester over in England's off-season. As mentioned, Ivan hated smoking and drinking. When he'd pick Lester up from the airport he'd say, 'You can't smoke in my car.' But when Ivan went over to England, Lester would pick him up and the first thing he'd do was light up a cigar. I haven't had much to do with Lester since those days, but one of the big thrills when I rode my 2000th winner was getting a card from him. I was surprised he even knew about me getting the 2000 and touched that he had gone to the trouble of sending a card. It read:

Dear Noel, Just a short note to congratulate you on your 2000th win, very well done, and also more importantly on your coming wedding.

Lots of Luck. Best Wishes, Lester.

George Podmore was a good mate during my time in Singapore.

It was a great experience riding against guys like him, Lester, Ron Hutchinson, Chris Gwilliam and co. And Larry Olsen was there, too. He was always battling his weight, and I remember one day at the Regent he was in the Turkish bath trying to shed 2 kilos. As he wasn't riding until the last race of the day, he asked me to get him a bottle of champagne, so I did. He took off the weight, got out of the bath as silly as a chook, got to the races, rode the horse at the right weight, but he had to get someone to take the saddle off. He was that weak. He went back to Australia, gave up riding then made a comeback and won the Melbourne Cup on Kensei. He was a top rider.

Greg Hall was another Aussie jockey I got to know well. We had a lot of fun together and we still stay in touch and laugh over the good times we had in Singapore. He was talented, ruthless, a wild card. He was born on the same day as me but different year. We'd get back from the track, have a sleep, then at 11 am we'd meet at a bar with a few others from the racing fraternity and go on from there. When he'd had enough he'd say, 'I can't move. I'm a dog and I'm going to lie down and not move.' And he'd do it. I'd be trying to get him up before we got kicked out. He's a real joker, a really humorous guy.

When we were all riding in Penang, after trackwork we'd fill in the time water-skiing, fishing or just entertaining each other around the hotel we were all staying at. There was a Welsh jockey there, Taffy Thomas. We went out fishing and Taffy and the others were quite mullocked after drinking most of the day. We were coming back to the beach and Taffy decided to jump off and run up the beach. He's about as big as Bill Skelton — three foot nothing — and he jumped off the boat and disappeared. His wife was on the beach and she flew in to the water and pulled him out.

Actually, there's a funny story that concerns Taffy. It appeared in the *World Weekly News* in August 1981 and had me in stitches when I read it. The headline read: 'Child-sized jockeys end up in jail' and the story goes:

> Four tiny jockeys were locked up for two hours because cops thought they were kids joy-riding in a stolen car. Three police cars full of cops pounced on the jockeys as Taffy Thomas was driving his three pals to the races in Essex, England. Taffy was taken to jail along with Alan Bond, Paul Howard and Paul Merrin. There they sat in separate cells and missed races until they convinced the cops they were not children and the car was not stolen.

It still makes me laugh when I read it.

The local riders in Singapore–Malaysia were always praying. If they had a fall on a track they'd go and get the affected part blessed. On race morning they'd be praying for a good day; you would start to get more superstitious yourself. It happened with Bruce Compton. He wasn't travelling that good for a month so they asked him to sit in the bath of seven different flowers. What a surprise when he came out and rode a couple of winners each day straight after it.

I've always been a little superstitious. I believe in the one about black cats running across the road. I was told it is all right if they keep going, but if they change their mind and run back in front of you don't do what you were going to do. Also, I will never walk under a ladder. But after being up there for three years I started thinking like the locals. I went to see a medium and was told I needed some black fish so when I got back to New Zealand I bought nine Black Moor goldfish. Then I started to win some top races. Magic, mate, this must work for me.

One Saturday morning, one of the fish was upside down in the tank, so I headed straight down to the pet shop to get another. It started happening regularly and it was getting to me. Then my daughter had a party one weekend and I came back and all the fish were dead. I never replaced them. I'd had enough. The superstition was driving me mad.

I know a lot of people who are superstitious. Bruce Marsh always says number eight is his lucky number. I won the New Zealand Derby on Hail for him and it was number eight. Ivan Allan was also very superstitious. He used to always wear a light blue suit. It's amazing how it can rub off on you. I've got a lucky charm toy. I was going to the races one day and I could smell something had gone off, like a bit of fruit. Next door to it was this little wee toy that looks a bit like a wombat. I threw the fruit and the toy away, but then I realised it was one of the kids' toys, so got it back and it's been in my riding bag for 30 years. It's in my skull cap and it has been all over the world with me. I always double check that it's still there.

I also believe in the luck from four-leaf clovers. Bert Swney, one of the trainers, gave me one for when I was riding his horse (he probably has a paddock full of it). I put it in my lead bag and though his horse didn't win I ended up winning the Auckland Cup on Bodie. It's been in my bag ever since. When my son Troy was having his first ride I wrote a note and slid it along with a four-leaf clover into his riding bag. And sure enough he came out and won on his first ride, at Ruakaka.

You can say my time in Singapore took my belief in superstitions a bit further, but that and the winners and the money weren't the only things I got out of the trip. I made some really good friends during my three years there. PK Leong and his wife, Rina, were like family to me. I rode with PK and he always looked after me. He actually came out and did a stint with Jock after he finished riding to get a trainer's licence. He'd give you the shirt off his back.

A lot changed for me during that last year in Singapore. I had got married in January 1979 back in New Zealand to my first wife, Darrell, whose father, Sonny Pikimaui, was well-known around Central Districts as one the barrier attendants. I'd been to Perth to ride Teddy Doon in the Derby for Ivan Allan. Rogey — Graeme Rogerson — had won the Manawatu Sires' Produce Stakes with Teddy Doon, then took him over to Perth. At the same time I represented New Zealand in an invitation race there and ran third on Hands Up, came back, got married and we flew back to Singapore in time for the Singapore Cup.

I shouted Mum a trip to Singapore that year. All Mum had done was wash and clean and she never went anywhere. She had an older couple come up with her, too. I booked her into the Hyatt Hotel and I remember telling her that if anyone knocked on the door, not to open it because it would probably be touts — people who would take her on tours and rip her off. A little later in the day John, who managed the hotel and was a friend of mine, rang me to say: 'Noel, we've got a bunch of flowers and fruit for your mother, but she won't answer the door. She's just yelling, "Go away, go away."' I had to ring Mum to tell her it was all right to let him in.

Another day I took her to Bugis Street and she couldn't get over all the transvestites. She reckoned they looked prettier than the girls. Coming from Woodville and Palmy, she hadn't seen anything like it. And after a day's shopping she'd sit in the foyer of the hotel amazed to see all the people from different countries coming and going. It was a real revelation for her.

12

Longburn

January 1980 and I was back in New Zealand. I could have stayed on for another year in Singapore, but I was married and I was ready to come home and settle down. I'd decided I wanted a property and if I couldn't get one I was going to move to Melbourne to ride. Within a week or two a 10-acre property at Longburn on the outskirts of Palmerston North came up. It was ideal, with horse boxes, beautifully set up, but we couldn't take over for nine months, so we put a deposit on it and I still went to Melbourne.

That January was a good month all round. As well as finding the property, in my second week back I won the Wellington Derby on Lovelace Watkins for Graeme Sanders. Lovelace Watkins was owned by Graeme's wife, Gael, and I was down at the Trentham sales when I picked up the ride. Later that evening, after he had won, a South African, Cyril Hurvitz, offered $100,000 for him. It was a gentleman's agreement. Hurvitz didn't realise Lovelace Watkins was a gelding and the law prevented geldings being imported into South Africa. When Hurvitz found out, he stuck by his offer and sent him to Australia instead. The $100,000 was a record price for a gelding sold in New Zealand. Lovelace Watkins went to Colin Hayes. He won the South Australian St Leger and was third in the Adelaide Cup.

I also landed on my feet in Melbourne. I was riding for Colin Hayes, second fiddle to Brent Thomson, who was the stable's number one rider, but that didn't matter. I won eight races including a double one day at Sandown. I also won on Rang Again for Kevin Old, who later came back to New Zealand to train, and on Mysterious Ways for Colin. I rode five city winners and Jack Elliott, one of the big scribes in Melbourne, was giving me a million dollars worth of advertising.

Reading the papers it looked as though I was there to stay, but I was riding about 54 kilos, the same as Roy Higgins and Harry White. They were top riders. I couldn't think of getting any more rides than they were, so when I got offered the chance to ride for Bruce Marsh in Queensland over the winter I went there. That was my first time in Brisbane and it started me off riding at the carnivals in Aussie. I only rode a couple of winners that time, but the next year in Queensland I won the Prime Minister's Cup on Shamrock for Bruce Marsh. I'll always remember that because it was just after Natasha, my first daughter, was born, in April. And a couple of weeks after she'd been born I won the Ellerslie Sires' Produce Stakes, the big two-year-old race in Auckland, on Loughanure for Bill Sanders.

Shamrock was a good horse to me. I won my first ride on him at Trentham and rode him in eight of his 11 wins. My best New Zealand win on Shamrock was in the 1980 Avondale Cup, a Group One race, and I also rode him in his Hawke's Bay Cup win. As well as winning the Prime Minister's Cup, he was runner-up to Avitt in it the following year and he also won the O'Shea Stakes in Brisbane. He was by War Hawk II and they were good horses. Drum was by him, too. Chris McNab won the Auckland Cup on him and I was third in it on Northfleet. Before that he'd beaten me in the Waikato Cup when I finished second on Shamrock. I got to ride Drum three times and won the Harcourt Stakes on him at Trentham.

With the likes of Shamrock, over the years I've had the best of both worlds. I could ride here in New Zealand, get a good horse, go over and do the Aussie carnivals. The Melbourne Cup carnival has to be my favourite, but I do love going to Brisbanc in the winter. I've won big races in Sydney and also had a bit of luck in Adelaide. I won the South Australian Derby on Count Chivas for Don Sellwood. I'd won the VRC St Leger in Melbourne on Count Chivas the start beforehand.

I've also ridden in international invitation series in Australia. I still remember the one in Sydney. I was in a tight finish with Mick Dittman for second and he hit me over the arm twice right in the same spot. The bruise must have come up about four inches by the time I got back to the jockeys' room, and I said to Mick, 'Is this what you call foul riding?' I was just joking with him, but I have never been hit so hard by another jockey since I have been riding.

I've been asked over the years why I haven't settled in Australia. I like going there for the carnivals, but I love my life in New Zealand. I'm happy with the Kiwi lifestyle and it's a good place to bring up the kids. A couple of years after Natasha was born, we had Cushla, then Whitney was born in 1986 and Troy two years later. The day before Whitney was born I won the Lowland Stakes at Masterton for Ray Verner on Tri Belle, which means three girls. How appropriate is that? Whitney made it three girls for the family.

We had a lot of good times when I was living in Longburn. It was just a lifestyle block and we had the usual animals, a few sheep and ponies. We had a little Shetland pony named Atom and all the kids learnt to ride on him. Then we got another one called Muppet. He was hard to catch in the paddock so we used to hop in the old Morris Minor and round him up. He was great to use when we were breaking in weanlings.

Gus Clutterbuck and I got into breaking in horses for a while, but we only did it off and on for friends. We weren't totally committed, because it was too risky while we were still riding. Two of the best ones were for a Tauranga owner, Eric Pinker. We broke them in for Jock to train. He got them going, then the owner wanted them closer to him, so he gave them to Dave O'Sullivan. They turned out to be Eastern

Joy and Silver Tip; both won big races at Ellerslie. Eastern Joy won an Easter Handicap and Silver Tip won a Railway Handicap. They were hard work, though, and dropped us a few times.

Gus and I also had a go at buying weanlings and reselling them as yearlings. We went up to the Waikato sales and bought a weanling out of the Belle family. We paid $4000 and sold it at the Trentham sales for $22,000. Colin Hayes bought him and I think he won four or five races. We were over the moon and thought: *This is easy*. We were all keen and bought a Bellissimo weanling a year later for $16,000 and sold him for $18,000, so we came back down to earth. We didn't try it again.

Those were the days when the National Yearling Sales at Trentham were the big thing and Burnham Lodge at the course was always packed for the sales and races. All the trainers and stable staff and a lot of the jockeys and apprentices used to stay there for the race meetings as well as all the stud staff for the sales. It was a big party scene when everyone got together. I bet that old building could tell some stories. I can remember Lionel Clutterbuck, Gus' brother, coming home pissed one night and breaking into the kitchen for a feed. He set the fire alarm off. There was always so much going on there. You'd have people sneaking in and out of windows. Everyone has got a story about Burnham Lodge.

As well as trying my luck at pinhooking a couple of weanlings, I also bought a broodmare, Lilac, while I was living at Longburn. She was by In The Purple and was distantly related to Glengowan. Jock had trained her and she showed a bit of promise. I bred four foals from her and had two to the races and they both won. The first one was a gelding by Truly Vain, which we named Our Mzuri after a gorilla in the Melbourne Zoo. We'd seen a story about the gorilla and the horse was an ugly monster, too. It was before the Rules of Racing changed to allow jockeys and their wives to race horses. He was owned officially by my wife Darrell, and as she couldn't race him she leased him to Fiona McNab, Chris McNab's wife at the time. Chris has been a good mate of mine since he was an apprentice and he trained Our Mzuri.

Our Mzuri won first up at Woodville and I rode him. It was like winning the Melbourne Cup. My first horse and he's a winner. And being at Woodville, my home town, made it a big occasion. We got an offer of $60,000–$70,000 from Singapore for him after that, but there was some good stake-money around here at the time, and Chris said he would go to open company. So we kept him in cotton wool, but the next start he ran second-last and was not worth ten bob. He had a phobia in the gates and became quite a rogue. In the end we gave him away. I learnt my lesson about offers: when there's good money on the table, take it.

And it was during the 1980s that I got landed with the nickname 'Handbrake Harry'. It was Jimmy Cassidy who started it all off. He was being interviewed on radio by Alan Bright, and it was just before Jimmy shifted down from Hastings to Awapuni and he was travelling down to ride for Noel Eales. Alan commented that Jimmy must have been doing a lot of travelling and it must have been expensive. Jimmy replied, 'When I'm down in Palmy I stay with Handbrake Harry.' Alan quizzed Jimmy further: 'Handbrake? Like a handbrake in a car?' Jimmy said, 'Yeah, Harry always leaves his run so late. When I go past I yell out, "Let the handbrake off, Harry!"' Everyone started calling me Handbrake Harry after that, but it has died down over the years. Most people just refer to me as Harry.

The Handbrake Harry story goes a bit further. Jimmy was talking to someone in the jockeys' room once at Melbourne and used the phrase 'Handbrake Harry'. Leading jockey Harry White came over to him and said, 'You don't even know me. What are you saying about me?' Harry White has always been known as Handbrake Harry in Aussie.

We had a lot of laughs and fun times and I made some really good friends in those days. I got to know Lucky and Gaye Haitana well and they've become lifelong friends. Lucky is like another father to me. He's had pubs all over the place and we'd go and catch up with them most weekends. A group of us jockeys would gather at his pub and we'd have a good time.

The White Horse Inn is the local pub at Longburn, and in those days when there were no TABs in the pubs the bookies operated. They were illegal, but they were all over the place. One day the bookie at the White Horse said to me he was going to Perth and did I have any Aussie currency. He wanted a grand. I'd just come back from Aussie so I took down the thousand Aussie dollars and he had all these notes wrapped up nicely and put them in my pocket. When I took them to

HANDBRAKE HARRY

the bank I realised they were all rust-stained twenty-dollar notes. He'd had them buried in a cake tin in the back yard. I was worried they were going to disintegrate.

Everyone used to bet with the bookie in those days, and even though the pub was supposed to be closed on the Sunday you'd go and knock on the back door and be let in. You'd say you'd be drinking with Father O'Flagon on the Sunday. The pub was jam-packed at times and the next minute the cops would be there and everybody was running and hiding in the rooms. It's funny when you think back on it.

It was good to just go down there and relax without being hassled. You knew where the locals were coming from and there was a lot of bullshit being talked, but you knew what to put up with. And there were plenty of laughs.

I was riding some good horses at the time, too. I'd ridden 54 winners in the 1983–84 season. It wasn't my biggest tally, but that season was when I climbed aboard the first of my three favourite horses, Goldie.

13

Goldie and Jack

Australia had its legendary horse and trainer combinations. The Vo Rogues and Vic Rails, Reckless and Tommy Woodcock . . . Well, for me, there was Goldie and Jack — Kingdom Bay and Jack Taylor. They were inseparable. Jack loved Goldie, or Dog's Breath as he used to call him at times, and so did I.

Goldie was, if I can use the term, a real gentleman. You could probably bring him inside your house. He gave us so much pleasure. Old Jack was a precious guy, a real character. When we were in Aussie with Goldie, Jack loved the Bundaberg Rum and he'd tell the press, 'If Goldie doesn't win today, I'll walk up Mt Egmont barefoot.' He told the media how he trained in Stratford so many feet above sea level and the story came out in the papers about this craggy-faced trainer from New Zealand who trains his horse on a mountain, so many feet above sea level. Old Jack left them thinking that. It made a good story.

Kingdom Bay was a tough horse. Jack gave him 11 starts as a two year old and he was going as well at the end as the beginning. Obviously, the horse just thrived on racing and Jack knew it.

My first ride on Kingdom Bay was a winning one, in the Wakefield Challenge Stakes at Trentham. Bill Skelton started off riding him and got a couple of placings before Tony Williams had a couple of rides and won a race at Te Rapa on him. But after my win I stuck with him whenever I could. We won the big two-year-old race at New Plymouth then ran second to Vin d'Amour in the Manawatu Sires' Produce Stakes. He was the type of horse who could beat a horse by a short margin and break their hearts. He won 13 races and never won by big margins.

He came back as a good three year old. We won the Hawke's Bay and Wellington Guineas then he lined up on the first day of the New Zealand Cup meeting in the open sprint and won that. I still remember that day. Straight after the race he started picking grass in the birdcage while I was taking the saddle off. He was that relaxed.

Four days later he won the 2000 Guineas. That day they had big wraps on Governor's Bay, but he not only beat him, he broke his heart. Governor's Bay was never the same afterwards. And, really, Goldie was lucky to even run in the race. On the Monday morning he had lumps all over his back when I went to work him. I touched him and his knees went to the ground. It was thanks to Noel Eales that he actually got to the races. Noel was a top trainer and he said to Jack that Goldie had an allergy and to give him a shot straight away. Luckily, he missed no work and bounced back to win the 2000 Guineas.

After that we got third in the Bayer Classic, but he didn't have enough weight for me in his next two starts. David Peake rode him and won both. He beat Abit Leica and some other top older horses in the weight-for-age at Te Aroha. I got back on in the New Zealand Derby and he went a top race for seventh. He'd jumped from two 1600-metre races as lead-ups to 2400 in the Derby then went back to 1600 just over three weeks later to win the Wellington Stakes. I remember in the Derby, Peter Tims said to me, 'Harry, I don't think I've got much. Just follow me and I'll give you a good run.' We got to the winning post and Timsy ran off and went over the outside hurdle fence. Back in the jockeys' room I said to Timsy, 'Thanks mate. I was thinking of following you, but I'm pleased I didn't.'

After winning the Wellington Stakes, Jack backed Goldie up a week later against the older horses in the Group I Jarden Mile, now known as the Thorndon Mile. It was on a slow track and he tried his heart out. He ran third, beaten two long heads by Atrapar. Jack gave him a couple more runs then decided to go to Queensland with him; he wanted me to go over and ride him. Back in that era it was common for New Zealand trainers to take Kiwi riders over to Aussie, but it has changed a lot in the last 10 to 20 years. A lot of trainers now use Aussie jocks and it has got to the stage they are bringing Aussie jocks over here to ride. But Jack wouldn't have done that. He was loyal and he knew what I thought of Goldie.

We went over to Brisbane and won the Black Douglas first up, and a few starts later he ran second in the Stradbroke Handicap to Canterbury Belle. She was a top filly who had won the 1000 Guineas earlier in the season. Grant Cooksley was over to ride Canterbury Belle and the night before Cookie and I were down in the sauna sweating our guts out. Cookie had to ride at 49.5 kilos. I thought if anyone can beat us it would probably be Cookie and, lo and behold, that's how it turned out.

Goldie never ran a bad race over there. A lot of horses get homesick, but not him. He never disgraced himself. He had five starts and his worst placing was a sixth in the Queensland Guineas. He ran third in the Ansett Cup, a Group Two race, and when he came home after the Stradbroke he just grew another leg, and it wasn't long before we were off again, to Sydney. He ran second first up in the Marton Metric Mile and a week later we were in Sydney.

I ran second on him to Roman Artist in the George Main Stakes in Sydney — Roman Artist only had 49 kilos and Goldie carried 57 — then next minute Jack decided he was off to the Cox Plate. I thought Jack was going to fly him down but, nah, he had him on the horse float. Jack and I came home just after the George Main and it wasn't until we got back to New Zealand that Jack realised the horse had stopped off on the way from Sydney for a night or two. Jack thought it was just a straight trip there and he didn't know where he stayed until he received the bill for accommodation. That was typical Jack.

Returning to scale on Saas Fee after winning the Singapore Gold Cup.
He began his career with Margaret Bull at Awapuni and became a star
in Singapore.

With Star Prince after winning
the Sultan's Gold Vase. He was
probably the best horse I rode
during my time in Singapore.

Butterfly Boy, one of my top
Singapore rides. They still
remember us over there.

Ivan Allan and me after yet another good win on the way to my premiership win in Singapore.

Standing with the world champion jockey Lester Piggott as we await the call-up to ride during my time in Singapore/Malaysia.

Jimmy Mulchand was like a father to me in Singapore. I can never forgive Ivan Allan for what happened to him.

I'm just finishing off my speech and about to cut my twenty-first birthday cake as Jock and Mum wait patiently.

You can't have a party without Baggy Hillis, the man who named the Wiki Waki Pa.

Above: Pat and Kath Courtney, who were like part of the family to me when I stayed in Melbourne.

Right: Don't know what my expression is all about, but it was always going to be a fun twenty-first with my mate, Big Paul Harris.

Horsepower of a smaller type. Taking the inside running on my Shetland pony with Dessie in the centre and Peter ready to come with the last run.

My sister Karen's first day of riding. She had plenty of support from Dessie, me, Peter and Jock.

7 July 1990 and it's Jock's sixtieth birthday party. Jenny and Karen are in front while standing behind (from left) are Peter, Jock, Mum, Johnny (obscured), Dessie and me. It was the last photo of us all together as Mum died just a few days later.

Sea Link is in full flight as we charge to my 1000th win in New Zealand. It was 27 October 1990 and I went on to ride four winners that day.

Me with a cigar in hand and Gus with the Cup . . . we thought we were the new Robert Sangsters with the yearling we pinhooked at the Trentham sales.

What a day! Returning to scale on Our Mzuri at Woodville on 4 April 1989. I'd bred the horse and we owned him.

Sleeves rolled up and into the business as I urge Horlicks to victory over Bonecrusher in the Group I TVNZ Stakes at Ellerslie in April 1988. I was unbeaten in two rides on the Japan Cup winner.

See, I do ride trackwork. Riding Shamrock in work in Brisbane.

We ran seventh at Caulfield in a lead-up to the Cox Plate then ran into Roman Artist again in the Cox Plate. Rising Prince ended up winning the Cox Plate that year from Roman Artist and we finished seventh. He tried hard, as he always did, but it was just too much for him. Jack gave him another run on the last day of the carnival and he was seventh again on a heavy track in the Group One mile. A month later he had his last race and won the weight-for-age at Te Aroha. Unfortunately I couldn't be on him. I had to ride Kiwi that day at Trentham and David Peake rode him.

Jack O'Brien stood Goldie at his Sovereign Lodge Stud and he went on to be a top sire. He was champion New Zealand sire twice and left some good ones. Snap, his daughter, was the Filly of the Year and won three Group Ones. She won the 1000 Guineas and the New Zealand Oaks. Another good one was Kingston Bay, who won the Chipping Norton and Canterbury Guineas in Sydney. And there was Lady Madonna, who won the Telegraph. It was good to see him leave a lot of winners.

I got to ride quite a few of Goldie's progeny and when I hopped on them the quiet ones were just like him. He was so laid back. And when I got my broodmare, Lilac, I bred one by him. That was Smart Myrtle, and Darrell and I raced her. Murray Baker trained her for us and I won a race on her at Otaki which was a special thrill, especially with her being by Goldie.

Goldie ended up standing at Trelawney Stud and he lived until he was 21. He's buried alongside Foxbridge and Alcimedes, two of Trelawney's great sires. He'll always be special to me. Thanks for the memories Goldie.

14

Poetic Prince and Wheels

We've accused the Aussies of all sorts of rorts, especially since the under-arm bowling incident in cricket. We've got a friendly rivalry, Aussie and New Zealand. We love to beat each other. But there are times when it goes beyond that. Don't get me wrong. I love the Aussies and their sense of humour. I'd adopt one! But I've had my own bad first-hand experience and it still stings.

It happened with Poetic Prince, the best horse I've ridden. It was in the 1987 Caulfield Guineas and we won it fair and square. A protest was put in, alleging that we'd interfered with Marwong and it had cost him the race. There's no way Marwong would have beaten us that day. I couldn't believe it when they changed the result, promoted Marwong to first and relegated us to second. It was so unjust. Geoff Murphy, who trained Marwong, was dying of cancer and to me it was like a sort of sympathy call.

They said to me if I had ridden the horse out and won by four lengths instead of a length there's no way they would have changed it. But Poetic Prince, who raced as Our Poetic Prince in Aussie, had just run a race record, so how fast can a horse go? To lose a Group One race like that stinks. The result should never have changed, and to this day even Aussies keep reminding me of how wrong it was. Poetic Prince won four Group One races and it should have been five. The Caulfield Guineas should have been the first one.

Poetic Prince and Wheels

After Goldie (Kingdom Bay) retired, I was wondering whether I'd find one to replace him. I was riding some good horses at the time, but nothing really special. Then only two years after Goldie along came Poetic Prince. John Wheeler — 'Wheels' — was training in partnership with Ian Adams at the time and he came to me one day and said, 'Harry, this horse is not learning anything going to the front. You need to ride him and get him to relax in behind.' What a pick-up ride for me, and from there on it never looked back. I ended up riding him in 25 of his 36 starts and won 12 on him. He won almost $3.5 million in stakes.

My old mate Earl Harrison was the first jockey to ride Poetic Prince — I bet a lot of people don't know that. It was at Auckland and he ran off but still finished third. David Walsh then won a couple on him and Garry Phillips won one. Wheels then took him to Queensland and Walshy finished sixth on him in the Castlemaine Stakes.

My first ride on Poetic Prince was in a three-year-old race at Foxton and he bolted in. We then went to Te Rapa and beat Weston Lea and Young Indian in the Cambridge Breeders' Stakes. I knew then he was something special. Weston Lea was a very, very good horse. He was all the rage for the New Zealand Derby after he'd won the 2000 Guineas and Avondale Guineas. He was on a winning streak, but he broke a leg in an exhibition gallop at Te Awamutu before the Derby. Laurie Laxon trained him and he still brings his name up when he talks about top horses he's trained. Young Indian was a good horse, too. He went on to win the Bayer Classic.

I won again on Poetic Prince at Waverley then Wheels ran him in an open sprint at New Plymouth. He only had 51 kilos so Garry Phillips rode him and won. It was then off to Aussie and I was back on. It should have been five wins in a row, but for that shocking relegation in the Caulfield Guineas. *Don't get me started on that again.* Not only did he lose the race, but I copped a suspension, so it was a double whammy for me. Poetic Prince went on to the Cox Plate a fortnight later and he had only 48.5 kilos so I was never going to be on him. Garry Phillips rode him and he went a good race for second to Rubiton.

I was back on when he had his next run in the Group One VRC Derby and he ran fourth to Omnicorp. The Aussie media came out and said he wouldn't stay because he didn't win. It was a big call. He'd run against the best three year olds in Australasia and had just missed a place. I knew he could stay and it shoved it right up them when he came out and won the Tancred Stakes a couple of seasons later.

Wheels freshened Poetic Prince after the VRC Derby and before we went back over to Aussie he won the Otaki Weight-For-Age, beating two really good horses, Westminster and Courier Bay. He had a couple of placings on that Brisbane trip and Garry Phillips rode him in the Stradbroke when he ran fifth. That was around the time my son Troy was born, so I was back here in New Zealand. It was the last time anyone else rode him.

Poetic Prince came back better than ever as a four year old and should have been unbeaten right through to the Cox Plate. First up I won the Foxbridge Plate at Te Rapa on him. That day when he hit the front I thought he'd win by five lengths. He just went whoosh and I was sure we were going to blow them away, but then he thought he'd done enough and pricked his ears. It was the same as when we were relegated in the Caulfield Guineas.

Wheels then took him to Hastings and we easily won the Byerley Thoroughbred Stakes, now known as the Mudgway Partsworld Stakes. It was then off to Aussie and he won the Feehan Stakes in record time. That was three wins in a row and he should have won the next one, the Caulfield Stakes, too. He got beaten by Sky Chase and I blamed Wheels that day. He wanted me to go to the front on him, though I thought it was an odd instruction. I did and I got taken on by Wayne Treloar on Imposera, who dropped right out. Poetic Prince was a sitting duck. If he hadn't gone to the front he'd have won. I'm sure of it.

But I got payback in the Cox Plate. Imposera came out a week after the Caulfield Stakes and won the Caulfield Cup at 50 to 1, then backed up in the Cox Plate. We trailed her the whole way in the Cox Plate. She'd got me beaten in the Caulfield Stakes but won me the Cox Plate. She just moved at the right time for me and I got a beautiful run through. There was no way Poetic Prince was going to be beaten in the Cox Plate that year. He beat Horlicks and Bonecrusher and everyone knows how good they were. Both champions, but they weren't up to beating him that day. It was a great day of us Kiwis.

The big story on the morning of the Cox Plate was the scratching of Vo Rogue. Vic Rail, his trainer, was adamant he wouldn't be able to show his best on the track, which was rain-affected. Even after it had been upgraded from dead to good after race three he still told the media he was glad he scratched Vo Rogue. Even if he'd started that day he wouldn't have beaten Poetic Prince. Wheels had him at the top of his game. Poetic Prince had met Vo Rogue a couple of times beforehand. The first time was in the previous Cox Plate when Poetic Prince was second and Vo Rogue fourth. The other time was in the Feehan Stakes when we won and Vo Rogue finished third.

We clashed again with Vo Rogue again the following week in the Mackinnon Stakes and he got one back on us. He was second to Empire Rose, who went on to win the Melbourne Cup in her next start, and Poetic Prince was fourth. We ran into him again once more and he levelled the score. That was in the Australian Cup when he won from Super Impose and we were third. So the score ended up two all. He couldn't beat Poetic Prince at Moonee Valley, but Poetic Prince couldn't beat him at Flemington. He was a great horse and he just loved to freewheel out in front. When they talk of front-runners in Aussie he always gets a mention. In the Australian Cup, it was a top field and every horse was under pressure as he poured it on and just kept going.

That four-year-old season was a huge one for Poetic Prince. Before he ran in the Australian Cup he'd come back to New Zealand for three runs. He ran second in a sprint at Ellerslie behind Courier Bay, then we turned the tables on Courier Bay in the Lion Brown Sprint at Te Rapa. He just killed them that day. Then he ran in the Air New Zealand Stakes at Ellerslie and finished third to The Gentry and Maurine. He just couldn't win one at Ellerslie; he had four attempts and picked up three placings. It's a course that doesn't suit some horses and he was one of them. There was also the talk he was only good on left-handed tracks because in 10 runs he hadn't been able to win one clockwise. But that changed when he went to Sydney after the Air New Zealand Stakes. He blew that theory apart when he won the Tancred Stakes and Queen Elizabeth Stakes double.

That Tancred win was a great result and there were some fun times leading up to it. The local trainers, Kerry and Chris Jordan, and others, all met at the Park Royal for drinks at five o'clock after work. We had a good session then decided to go nightclubbing. We got to the nightclub and the bouncer wouldn't let us in, or more probably wouldn't let *me* in — I'd had a few. This guy said, 'Nah, mate, you can't come in here,' and I said, 'Fuck you, mate, when we win the big one, the Tancred, on Saturday, I'll buy this place and you'll be the first prick to lose his job.' I was still arguing with him as he went to hop into the lift. I had my finger poking out as the door closed and nearly took it off. Wheels was chuckling away: 'You told him, Harry.' We did win the Tancred, but I didn't go back there.

There was a lot of interest in the Tancred that year because of the English horses that were there. We had to gallop by 8 am and Wheels had jacked it up with one of the English trainers to work with his horse, the one Brent Thomson was riding. We'd had a big night out and I was riding Poetic Prince. Wheels was walking next to me and he said, 'Do you think we'll make it in time?' It was right on 8 am, but we went straight out and galloped him anyway. Afterwards I saw Brent and asked how his horse went. He said, 'We galloped phenomenal, mate,' and I said, 'Brent you couldn't have galloped that good because you've got a lot of crap on your face.'

Doc Chapman, one of the top trainers, had thought he'd fix these Kiwis. He got a letterhead from the Sydney Turf Club and wrote up a letter saying the trainer and the jockey didn't adhere to the rules and had galloped the horse when the track was closed and we would both be sent home. It looked really official, but Wheels was on to it and he put something funny up on the blackboard at the track in reply to the letter. We had the last laugh because we won the Tancred.

Doc Chapman probably came across as an arrogant prick to some people, but once you got to know him he was all right. He had a beautiful sense of humour. We used to go out for lunches in town, seafood, mud crabs and prawns. You could bet on those crabs. We used to buy betting vouchers and the proceeds were all for charity. Wayne Revell was strapping Poetic Prince at the time and his crab won. You got to keep the crab, so outside where we were drinking they had braziers and we threw the crab in. It must've been there for a few minutes when Wayne reached in to grab the crab and it nipped the end of his finger, drawing blood. He was jumping around and we were all falling about with laughter. Revenge.

The Tancred was worth a million American dollars that year and it was a wet track. Top Class, the English horse, was in front and when we made our run I caught the English riding style of his rider Walter Swinburn out the corner of my eye. I thought, *I've got you beaten*, then Top Class tried to come back at us, but Poetic Prince was just too good for him. It was a feather in our caps that day, beating the English horses.

It was a huge payday, too, because as well as the usual 5 percent riding a jockey gets from the stake-money, the owners of Poetic Prince gave me an extra 5 percent from both the Cox Plate and the Tancred. In New Zealand currency the two races worked out to be worth about $1.6 million each with the total winner's prize-money over $2.1 million. It worked out at just over $50,000 in each sling. Those two were the biggest slings I've received.

After the Tancred Stakes, Wheels backed Poetic Prince up nine days later in the Queen Elizabeth Stakes, another Group One, at Randwick. He was up against Beau Zam, and Bart Cummings came out in the papers and said Beau Zam had always beaten Poetic Prince and we wouldn't get near him. But doing is proving and that day Poetic Prince made Beau Zam look second rate. He was just cruising on the turn and when I let him go he won in a canter from Dandy Andy. Beau Zam was a battling third, about six lengths from us. Poetic Prince was such a pleasure to ride. A horse like him comes along just once in a blue moon and I've had only one blue moon in my lifetime.

Poetic Prince had been sold by his New Plymouth owners, Warren Bolton and Gary Pratt, to Stockwell Stud, but he came back to New Zealand and had a farewell at Otaki in the weight-for-age race, then raced at the Queensland Winter carnival before the stud took him over. That was a special day at Otaki. There was a huge crowd, everyone had come to see him win and he didn't let them down. It was great to see the crowd around the birdcage cheering him when he came back. He deserved it.

When you're riding top horses like him, you're waiting for them to go a bad one. You hope they don't run a bad race because they've been so genuine. But when they do you know there's a good reason for it. That happened with Poetic Prince during his last campaign, in Brisbane.

He went over after he won at Otaki and he should have won the Sir Byrne Hart first up. He finished second to Groucho and he was unlucky. But on that trip he showed he had got a bit colty. Around the stables where he was staying in Brisbane there was a mare and he started roaring. He finished down the track in the Rothmans 100,000 and the Fourex Cup and in his last race, the O'Shea Stakes, he again had his mind on other things. The coltiness had got to him and even at the barrier he started roaring. He must have thought: *I don't want to be a racehorse any more.* He was ready for stud. As a sire he left some stakes winners, but nothing even looked a quarter as good as him.

The word champion is used far too often. I don't take a champion lightly. Kingston Town is probably the best horse I've seen. He truly was a champion. I've ridden a lot of great horses, but in my eyes I have ridden only one champion and that's Poetic Prince. He could sprint, stay, wet, dry, you could ride him anywhere. Unfortunately, he was racing when Bonecrusher was still around and he didn't get the accolades he deserved. But he did get officially recognised for his deeds during that 1988–89 season. He was named the New Zealand Champion Sprinter, Champion Weight-For-Age Performer and got the big award, the New Zealand Horse of the Year.

Wheels also trained Rough Habit, and I got to ride him four times for a win and three placings. Three of those rides were when he was an autumn three-year-old and the other time was three years later in the Lion Brown Sprint at Te Rapa when he ran third to Veandercross.

Wheels and I have often talked about who was the better — Rough Habit or Poetic Prince. Rough Habit won 11 Group Ones and over $5 million in stakes and Poetic Prince had the four Group Ones and $3.5 million. I always say to Wheels to this day, 'Don't ever tell me Rough Habit is a better horse,' and Wheels says, 'I never will.' Most of Rough Habit's form was on softish tracks and he loved Brisbane. He was just a freak, but Poetic Prince was a champion.

15

Triumph and mourning

The year 1990 should have been a very special one for me. It was and it wasn't. It was the year I rode my 1000th winner and we had a huge party to celebrate and I won the Sydney Cup for my brother Johnny. But that same year I lost someone very special, my mother, Daphne Violet Harris.

Mum died on 10 July and it came as a shock to all of us. She had been in good health. When we had Jock's sixtieth birthday celebration she had pulled a shoulder muscle, across the shoulder blade, and she complained about pains there. She thought she might've done it picking up my nephew, Daniel. She was in a lot of pain and was taking medication for pain relief. It turned out to be more than that. It was the start of a massive heart attack and she died two days later.

We've never been a close family who would kiss and cuddle all the time. It was just how we were brought up. As Jock says, 'Kia kaha' — be strong. But you look back and think maybe you're too hard, too strong, and you had to fight your emotions. Jock was always the tougher one, but Mum had the softer side. It didn't come home to us all until we had a funeral. We had to sleep for three days in the marae and it was just a chance to grieve, to remember all the times we'd shared with Mum and what she'd done for us all.

I think it's a brilliant way, how Maori do it. Mum didn't want to be buried in the Maori way, but it was Jock's choice and he made the decision. Even Johnny, the hard task master he is, to come out and cry was a chance to grieve and show emotions. My youngest sister, Jenny, never grew up with Johnny — he was already away apprenticed in Hawera when she was young. To see him crying was an experience for her. She only knew of his hard side.

Jock was still trying to be strong at the funeral. That's Jock. It wasn't until some time later that he talked more and more about Mum and we saw that side of him, how he was missing her. 'Daphne Violet would like this and she'd love to have been there', and so on. I was thinking *It's a bit late for that now. When you get up there she'll be ripping your ears off!* Jock has mellowed a lot since Mum died. We know he misses her and we all do. She was a special lady and we all loved her so much. But that's life. You've got to move on, but you never let your memories go.

It all came back to me again when a videotape about my 1000th winner was made and friends and family were interviewed on it. Dessie came out with the comment about how sad that Mum wasn't there to see me get my 1000th win. He's sitting in his courier van and you can see the tears in his eyes as he's thinking of her. Yeah, it was sad. You know, 1000 winners in any jockey's eyes is a great achievement, but it would have been even more memorable if Mum had been there to see it. I know she would have been so proud of me. She was proud of us all.

I've got many happy memories of Mum and I was glad we got her up to Singapore. She loved that trip. The times I used to come back and tell her about Singapore, then she got to experience it herself. I used to tell her: 'Over there with the Chinese, the more mess you make during a meal, the more you're enjoying it. If you go there and have dinner and leave a clean table you haven't enjoyed it.' Mum would say, 'If you make a mess at my table, I'll put newspaper down instead of a tablecloth.'

The year had started off well for the family when I won the Anniversary Handicap at Trentham on Go Bush, who was trained by Johnny and part-owned by Jock. He was a good old horse who won 16 races and I rode him in 12 of those wins. He beat two top horses, Fun

On The Run and Olga's Pal, in the Anniversary and later in the year, a couple of months after Mum died, Johnny took him to Sydney for the Doncaster Handicap. I went over to ride him and we won the Shannon Quality, a lead-up to the Doncaster at Rosehill, but he finished down the track in the Doncaster. He should have won a Winter Cup at Riccarton. He was second twice and the first time he was just beaten by Rongonui.

The biggest thrill for us all came when I won the Sydney Cup on King Aussie for Johnny. He was raced by six former Westfield freezing workers from Auckland. He'd originally been leased to a guy nicknamed Aussie Ken, but he did a runner back to Aussie still owing Johnny some money for training. That's when Johnny got the syndicate together, and they had a lot of fun with him.

Johnny sent King Aussie to Sydney in 1989 and won the Tatt's Plate at Randwick. Jimmy Cassidy rode him that day and he rode him again when he won the Chairman's Handicap the following year. I then got on him in the Sydney Cup. The track was heavy and I thought he was getting bogged down near the 800 when Sydeston, the favourite, came up alongside, but he soon dropped off and I was confident after that. He won by five lengths and the owners gave me a $30,000 sling. It was a huge result and it was great to win a Group One for Johnny. King Aussie then went on to run third in the Brisbane Cup.

We had a good celebration after the Sydney Cup, but it was nothing like the party we had for my 1000th win. I didn't know it was happening. Darrell had organised it all and when I walked into the Longburn Hall it was great to see all my family and friends. There were some faces I hadn't seen for years. They'd come from all over the country and it was like a big reunion.

I still clearly remember chasing my 1000th win. I got to 999 wins on Jongleur at Trentham then had to wait a fortnight to get number 1000. I had so many seconds between times it wasn't funny. Then the big day came at the Feilding meeting on 27 October. I won the first race on Sea Link, who was trained by Sandra Glennie. It was a relief to get my

1000th win, but then I came out and won the next three races as well. That's just how it goes sometimes. You get frustrated waiting for it to happen, then you get a run of winners.

It was an honour to join the New Zealand 1000 winners club, being up there with such great jockeys as Bill Broughton, Jim Ellis, Grenville Hughes and Bill and Bob Skelton. I was the tenth jockey to ride 1000 and I was still riding against four of them — David Peake, Garry Phillips, David Walsh and Maurice Campbell. I remember Grenville Hughes congratulating me afterwards and saying, 'Your next 1000 will be the hardest.' I never thought about it much at the time, but how right he was.

Grenville was a gentleman and had a lovely way with horses and the things he used to say. He said to me one day, 'Noel, with horses, just treat them like your girlfriend and just cuddle them up and be kind to them.' No truer words have been spoken. Be kind to a horse and you can get that much extra out of it. Grenville showed that time and time again, and he was always hard to beat in a finish. He'd often outfox riders, making you think he was beaten, then he'd get in the winning stride. I've always believed if you're kind to horses, it's amazing what they'll do for you. But if you start bullying them and goading them, things will go wrong. You need to treat horses like human beings. Treat them like you'd want to be treated. They've got feelings, too.

Bill Broughton and Jim Ellis were before my time, but I rode against Bill and Bob Skelton — more so against Bill because he was based down in Central Districts. Bill was great. He'd always give you advice and he'd never blow his top. Jockeys are known for swearing, but not Bill. The worst thing he used to say was 'basket' — 'You blummy basket' — if he was angry in a race. Other jockeys would rip your head off with foul language, but Bill was polite.

It took me 20 years to get my 1000 wins in New Zealand. It would have come a lot sooner but for the three seasons I spent in Singapore and the trips to Aussie. And these days jockeys are able to get there even quicker with all the race meetings; there are a lot more opportunities. When I started out there were only a couple of meetings a week and there were a lot more senior riders about, so it was tough competition for the good rides.

One of the biggest changes over those 20 years was females becoming jockeys. They'd been working around the stables for years and riding trackwork. I was riding over in Singapore when Vivienne Kaye, the first of the females to be licensed, had her first race-day ride at Trentham on 15 July 1978, the same day another four female jockeys started off down south, including Sue Day, who later married David Walsh. A week later Sue became the first New Zealand female jockey to win a race.

When I came back to New Zealand Linda Jones had already made her mark as the top female jockey. In her first season she'd won the Wellington Derby on Holy Toledo and ridden four winners in a day at Te Rapa. She got all the headlines. She'd been in racing all her life and was a good rider, but then again she was lucky to have the backing of her husband Alan, who was a driving force in the push to get female riders licensed. He's a top trainer and she had the cream of his team to get her going.

Cherie Saxon and Diane Moseley had done well, too, and Maree Lyndon was just starting off. Maree was apprenticed to Bruce Marsh and I probably saw more of her riding than the others. She was tough and she wasn't backward in coming forward with what she wanted and had to say. I think it was her attitude: 'I'm as good as you blokes.' She proved that she could compete on the same stage and I admired her for that, but I didn't like her rudeness. I've always said dealing with the owners and the trainers is part of longevity in riding and Maree might have shot herself in the foot with her attitude at times. But she did very well for the time she was riding. She won a New Zealand Cup (Sirtain) and an Auckland Cup (Miss Stanima) and did well in Aussie, too. She was the first female jockey to pick up one of the major cups in Australia when she won the Adelaide Cup on Lord Reims.

I didn't have a problem with females being apprenticed. Jock always believed in them. He said that women get on well with horses and around the stables they're kinder. I wasn't going to judge them until they got out there and started doing it. It took a lot of years before they made a real impact, apart from some of them, but as time has gone on there are a lot more riding and doing well. Now there are nearly as many female jockeys as male ones.

The only time I opposed them was when Napier Park wanted to have a female riders-only race at Hastings. I told them I wouldn't be riding at the meeting because I thought it was sexist. We had accepted the female riders as being equal, and I didn't think it was right they should have a race for them only. The club wasn't providing a race for male jockeys only. I realised it was a gimmick, but if one club runs one, other clubs might follow suit. I made my stand and in the end the race didn't go ahead. I wouldn't have minded if it had been a series of female riders against male riders.

Jock was right behind my sisters Karen and Jenny giving it a go when they decided they wanted to be jockeys. Karen rode a few winners, but I felt sorry for Jenny. She didn't have many rides and, though she picked up a placing, her career didn't take off. She was a bit weak and she got a hard time from the stewards. Being a Harris, there was a lot of pressure on her after the success we'd all had. She loved horses and had her heart set on being a jockey, but it didn't work out for her. I know Jock is proud of the fact we all rode.

I remember the day Karen had her first ride. A photo was taken of the group. Karen with her saddle, all ready for the big moment, and Dessie, Peter, Jock and I. Johnny missed the photo. He was training at the time and he gave Karen her first winner, Sabios, at Hastings. Karen beat Nigel Tiley, one of our top riders, then she won soon after at Otaki on Finlay for Jock, and Dessie was on the second horse. Karen rode five winners and four were for Jock.

There were a lot of male jockeys that were anti-women riders and there are some even now. In those early days a lot of them would say things like, 'We'll put the heebie-jeebies up her' and they were targeting them. You're going to get a lot of men that are never going to change their opinion, but to me the women were capable. The only thing I didn't like was that some of them used to go into the judicial room and start crying and maybe had a bit of favouritism as far as penalties go. You don't see male riders doing that. I used to say to the committeemen, 'If I start crying will you give me a lesser penalty?' Women come into a predominantly male domain, so they've got to put up with the shit, too. It's different now. There are so many of them they're treated as equals.

Over the years we've had the likes of Lisa Cropp, Linda Ballantyne, Cathy Treymane, Kim Clapperton, Trudy Thornton and Sam Spratt. Lisa Cropp has got into a lot of trouble at times, but she is a gifted rider. The way she rides on a loose rein has got me, but she's had the success. She's like a tomboy and can give as good as she gets. A lot of the female jockeys just want to be one of the boys, getting out there and doing the job. And some of them can hit a horse probably harder than a lot of male riders.

I take my hat off to Sam Spratt. She's one in a million, and you've got to love her. She had a bad fall at Wellington and they were going to write her off, but she came back better than ever. She can't even remember anything about that fall. She's got a beautiful seat on a horse and she's got a great personality, always bubbly, and you can't knock her. She's got that X-factor.

Most women are kind, get on better with horses than blokes, and in winter they do really well. Most male jockeys will whip the horses whereas female riders tend to go with the Grenville Hughes style and just balance them up, cuddle them through the ground. And that's why apprentices ride more winners in winter than summer. The wet tracks mean the horses go slower and there's more time to think, but mainly it's all about just having the horse balanced in the ground.

There are so many female riders in New Zealand now, but in Australia they're still not really accepted the same as they are here. Over here a lot of them do ride well. The ones that seem to do best are the ones who are more like men in their aggression and I don't mean with the whip.

16

Turn those lights on

A big change for the New Zealand racing industry during the 1980s was the introduction of night racing at Avondale. I went up to the very first meeting at Avondale on 1 April 1987, and I'll always remember it. I'd never ridden under lights before and I didn't know what to expect. I had quite a few rides on the night and it was an eerie feeling. I just couldn't give it a yes or a no for while. I didn't know what to think about it, apart from it making a hell of a long day for everyone. Night racing fizzled out in the end, and what probably didn't help was being at Avondale. It was such a big course and night racing is better on a smaller, tighter track. Look at how well it has worked in Aussie at Moonee Valley.

My main ride at that first meeting was Palliser for Murray Baker in the last race. He was a promising horse and I thought he could win. I'd won three on him, including a Group Three race at Trentham. That night he did it easily and, being a late finish, it took a while for me to wind down. I'm not someone who can just go home from a race meeting and switch right off and hit the sack. It started with a few drinks with Des Coppins back at his hotel, and I continued celebrating well past the early hours of the morning with Wally (editor of this book). I was staying at Wally's place and by the time we called it quits the birds were chirping outside.

No sooner had I got home than Murray confirmed Palliser would be going to Sydney, so 10 days later I was over there, riding him in the Carringbush Cup at Rosehill. It's a lead-up to the AJC Derby and it's now known as the Tulloch Stakes.

Joindre was all the rage in the race. He'd come from Perth, where he'd won the Australian Derby and the Western Australian Derby. He was unbeatable as far as the press were concerned and I remember just thinking I'd ride Palliser (renamed Our Palliser in Aussie) how he normally races, just leaving him alone early. In Australia they go a lot harder in their races and I just bided my time at the back. I was last on settling, stuck to the fence into the straight and started making a little bit of ground. Halfway down the straight we were about midfield. The next minute I clicked him and I could just feel the power I had under me. It was just a matter of angling him out three or four horses. We had that roll on and he really flew and got up to beat Joindre on the line. It was an unreal feeling. Before the turn I thought if he ran midfield it would be all right.

The win was unbelievable. It stunned commentator Johnny Tapp. As we grabbed Joindre right on the line he said, 'I'll never say a horse is home again as long as I live. He was 4/1 on, Joindre, 100 metres out, when he stormed to the front and Our Palliser is the last horse I'd think would get him.' Tapp then just kept on about the win. He said something like: 'I'll be a monkey's uncle. I nearly fell out of the box. Our Palliser? Never heard of him. A New Zealander, blimey they're good these Kiwis.' He was totally stunned. And I'll always remember Bart Cummings after Palliser won. He said: 'Palatable (Palliser's sire) . . . where are these horses? Where do they come from?' because he was so impressed.

The Carringbush Cup was a Group Two race, but Murray Baker has listed it among his Group Ones on his website, with the comment it was a Group One winning ride. I'm proud of that.

I was riding quite a lot for Murray at the time. I'd won the 1985 Wellington Derby and New Zealand St Leger on Sir Vigilant and over the years I've won a heap of big races on his horses. Jeff Lynds was also training at Woodville during those days and I did a lot of riding for him, too. I won the Ormond Memorial Gold Cup, which later became the Kelt Capital Stakes, on Secret Seal. And it was in that period I also got to ride Horlicks. I think Lance O'Sullivan was either suspended or hurt and Dave O'Sullivan got me to come up to a Matamata meeting and ride for the stable. I rode two of the stable's best that day, Horlicks and Mr Tiz. Not bad, eh?

Two champions and I got to ride them both. They weren't champions at that stage, though, both just young horses. Horlicks had raced half a dozen times and won a couple, and Mr Tiz was only a two year old, having his second start. In Mr Tiz's race, the gap was closing and I was half a length through. He buffeted his way through the rest of the way and got up to win. But he was relegated to third; I just couldn't believe it, because he'd won so nicely. Nothing was going to beat him. I told Dave there was no way he was going to be beaten. I think Dave might have been on the Matamata Racing Club committee at the time and I was waiting for him to blow up a bit, but he took it on the chin.

What made it worse was I copped a six-day suspension. Afterwards the stipe said to me, 'We don't stand bulldozing up here,' and I said, 'Well, if that's the case I will never ride here again.' I did relent to come up just for the Breeders' Stakes meetings. I'd won the Breeders' Stakes the previous year on Scotch And Dry for Wheels, who was training in partnership with Ian Adams at the time. It's funny how things work out. I thought *Bugger Matamata*, and then look what happened — I end up shifting up there and it's my home now.

Horlicks won easily that day in a Class Three 1600 metres and she impressed me. I said to Dave afterwards, 'This mare could be anything.' I was lucky to get to ride her once more and that was in the Group One TVNZ Stakes at Ellerslie the following year. By that stage she'd won eight races, and had just finished second to Bonecrusher in the Group One Air New Zealand Stakes and won the Awapuni Gold Cup. It was a top field in the TVNZ and I picked up the ride because Lance was hurt. I soon noticed the difference in her. She'd virtually grown another leg since I'd won on her at Matamata. She'd improved out of sight.

I urged her forward on the home turn and I remember halfway up the straight when I went for her I nearly lost my whip. I've got a photo that shows me with the reins apart and I'm right at the back of the reins. It wasn't what you'd like to see in a Group One race, losing your stick or losing your reins. But I was able to keep going and she was just too strong that day. Most people would expect you to go out there against Bonecrusher and run second at best, but she had improved so much. She really wanted to win and we got there by about three-quarters of a length. It was great to give Graham de Gruchy his first Group One win as an owner. It was a big day, too, for Dave and Paul O'Sullivan because they also won the Sydney Cup with Banderol.

I never had the opportunity to ride Horlicks again, but I clashed with her a few times. I got the better of her when I won the Cox Plate on Poetic Prince. She went on to win the only two runnings of the $1 million DB Draught Classic at Ellerslie and showed the world how good she was by winning the Japan Cup. She was a champion stayer and I was lucky to get the chance to ride her. I've even got a better record on her than Lance O'Sullivan. Two rides — two wins. You can't beat that.

I should have been unbeaten on Mr Tiz, too. I never got to ride him again after being relegated at Matamata. And what a good horse he turned out to be. He won seven Group Ones and proved he was a champion both here and in Australia. He won the Railway Handicap three times, the Telegraph Handicap twice and the Lion Brown Sprint, and what an amazing run he put up when he won the Galaxy in Sydney. I've won other races for the O'Sullivans over the years, but haven't had a great deal of rides for them. I've won the New Zealand St Leger four times and two of them have been for the O'Sullivans, on Sunray and, a couple of years before that, Forfar.

About five or six months after I won the TVNZ Stakes on Horlicks I had a lucky escape in Melbourne. It was at Caulfield and I was riding Flying Luskin for Wheels. The race was the Royal Show Stakes, a Listed event, and I was in a tight finish with my mate Greg Hall on Ebeli Show. We'd got to the line and he'd just beaten me. Just past the winning post at Caulfield there is quite a sharp turn. I had a light saddle on and it started slipping around to the side. I was coming off and automatically Greg just reached across and grabbed me by the shoulder and pulled me back in the saddle. I joked to him later that if I had got up and beaten him he wouldn't be touching me. It was just instinct on his part.

I remember riding a horse at Hastings years later and the outside rein broke and I was trying to steer on the one rein. Luckily, the horse wasn't pulling. I got to about the middle of the track and came around the turn and thought I still had a chance of winning so I thought: *Bugger it.* I pulled the whip and rode the horse out to the best I could and ended up running third, but then I had trouble pulling up. Darryl Bradley rode over to help me by directing my horse into the fence to slow it down. Just as he did it, his horse shied and he got dropped.

You do what you can to help other jockeys in trouble, but I think a lot of these young apprentices haven't got any idea how much trouble you can get into. You try to help when you can, but if you can get an edge in a finish you take it. When I was young, one of the tricks was to get up as close to the other jockey as you could if he looked like beating you and give him a whack over the toes with your whip. He'd lose concentration for a brief second or two and that could be the difference between winning and running second. It had to be a tight finish and you couldn't be seen to be doing it on purpose. A lot of us young kids used to do that in the old days. We learnt it off guys like Herbie Rauhihi. We started doing it to each other and it was just lucky the films weren't as clear as they are now because half of us would have got holidays. We all probably won a few races that way.

It's a bit like yelling to another jockey when it gets tight. The jockey loses concentration for just a stride or two, but you don't touch the other jockey because it then becomes foul riding. I was actually charged one day in Christchurch. The horse had come from behind me and I hit it over the head with the whip. It wasn't intentional. I didn't even know it was so close. Jockeys have got certain actions with their whips and it is not the fact that you are reaching out to hit others. They are just coming up in your space and you have to be careful.

One of the strangest things that happened to me in a race was the year I dead-heated with David Peake in the premiership. It was the last month of the season, at a Foxton meeting. I was riding Quelani, a three-year-old colt trained by Percy Burgess. It was a division race. We were in the first division and one of the favourites. I had quite a tussle up the straight with Don Foley on one of Gordon Ryder's horses, a four-year-old mare named Extra Grace. I think I had them beaten and about 200 metres out his mare reached across and grabbed my horse's bridle. I was quite stunned. I stopped riding and we got beaten. I've ridden thousands and thousands of horses and to this day it has never happened to me again. I know of colts trying to savage fillies in a finish, but never a filly or mare having a go at a colt. When I pulled up, I never thought to mention it because it wasn't something Don had done. But then the stipe George Tattersall asked me if I was going to protest. I said, 'Mr Tattersall, what do you mean?' He said, 'That horse grabbed you.' He'd seen it and the stipes put the protest in. It was upheld.

George Tattersall was a good stipe. He'd go up to the old man if anything was wrong. If I didn't ride a horse out properly he'd go to Jock and say, 'Tell Noel this is what I expect,' and he'd explain everything. There was none of this standing over jockeys with that 'I've got the authority' sort of act. He'd come up to you and warn you and if he had to put you out he'd even say to Jock, 'I can't help it, but your son has got to go.' He was fair to everyone. He'd been a good jockey and he knew what he was talking about. I respected him.

When Mr Tattersall moved on, there were Greg Humphries, Noel

McCutcheon and George Lawson, who were the stipes down our way before George shifted to the Waikato. One incident I had with Greg and Noel was with a horse called Atrapar, who was trained by Bill Calder. It was back in December 1983 when Jimmy Cassidy won on him at Trentham and he ran around. The stewards advised Bill that he had to pass two trials before he raced next. He did that, but he was still a concern, so the instruction from Noel McCutcheon was for the next three races he was not to be hit behind the saddle. I happened to ride him in the next start, which was a fortnight later and again at Awapuni. Greg Humphries was in charge on the day and he said to me the Thursday beforehand, 'If you don't ride this horse with a stick I am going to charge you,' and I replied, 'Mr Humphries, the officials have already given me a letter saying I don't have to use the stick.' He just said, 'Well, you try me.' He wasn't happy.

On the day, Atrapar got beaten for third by a nose. Greg Humphries charged me and he also charged Bill. It was all done wrong, because Noel McCutcheon should have been there to back up the letter. The judicial committee found that we both had acted in 'an honourable and honest manner' in that we raced Atrapar in accordance with the 'advice and direction of Mr McCutcheon', and both charges were dismissed. But the judicial committee went on to say in its report that it was 'most concerned that the instructions of Mr McCutcheon may be seen to be in conflict with the Rules of Racing'. I felt we had been the meat in the sandwich. It was bad that the two stewards were fighting over the issue and it hadn't been sorted out beforehand.

Greg Humphries charged me another time for my ride on Shamrock before he won the Prime Minister's Cup. It was over 1600 metres at Awapuni and he was going to charge Bruce Marsh, too. The charge against Bruce was dropped, but Humphries proceeded with the charge against me. He then brought Arthur Bird, one of the older stipes, into the room and asked what he thought of the ride. Mr Bird looked at the film and said there was not a case to answer, so they dropped the charge. It had just got to the stage that I felt Greg had been picking on me as a steward. Shortly after that he finished as a stipe. It was quite a shame, because I think he was good for racing in general.

Greg also started up a jockeys' rugby team and he wanted to be the coach. It wasn't going to work, especially when you had to work on race day with him being a stipe and us jockeys. He ended up managing the team. It was a racing 15 consisting of stablehands, blacksmiths, jockeys and the like, and it was well organised, with lots of functions.

The whole idea stemmed from when Jock was an apprentice. They used to play different jockeys' teams from around the area. But for us it got to the stage where we were playing the Wellington wharfies and prison guards. It got quite serious. People were betting on it, and a lot of the jockeys were getting hurt. I remember Tony Burridge started throwing a few league players in the Hawke's Bay team and they'd come down and play the Manawatu jockeys. It was a real grudge match and got out of hand. We wanted only jockeys' teams, but the size of the players got bigger and bigger. While it lasted it was a lot of fun. I scored a few tries, but I got pushed out more than I scored. Every time I scored a try the crowd was still clapping on the Monday morning!

We used to go down to Christchurch to play their jockeys' team. On one trip we went down on the ferry. It was at Grand National time and I was to ride La Foudre in the Winter Cup for Evan Rayner. She had 51 kg, which I could do by taking a few kilos off. But on the way down we had a few drinks and that led to more. I didn't turn up to ride the horse. Evan went up to Dessie in the jockeys' room and said, 'If I see your brother, I'll knock his head off. He'll never get another ride from me as long as I live.' Russell McAra ended up riding her and she finished sixth to Shifnal Chief, who carried 62.5 kg that year. I did apologise to Evan. We patched things up and I've ridden a lot of winners for him after that. One of them was Higgins in the Wanganui Guineas.

I hate letting people down and I haven't done that since that day. I still feel it when I see Evan and I think of La Foudre. In those days jockeys didn't have to be declared for races and a lot of times you sat in the jockeys' room and trainers would throw the colours in. Whoever grabbed them could ride the horse. But I still feel guilty that I'd been confirmed for La Foudre and didn't turn up. It wasn't professional.

One thing with the racing game, it takes all sorts to make it work. You hear all about the big guns; they get all the attention. But it's the little people in racing who make it tick, too. I remember Mrs Manapori, from Patea. She had a horse called Rongomai and one day she rang me up: 'Mr Harris, can you ride my horse at Palmerston?' I replied jokingly, 'Mrs Manapori, it will cost you some puha and pork bones and I'll certainly ride your horse.' I love a good feed of pork bones and puha.

That Saturday she arrived at the racecourse with the colours on a coat hanger, along with a large bag. I opened it up and it was full of about 200 pork bones and bunches of puha. I told her I was only joking when I'd asked for it. It would have been different had I won on the horse and she'd brought it along as a sling. As it turned out, I did win on Rongomai that day. It was a Marton meeting and I also won on him at Trentham a couple of months later. It was so precious what she'd done. She was such a loving person. She used to bake me cakes and send me whitebait. It meant a lot winning a couple of races for her and her husband, Taka. Rongomai loved the mud up to his knees, but on a firm track he just about needed another lap to catch up.

It was a few years after riding Rongomai that I got involved with Australasian Breeding Stables (ABS), doing a lot of the stable riding. Malcolm Smith had been the trainer when it started up, then Chris McNab took over the training and Rob McAnulty was manager. The company bought Always Summer, who had been a good winner for Don Grubb. She stayed with Don until Chris took her to Australia and I went over to ride her. I'd won the Whyte Handicap at Trentham on her, and in Aussie she ran third in the Craiglee Stakes and fifth to Bonecrusher in the Underwood Stakes.

Though Chris was employed by ABS, he could train some outside horses and one of them was Latitude. She was a good mare, good enough for Chris to take to Hong Kong for the Cup. I rode her in the Cup and she ran second to Grey Invader, who was ridden by another Kiwi jockey, Gary Stewart. It was an all-New Zealand finish that year with Grant Cooksley running third on St James.

On that trip we got friendly with our chauffeur, Eddie, who took us everywhere. He was paid to do it by the club, but he went that bit further to help. He'd take us around all the shops and show us where to go for cheap buying. He was a great guide. One night Nigel Tiley, who was riding up there on contract to the Hong Kong Jockey Club, had a party and we went along with Eddie. Nigel didn't want to let Eddie in because he was a driver, but when we told him to 'stick' his party he relented and Eddie joined us. We had a big night.

Eddie became a good mate on that trip and when it was time to be dropped off at the airport to come home Chris and I gave him $500 because we felt sorry for him. He was thrilled. Then he went on to tell us that he had got HK$44,000 off the trifecta in the Hong Kong Cup by coupling up the three Kiwi horses! You should have seen the look on our faces.

17

Mac arrives in town

After riding Kingdom Bay and Poetic Prince, I knew it would take a very special horse to join them on my top list. I'd ridden some good horses both before and after the pair, and when I climbed aboard 'Mac' for the first time in the Queensland Derby he was another good one. But what he did from then on made him a sentimental favourite, a crowd pleaser, and put him right up there as one of my top three horses. He'll always be special to me.

Mac was the stable name for Castletown and what a horse he turned out to be. He had got the nickname after MacGyver, the guy in the TV series, because they thought he could do anything. Talk about a nickname suiting a horse. He won twice as a two year old and raced every season through until he was eight. I've always believed with a top horse you've got 18 months to two years at the top then 90 percent will fade. He was at the top for at least five years, with 103 starts, and I rode him 74 times.

I said I would go anywhere to ride Castletown and I did. From that first time when we ran third behind another couple of Kiwis, Rough Habit and Ray's Hope, in the 1990 Queensland Derby I was only off his back in six of his races and three of those times were at the beginning of a campaign when the decision was made to go for an apprentice allowance. And in all that time I missed only one winning ride on him, in the 1991 Trentham Stakes when Roy McKay filled in for me as I was suspended.

I'd ridden for Castletown's trainer, Paddy Busuttin, a fair bit before then, though Garry Phillips was the stable jockey for a long time, then Roy McKay. Paddy raced him with Barney McCahill, a real character of an Irishman, and Kevin Morris. Barney had bred the horse and he'd had a fair bit of luck as an owner, especially with McGinty, who was also by the sire One Pound Sterling. McGinty was raced by Barney and commentator Keith Haub and won six Group One races, three on each side of the Tasman, and he would have been New Zealand's best chance to win a Golden Slipper. He beat Marscay in the lead-up then broke down before the Slipper; Marscay came out and won it. McGinty was a little champion.

Little did Barney know that he had another star on the horizon with Castletown, a horse who would also win six Group One races. It certainly didn't look that way at the start when Castletown finished last in his debut at Wanganui. Paddy had stables at Foxton and Riccarton, so he sent him south and he quickly turned around his form. David Wadley won the next two races on him and as a three year old Castletown first caught my attention when he ran third to Finnegan Fox in the Group One, Two Thousand Guineas at Riccarton. After that Paddy set him for the New Zealand Derby, and my mate Bruce Compton picked up the ride when he won at Avondale in the lead-up to the Derby. He then came out and won the New Zealand Derby. That was the only one of his six Group One wins I missed out on.

Bruce was able to stick with Castletown for a while after that, and Paddy had no fears about taking on the best weight-for-age horses as a three year old. Castletown ran second in the Air New Zealand to Riverina Charm, who had won the One Thousand Guineas in Melbourne and the Rosehill and Canterbury Guineas in Sydney, and third to Horlicks in the second of the two $1 million DB Draught Classics at Ellerslie. Bruce then went over to Sydney with him and they ran fourth in the Canterbury Guineas, Rosehill Guineas and AJC Derby. Michael Pelling picked up the ride when Paddy took him to Brisbane and finished third in the Queensland Guineas and Southport Cup and fifth in the Grand Prix Stakes. Then it was my turn. I can't remember how I picked up the ride in the Queensland Derby; I was just there at the right time — and what a beautiful pick-up ride.

It was a heavy track for the Queensland Derby and he tried hard. He'd had a long season and to finish third to two good horses was a top effort. Rough Habit went on to become a legend in Queensland with his three Doomben Cups and two Stradbroke Handicap wins. He even got a bar named after him. And Ray's Hope came home and won two Group Ones, the Easter Handicap and the New Zealand Stakes. But Castletown got his reward at the end of the season when he topped the Three-Year-Old Free Handicap.

I wasn't available for his first race as a four year old and Peter Johnson got the mount. But two starts later I got my first win on him at Trentham and later that month we finished second to another of Paddy's horses, Coconut Ice, in the Avondale Cup. Just after that I got suspended at Wanganui for having a bit of a tacking duel with Garry Phillips. I was put out, so I appealed and got back in to win the Queen Elizabeth Handicap on him. I appealed because I didn't want to miss the Auckland Cup, and as it turned out he got beaten anyway (fourth behind Star Harvest). But the stipes appealed the decision and I appealed it again and they finally gave me more time. The suspension meant I missed out on the first two days at Wellington. It cost me the Oaks on Let's Sgor and the Wellington Stakes on Steineck, both for Murray Baker. That's when Roy McKay won the Trentham Stakes on Castletown. I probably lost about $15,000 in riding fees through the appeal, but at least I got back for the Wellington Cup. I thank my lucky stars about that.

It was a close call in the Wellington Cup. Castletown had easily beaten Shuzohra in the Trentham Stakes, but she put up a good fight in the Wellington Cup. There was only a half-head in it at the finish. But a win is a win — that's all that mattered. I knew then he was a star. That autumn we went over to Sydney and he had five runs; he got better the more Paddy gave him. He was third in the BMW to Dr Grace and two starts later he was narrowly beaten by Just A Dancer in the Sydney Cup. But we turned the tables on Just A Dancer in the St Leger, and that's what probably won him the New Zealand Champion Stayer of the Year award that season.

From then on it was a case of always having your passport ready. You just knew there'd be another trip to Aussie with Castletown. Sure enough, after he won the first running of the Kelt Stakes and beat Surfers Paradise we were back on the plane and off to Melbourne. He didn't win on that trip, but he didn't do badly. He was sixth in the Caulfield Stakes, fifth in the Caulfield Cup and Mackinnon Stakes and got wiped out by the winner Let's Elope in the Melbourne Cup.

I always used to stay with Kath and Pat Courtney in Melbourne. They were wonderful to me and made me feel so welcome. Just before the Cup that year we went to the markets in the city. Their son Barry, who was riding at the same time, said, 'Hey, Harry I've found this T-shirt that would suit you.' The words on the front of the shirt said: 'Nobody upsets this little black duck' with a cartoon of a stern Daffy the Duck. I wore it to trackwork and it got a lot of mileage at the 'Breakfast with the Stars'. Everyone had a laugh and said it suited me to the ground.

Paddy brought Castletown straight back to New Zealand after that 1991 Melbourne Cup and ran him in the Waikato Cup. Empire Rose had come back from the Melbourne Cup to win the New Zealand Cup, and we thought he was tough enough. But it didn't work out. He pulled a muscle and was sore afterwards. That was the year he bounced back to run second behind Just A Dancer in the Queen Elizabeth Handicap — there was only a nose in it — then we won the Auckland Cup.

I'll never forget what I had to go through that Auckland Cup day. I'd ridden at Wairarapa the day before and my gear had got wet. I washed some of it, and put my saddle and boots in the hot water cupboard to dry. In those days nobody really worried if you went out for a few drinks the night before the races so we decided to go down to the White Horse Inn, our local at Longburn. I was just going to have a quiet night, just a few drinks, but it ended up two o'clock in the morning, seeing the New Year in. Next morning, hung over and with a seven o'clock flight to catch, it was rush, rush, rush. I grabbed my riding bag and it wasn't until I was on the plane that I realised I had left half my gear at home. There was nothing I could do about it so when I got to the track I went around the other jockeys borrowing gear. I got a saddle off Jock Caddigan, skull cap and boots off Johnny Hayes and rings and towel off Roy McKay. I did have the silks and my whip. And to make it worse I had to take off two kilos, so it was straight into the sauna.

But it all worked out well. Castletown came out and beat Lurestina in the Auckland Cup. It was my first win in the race, although I'd been placed in it four times before. I was third on Fountaincourt and Northfleet, who was then trained by Paddy, and fourth on Sanyo and Castletown (the previous year). It was my biggest win in New Zealand and I knew he'd be hard to beat, but I was worried when I was back on the rails with Melco having put a big break on the field. I tried to get off the fence at the 1000, but got pushed back on and the field started to pack up in front of me. I knew there was no way I could win if I tried to go through them. I was able to get around them before they fanned out. Melco was still well clear, but I knew at the 200 I was going to catch him.

Castletown used to get back in his races, even with a lot of weight on his back, and not many horses could go around and win like he could. Other horses you've got to try to ride for luck. He got rolling and he got past that pain barrier. That was the beauty of him. And he was the type of horse you could freshen up and he'd go a big race over 1400, like he did one year when he ran fifth to Surfers Paradise in the weight-for-age race at Hastings.

That Auckland Cup win put Paddy in a select group of trainers who had won New Zealand's three big cups. He'd won the 1988 New Zealand Cup with Gallipoli, and Castletown had won the Wellington and Auckland Cups. Of course there was more to come. Castletown was at his peak and he went on to win the Trentham Stakes, then killed them in the Wellington Cup, winning by five lengths. They had some rain and he didn't mind it, but when he went to Aussie and raced on wet tracks it was a little sandy for him. He had such a long stride that the sand was shifting, and he wasn't that comfortable; he got a bit more grip here.

The passport was out again soon after that and we were back in Sydney for the Sydney Cup. Castletown had gone all right in the lead-up races, the Ranvet, BMW and Chairman's Handicap, but he had 59.5 kilos in the Sydney Cup and I thought it would probably be too much for him. Eagle Eye was in the field with only 52 kg. I knew how good he was because I'd won the Bayer Classic on him and run second in the Two Thousand Guineas. I'd ridden him right through till he got to Aussie then I had to stick with Castletown. Grant Cooksley picked up the ride and won the Ranvet on him and finished fourth in the BMW and second in the Queen Elizabeth. I'd told Cookie early in the carnival that I thought Eagle Eye could win the Sydney Cup.

Cookie has been a good mate of mine and I remember he was inside me and had a handful of Eagle Eye. He was travelling that well, better than I was. I could've stopped him from winning by holding him in, but then I spotted Just A Dancer out of the corner of my eye. Just A Dancer and Castletown had reversed the tables so many times and I didn't want Just A Dancer winning the Cup. I relieved the pressure and Cookie won the race. Castletown finished third and Just A Dancer was fifth. It was a huge run from Castletown under his weight. Only good horses can carry that weight over 3200. Cookie didn't want to admit he got out because of me, but he understood.

Though we had no luck in Sydney, it was a different story for us in

Melbourne during the spring. Castletown had left New Zealand with a third behind Veandercross in the Kelt Stakes and first up he struck a heavy track at Caulfield in the Group One Caulfield Stakes. About 1000 metres out I'd dropped off them and I was going to pull him up, he was travelling so badly. So I angled him out to the middle of the track, and he picked himself up and got home to win by three-quarters of a length. It was unbelievable.

The funny thing is a week later Shane Dye asked me how far out I went on the track. I told him out to about the middle. The track had stayed wet, so Shane had decided to go wide on Veandercross in the Caulfield Cup. He went out, and out, and I went to follow him on Castletown and then changed my mind. I knew the track wasn't as good out there as in the first week. I could've followed Shane out and he wouldn't have been the only one out there. He got beaten a short half-head by Mannerism and he's still criticised for the ride to this day. If he'd won, he'd have been a champion, but he got beaten and he's been called a mug. They all talk about the day Shane Dye murdered Veandercross and threw away the Caulfield Cup. To think I could have been sitting out there with him.

Castletown finished seventh in the Caulfield Cup and Paddy decided to press on for the Melbourne Cup again. I thought that was the year I was going to win the Melbourne Cup. I was travelling sweetly across the top on Castletown, just cruising, going beautifully. The next minute Greg Hall passed me on Subzero as if I was tied to a post. My dream was short-lived. My blood pressure had risen about six feet and I'd been thinking, *Wow, today's going to be the day*, and as quick as I thought that Subzero ruined it all. Subzero went on to win from Veandercoss and we finished up third. It was still a good run, but no dream result for me.

Paddy and I did a lot of travelling together with Castletown and we had plenty of laughs along the way. I remember the flights to Aussie. Most of the times I'd be wasting and Paddy would be sitting next to me when the meals were served. He'd eat his and ask the stewardess to put mine aside for him, too. I'd be sitting there doing crosswords and trying not to think of food and he'd be scoffing away. Paddy would think it was a great joke.

Castletown had another go at the Auckland Cup after Subzero's Cup, but we got wiped out by Lance O'Sullivan on the winner Ligeiro. I was just starting to make a run and we got hammered — we weren't the only ones. I still can't believe the placings didn't change that day. Lance should have lost that Cup. Once Castletown got stopped it was hard to get him going again. But luck turned around two starts later when he won the Trentham Stakes again, then Fosters jinxed him in the Wellington Cup. Fosters sponsored the Cup and the managing director Richard Holden decided to put out a big photo of Castletown with back-to-back Cup wins. There were the 1991 and 1992 finishes and a gap for the 1993 one. Instead of a winning shot in 1993 there was a question mark. Pre-empting things didn't work. Horses are like humans and they can have an off day, too. That was his off day.

But just as he always did, Castletown bounced back to earn another trip to Aussie. He ran third to Calm Harbour and Solvit in the Kelt Stakes. Solvit went on to run second behind The Phantom Chance in the Cox Plate and win it the following year, when he just beat Rough Habit. And Calm Harbour was a top horse in New Zealand, so the form from the Kelt was strong.

Castletown didn't really fire in Melbourne that spring, however. His best placing in four starts was an eighth in the Caulfield Cup and he ran tenth in Vintage Crop's Melbourne Cup. Yet he came back and ran third in the New Zealand Cup straight after the Melbourne Cup, and when he ran fourth in the Trentham Stakes a couple of months later I knew he'd be hard to beat in the Wellington Cup again. He was fit and the weight (58 kg) didn't worry me.

I'll never forget the atmosphere that day at Trentham. Rod Stewart and Rachel Hunter attended. The crowd was huge and it was a great sight when I looked across heading down to the start. When I did the preliminary on him I was confident that he was as good as he had been since I'd been riding him. The build-up was great and you could hear the crowd roar when we went past the winning post the first time. When he hit the front in the run home it seemed the whole crowd was behind us. I knew 200 metres out we were going to win. It was just a case of keeping him going. The noise from the crowd was deafening, but I didn't mind. They'd just seen something special. It wasn't until I heard Tony Lee's commentary later on that it struck me even more: 'The dream bursts into reality.' It was one of the great calls and it made the hairs on the back of my neck stand up.

There was a lot of hype around about how Castletown was trying to become the first horse to win three Wellington Cups since Great Sensation won it from 1961 to 1963. Everyone knew they'd just seen history made, and at the presentation Rachel Hunter said, 'If this horse ever needs a home, he can come and live with us.' I just said to Rachel, 'The jockey and the bridle go with the horse.' It was an amazing day. Castletown had brought a lot of people out to the course and they'd got what they'd come to see.

Paddy had tears in his eyes after the race. He'd downplayed Castletown's chances in case he was beaten. He said he had his heart in his mouth when Castletown hit the front 300 out, then he let rip, yelling, 'Go Mac, Go Mac.' Castletown lived up to his nickname that day. It was his thirteenth start at 3200 metres and there would be very few who have done that. So much for 13 being unlucky.

It was a great scene when Paddy rushed out to lead Castletown back with Rata Prince. I looked down and they were hugging each other. The win meant more to them than anything. They'd always believed in Castletown, just as I had, and they'd been through his ups and downs, too. This was a dream come true.

Rata had been Castletown's constant companion, his best mate. Without Rata around, Castletown would get homesick. Rata really loved that horse. I remember Rata saying nothing came before Mac and that he was a bit like a drinking partner. He also made the comment that Mac had a great sense of humour and was like a human with a couple of extra legs. Rata had his own way with words. He'd been with Castletown since the horse was a three year old and he missed seeing him race only once.

Rata was a real character of a bloke. He'd dress up in something colourful and out of the ordinary. One year it was a flashing tie, pink waistcoat and black striped trousers. He had a waistcoat and matching bow tie for that third Wellington Cup and apparently he'd won a prize for the most outrageous outfit at an Otaki meeting just beforehand. He also had one bucktooth in front and gaps everywhere else. He was given $3000 to get a new set of teeth and we'd be out having a few drinks but he never had them in. He wanted to look after them. That was Rata. He'd never even touched a horse before he went to Paddy's stables and went on to become the stable foreman. He drifted out of racing, but he's often talked about. Whenever we think of Castletown we think of Rata.

The day after we won the third Wellington Cup I had to go and ride at Foxton races. As you'd expect there was a big party to celebrate the win and we didn't get home until about three or four in the morning. I arrived at the races and while talking to Paddy I walked out to the horse, jumped on and, hello, it wasn't my saddle. I then realised I'd jumped on the wrong horse. I was riding one for Murray Baker and not Paddy. The crowd clapped and cheered. I'd been talking to Paddy, so naturally thought I was riding the horse for him. I was still on a buzz.

Castletown went back to Sydney and Brisbane after the Wellington Cup, but he never won another race. It's as though he threw everything into winning that third Wellington Cup. He was retired after he ran in the New Zealand Cup again, in 1994. He was going so sweetly at the 1200 I thought he'd make a clean sweep of the Cups. But on the home turn he went from feeling terrific to terrible. He'd strained a suspensory ligament in his near foreleg. He pulled up sore that day, but at least he was in one piece. It was an emotional day for us all. He'd won almost $2.5 million in stakes and given us so many highlights. He'd raced in 40 Group One races and 30 others at Group level and contested 15 races of 3200 metres. I remember Paddy making the comment to the reporters: 'It doesn't matter how long I train for, I'll never get another one as professional and honest.'

I've seen Castletown since he's been in retirement. A few years ago Paddy and I went out and saw him, and we both hopped on his back. He was looking good and acting like a two year old. He remembered me.

18

Life-changing

With my third Wellington Cup in the trophy cabinet, I headed back up to Singapore later that year. It was just for a weekend, but it was 14 years since I'd been back and I was looking forward to it. I went in feeling fresh and ready to go. I rode four winners and three placings over the weekend, made some new contacts and got reacquainted with some of the older ones. It was a successful trip all round.

Back home I'd had more Group One success to go with the Castletown highlights. I'd teamed up with Murray Baker's top filly Staring and won the 1992 New Zealand Oaks and 1993 Bluebird Foods Classic. And in 1995 I got the opportunity to ride another Group One winner for the Sanders stable. Graeme had the smart filly Ballroom Babe and I picked up the mount in the Manawatu Sires' Produce Stakes. Her regular rider, Gary Grylls, was riding in Sydney that day. It's a race I'd tried to win and I'd come so close, but just couldn't get it. My first placing in it had been 23 years beforehand, a third on Slips, and I'd finished close seconds on Loughanure, Kingdom Bay and Glorious Way, and had also been second on Straight Order and Centime. I thought surely I'd win it soon.

Ballroom Babe was the only horse to beat Our Maizcay in New Zealand that season. That was in the first two-year-old race at Wanganui and Our Maizcay then went on to win seven in a row before Grant Searle took him to Aussie for the Golden Slipper. He ran huge races in Sydney against a top lot of two year olds. He was second to Strategic in the Skyline Stakes, second to Octagonal in the Todman Slipper Trial and he ran a great race for fourth to Flying Spur and Octagonal in the Golden Slipper Stakes.

Ballroom Babe had also continued winning after she beat Our Maizcay, but then disappointed when she ran fourth in the Matamata Breeders' Stakes on a hard track. Graeme said she had a few niggling problems that day at Matamata and he was confident she'd be hard to beat in the Sires, but given how my luck had been in the race I wasn't going to get carried away. I shouldn't have worried. I took her straight to the front and she cleared out to win by 14 lengths! I wasn't aware of the gap she'd put on the field. I was too scared to look around, worried something might be charging home to beat me yet again, and when I got to the finish I was amazed to see how far back they were. It was a heavy track and my concern had been that she mightn't be seasoned enough, but she was a natural in it. Gryllsey was back on her when she won the Ellerslie Sires' Produce Stakes next start on a slow track by nine lengths, and she later won another Group One, the Captain Cook Stakes at Trentham.

Soon after my Sires Produce win I headed over to Aussie to ride Count Chivas for Don Sellwood. We ran second at Flemington then won the VRC St Leger and went to Adelaide and snatched the South Australian Derby. Count Chivas was a horse with a good finish and he showed it in the Derby at Morphettville. That was a big day for the Kiwis. Jeremy Walsh won a stakes race on Our Marquise for Laurie Laxon and Brent Phillips won the two-year-old race on Big Twister for Dick and Chris Bothwell. I went on to have a couple more placings that year on Count Chivas, but after he failed in the Turnbull Stakes I lost the ride. Rod Griffiths came out and ran second on him in Doriemus' Caulfield Cup, then he ran down the track in the Melbourne Cup before winning the Sandown Cup. I did finally get back on him, but that was at the end of his career. Time had caught up with him, but he was still competitive. I rode him in his last four starts for a second in the Feilding Cup, a third in the Counties Cup and fifths in both the Kelt Capital Stakes and Manawatu Cup.

Sure, I'd been disappointed to lose the ride on Count Chivas in Melbourne, but it's all swings and roundabouts in racing. I've always believed you have just got to take it and move on. Sometimes they come back to you, other times they don't. I lost that ride, but I picked up a good one on Clear Rose for Laurie Laxon. She was raced by Laurie and the Vela brothers, Peter and Philip, and a Hong Kong owner, Ad Leung, and she turned out to be a top filly. She'd only won a two-year-old race when I got to ride her for the first time in the Desert Gold Stakes at Trentham, but I knew straight away she was something a bit special. She bolted in by five and a half lengths. She then went down to Riccarton and showed that same acceleration when she won the Group One, One Thousand Guineas.

It was my second win in the race and it came 19 years after I'd won it for Bill and Graeme Sanders on Porsha. It was also a big thrill for the Velas. Laurie had given them their first Group One win in the One Thousand Guineas back in 1981 with Noble Heights. It was good to win the race for Laurie, too. I've known him for years. In fact, when Jock was training Far Time and my brother Johnny won the first international race at Te Rapa on him, Laurie was the strapper. Back then Laurie was an amateur rider.

Clear Rose had been a temperamental filly, but I was getting on well with her. We went on to win the Eulogy Stakes and that was a huge effort. She was on the wrong foot when the gates opened and lost a couple of lengths. I was forced to make my run three-wide from the 800, and to make it worse I got my stick caught in her mane; I was only able to hit her twice in the last 50 metres. We got home by a nose that day and Laurie stepped her straight up from 1600 to 2400 metres in the New Zealand Derby. Roysyn won the Derby that year and I still believe I should have won it on Clear Rose. Two horses fell in front of her and she jumped one of them. To get up for second was an unbelievable run.

Things had changed in my life during the time I was riding Clear Rose. A week after I won the One Thousand Guineas, Darrell and I split up. My weight was stuffed and I was under a bit of pressure financially. We'd had the good payouts from Poetic Prince, but soon after that the government brought in a provisional tax on any Aussie earnings. In the meantime we'd probably spent about $60,000 renovating the house, extending it because of the four kids. Then I copped a $30,000 tax bill and another $8000 penalty tax because my accountant hadn't been aware of it. That was on top of the other tax I'd paid.

Sure I'd had some good payouts with Castletown and had some other big wins, but it was all getting on top of me. I did a couple of trips up to Singapore–Malaysia to try to earn a little bit extra, but for a few years I found it very hard to get ahead. I ended up having a good season then going nowhere. I was in a rut and my weight was a problem. The harder I tried, the worse my weight got. In fact, I thought quite a bit about just giving up. But I knew if I gave up I would never make a comeback. I would have walked away from riding for good, as I don't believe in comebacks. The expectations on me with a family and everything were coming to a head. It was because of the family I kept going.

I gave up smoking for a year and at the time going cold turkey didn't worry me. I love my coffees. I used to have about 100 coffees a day. One day I found decaffeinated coffee in the pantry. I quizzed Darrell about it and she said I'd been on it for the last three months. So not only was I lacking nicotine, it was caffeine as well.

I was a shit-head to live with. I got angry quickly, just snapped and everything built up. I'm one of those guys who won't go and discuss problems with other people. I kept it all to myself. I always thought: *I'm the provider; it's up to me.* It was the way I'd been brought up. I knew I was in a rut and I had to get out of it. It gradually got worse between us and in the end it came to a head. We decided to split up.

Wasting had made it even worse. It's a problem most jockeys have to deal with. You've got to try to live a normal life. A jockey has got to keep the trainer happy, the owners happy, punters happy and so on. That stress goes on top of life's normal ups and downs. It's an added strain when you're not eating and drinking week in and week out. You've got to be focused. There's nothing worse than being dehydrated. I can probably go a week without eating, but it's the fluid that gets you. Mentally, it's not good. It got to the stage with my wasting that I'd be having to take off nearly 3 kg every time I rode, and that was twice a week.

In any split up, you go through some rough times, but eventually you move on. The kids stayed with Darrell, and I remained in our home at Longburn until it was sold. Dessie shifted in with me. He'd just split up from his wife, too. It was a period in racing when there were a lot of marriage break-ups down our way. They weren't linked, as far as I was aware! It just happened that way. I never lost contact with the kids, and they were around the corner, virtually. Later on, when I shifted up to Matamata, Troy moved up and lived with me and the two older ones, Natasha and Cushla, lived in Matamata for a while.

It was a big change for me being single again. I'd been married almost 17 years. In the next few years it was almost like going through my apprenticeship again to get back on my feet and set my direction in life. That's the way I looked at it. I had to decide whether I wanted to keep riding. I had time to think it all over, then things just started clicking into place. One door closes, another one opens. With my marriage I felt the expectations were on me. And I was a prick to live with, I don't mind admitting that.

Financially, I plodded away and gradually got back on my feet. I ended up finally selling the farm in December 1998, just over three years after we split up. In hindsight I should have let it go a year earlier and I'd have made $100,000 more. The market was solid and I got offered good money for it. The guy who made the offer heard I was going up to Singapore to live, but I was only going short term and I didn't know what to do at the time. In the end I sold when the market had dropped, but I'd decided to cut my losses and move on.

Though I felt I was in a rut, I didn't show it on race day. After parting ways with Darrell, I kept riding winners and ended that 1995–96 season with 74 wins to finish sixth on the premiership behind Chris Johnson. My mounts earned over $785,000, so my 5 percent of that helped. And it was in that season I climbed aboard a very good horse, Chatham. He could have been something special if he'd stayed sound.

Sue Walsh, a top horsewoman who had been a jockey and was David Walsh's ex-wife, trained Chatham, and the first time I rode him was at Foxton in a welter. He'd won his second start at Awapuni and he made it two on end that day. The way he finished it off I knew he was pretty good. Brian Hibberd was fourth on him in the St Leger, and I was back on the following season. I had four rides on him for three wins and a third. He won four in a row and I rode him in the last couple. In the last win he simply bolted in by six and a half lengths and beat Lady Dahar, who had won the St Leger the year before.

Chatham was off the scene for a year, but second up he showed he was coming right when he flew home for third in the Rotorua Cup. Sue took him to Brisbane and I rode him in his three runs and won second up in the Eagle Farm Stakes. That day we beat Cronus, who was going for the Brisbane Cup. Cronus was Roger James' good stayer who had won an Adelaide Cup and went on to win a Chairman's Handicap and Prime Minister's Cup in Queensland. The plan from then on was to get Chatham to the Melbourne Cup. After I won the Taranaki Stakes on him, beating Group One winner All In Fun, we looked as though we were on the right track.

Sue ran him in the Geelong Cup, hoping to qualify for the Melbourne Cup, but he missed the start. I don't know why he did it. He just stood there when the gates opened then jumped sideways. I had to ride him for luck after that and he came home well, but he was never really a realistic winning chance after the poor start. He then ran fifth in the Saab and that was the end of the Melbourne Cup dream. He broke down and though he was tried again briefly he never came back. I felt he had so much natural ability and that bit of brilliance needed to win a Melbourne Cup. On ability, I really don't know how good he could have been. On his day, with everything going right, he could have won anything.

Around the time I was riding Chatham through the grades, I headed over to Melbourne to ride The Bandette for John Wheeler. I've kept scrapbooks over the years with both the good and the critical write-ups and there's one article which appeared in the *Sunday Telegraph* just before I rode The Bandette in the 1996 Melbourne Cup that always makes me smile. To some people it looked like the writer, Mike Colman, was having a real shot at me, but I liked the way it was written. It was a story about the difference between me and Darren Beadman, who had just found God. It was titled 'Wild and Mild' and in part it reads:

> Run your finger down the field list for the Melbourne Cup and you've got Beadman, the Hallelujah Kid on the aptly named Saintly. A little bit further down and there's the Kiwi hoop Noel Harris on the equally aptly named The Bandette.
>
> Says Beadman of his evangelical fervour, 'I believe it is what God wants me to do. I like to see where I get my blessing from and who is the provider.'
>
> Says Harris: 'I do love a beer.'
>
> Beadman says he speaks out in the hope that others might 'see the light'. Seeing the light — particularly the early morning light — is something Noel Harris is not too fussed on. 'I don't ride trackwork unless I feel like it,' he says. And most days, unlike Beadman, he doesn't.
>
> Friday was a case in point. Anyone waiting for Noel Harris to do a few circuits of the track at dawn's early light was waiting in vain. As was his landlady, who left the porch light on all Thursday night.

'Met a few Kiwi mates,' he said when he arrived home around 10 am. 'Had a bit of a look around, checked out the nightspots.'

But Harris, who sports a ponytail and two earrings, does admit to having something in common with Beadman, whose good looks have earned him the nickname Tom Cruise.

Commenting on a report that Beadman uses his time in the sauna to pray, Harris says he too prays in the sauna. 'I pray the bloody power shuts off so I can get out of there,' he says.

Chalk and cheese, one might say, of the two. Beadman describes his life as having 'turned 180 degrees since I became a Christian.' Harris sums himself up as the Wild Man of New Zealand racing.

But come 3.20 Tuesday they will be as similar as the closest of twins, riding in synch to a common goal: The Cup.

The story went on to outline our backgrounds in past Melbourne Cups and how life had changed for Beadman since he turned religious and how the other jockeys handled it. The story goes on:

'Now because of the life I lead and the success I have had, other jockeys come up to me and want to talk about God,' says Beadman. 'They realise something is happening right for me.'

Odds of Noel Harris being one of those approaching Beadman are long, but he does admit to making some sacrifices in the lead-up to the Cup.

'I get off the beer and switch to the wine,' he said. 'It's better for the weight.'

Other than that, they are just two gifted, successful professionals who go about life their own way.

Across the bottom of the page was the heading: 'Racing's odd couple chase the greatest prize on the turf calendar'. I find it very humorous and it didn't offend me at all. As the writer said, Darren and I are like chalk and cheese. We go about things differently, but in the end we both want to win races. We both wanted that Melbourne Cup and maybe God was looking down on Darren. He certainly didn't help me. Darren won the Cup on Saintly and I was down the track on The Bandette. Mind you, it wasn't a bad carnival for me. I'd won the Quick-Eze first up in Melbourne on The Bandette and finished second on him in the Werribee Cup. Thank God for those pickings.

19

Wake-up call

God was a turning point in Darren Beadman's life and he says it helped him win the Melbourne Cup on Saintly. Riding a horse with that name was an omen in itself. Well, my turning point came about seven or eight months later in Queensland. I had been riding everywhere and kicking home winners. I was just floating along, taking every day as it came. And as I'd done most years when I could, I headed over to the Queensland Winter Carnival. But this time it was different and even my family and closest friends don't know what went on.

I thought: *Oh well, I'll pick up a few rides, so be it. If not . . .* And off I went. I might have had two or three rides, but I wasn't chasing any and I didn't care. I just booked myself into a $40-a-night motel down the Gold Coast and it was like nobody knew where or who I was. I just let loose and lived as though there was no tomorrow. Every night I'd be out hammering myself on the piss. I was just drinking with a crowd I didn't know, and they didn't know what I did. It was like living a normal life away from racing. I did run into a few people who knew me, but I just didn't care at that stage what people thought. I was just ordinary Joe Bloggs going to the pub.

It got to the stage where I'd be going out about 9 pm and wouldn't be getting home until three in the morning. I'd sleep all day until about five or six o'clock then get up, have a shower and do it all over again. Pubs, nightclubs . . . everywhere. After about a month it got quite scary because here I was trying to go to bed when everyone else was starting to get up. One night I had $1000 on me and I put $500 in my pocket and went out and when I got home I had no wallet. I'd been robbed. Just as well I didn't take the whole $1000. I had to ring up later that day and cancel my cards and go into Brisbane to get a new American Express card. I was lucky I had kept the $500 back in the motel unit; otherwise I'd have woken up with no money at all until my new card came through. When I finally did get home from Brisbane I got an envelope with all my cards, American Express, my birth certificate and driver's licence I had in my wallet, but no money mind you. It just had a smiley face on it and the words 'Have a happy day'.

When I think back I could easily have been bashed or worse. Nobody knew where I was or who I was. They say people can vanish off the face of the earth. All that my family knew was that I was over in Brisbane somewhere. I just kept to myself. I ate bugger all. I picked on a bit of seafood — prawns and a bit of fish, or something like that. I only ate like a sparrow and that was just as a late lunch, then I went drinking beer and got on to the spirits. It just killed my appetite. You see these druggies and alcoholics; they get that light, don't they? Food is the last thing they feel like. I probably lost about four or five kilos and I was feeling a bit weak. It got to the stage where I was trying to make myself eat, but it would make me feel sick. Once I had a couple of beers that would take over.

I was locked up one night. I'd been staggering down the street and the cops wanted to know where I was staying, but they couldn't understand me so they just put me in the holding cell overnight. I went to the races a couple of days later and Reid Sanders, the stipe in Queensland at the time, said to me, 'I was talking to a copper mate of mine and they said they had a bed for you the other night.' I was surprised he knew.

Some people might say I was finding myself. But the truth is I was nearly falling off the planet. By the end of a month or so it actually frightened me, but it did me more good than harm. It was a wake-up call, a scary one. In the end when I did try to go to bed at 10 pm instead of going out I couldn't sleep. I'd be buzzing and I'd still be awake at 2 am. It took me a good week to get back to reality. I thought: *This is not me. It's not the way I've been brought up.* I know of jockeys who went right off the rails and didn't come back. They probably didn't go to the extent I did in a short time, but they wasted what they'd had and where they could've been.

When I did get my shit together and came home it was good to be back in New Zealand. I went back to my place in Longburn and straightened myself up a bit and started living normally. I didn't tell anyone what actually happened to me, not even my family. It was something that I went through that I was probably pleased but scared about, too. It served as a warning, and no one really missed me anyway.

The experience was something I had always kept to myself until I met my future wife Kylie. It's great to have someone that you trust, love and can confide in and, most of all, be understanding. I found that in Kylie. She was the first to know about all these things in my life, things I had kept to myself. She understands me and knows what I've been through. Once I told her about my Brisbane 'time out', I felt a weight lift off my shoulders. They always say it's good to talk to someone. I'd known that, but it wasn't easy for me until I met Kylie.

By now you'll have realised I enjoy a drink. Don't get me wrong. I don't have to have one every day. I'm not an alcoholic, but it's good to relax with a drink or two. That will probably never change, but I'll never again go through what happened in Brisbane that month. That was a turning point in my life.

After I've been wasting all I want to do is have a drink and when I have a couple of beers I lose my appetite, even though I haven't been eating for a week. I can eat the next day. The first thing some jockeys do is eat; they've got to eat, but because they've been wasting, the constitution is small. Their stomachs have shrunk. They might have a steak and it will fill them up, but I just have a few beers. I know I should have something to eat before I drink, but I go straight to the alcohol. It hits me like lightning.

It's the same after a race day. When I've finished riding I just want to sit down and have a drink and get away from it all. If I go to the pub all I feel like doing is getting a loud speaker, going through my rides and how they went and then saying, 'That's it. I don't want to talk about the races any more tonight.' If I tell one person then I'll be telling 20 or 30 during the night. Sometimes it gets to the stage when I'm sitting down, having a couple more gins, and telling people to fuck off and leave me alone. My day's racing is over. Talk about rugby, league or anything but not horses. I just want to relax and switch off.

It's the same for most people after they finish a day's work. They don't talk about their work, and they have a life outside of it. It gets worse when I ride winners, especially big winners, and go out. Everybody wants to be there with me. Some jockeys love it, being the centre of attention. And when I was younger it didn't worry me.

When I win a race and run into the connections I appreciate they want to know about their horses and have us all celebrate together. That's fair enough. I go along with that, but sometimes I might disappear — not meaning to be rude, but just wanting to get away from talking about horses for a while. I've got the rest of the week for that. Other times I get caught up in the celebration and I end up writing myself off, and a lot of people have come to the conclusion that it's just me. And when I do have a few too many I start mumbling anyway and nobody can understand me. But, for me, it's my way of having a release and not having to answer to anybody.

My perfect night out is having a few drinks and a bit of Chinese food with friends. With Chinese food, there are so many dishes you can pick and eat all night. I can just sit back and relax. It's just what I feel like after a day's riding. It's either that or a relaxing night at home. It's a bit different when you're young. I've been through that and I just like to think I've matured. *Yeah, right*, I hear some of you repeating the popular phrase from the Tui beer adverts. But it's true.

Most of the time, sober or drunk, I talk with my hands. I know what I'm trying to say, but I'm trying to express myself. It got quite bad there for a while with poking my finger out and saying 'fuck you' when the other person wasn't really listening. I get frustrated trying to make my point. Dessie actually made a key ring. It's got Handbrake written across it with my mobile number and it's a hand with the first finger pointing out. There's quite a few of the key rings around the racing people. Some of my friends will say, 'Oh here's Harry,' and they'll point and say, 'Fuck you,' then laugh.

Another thing I'm known for is a bit of pole dancing when I've had a few. It all started when my mate Lucky Haitana had the Cue Bar in Matamata. I'd had a few drinks and I said, 'See that pole over there. I'm going to go and dance with it. I don't have to shout it a drink, it doesn't argue and it will be there tomorrow.' So I started wrapping around the old pole for a joke and next minute, you wouldn't believe it, half a dozen blokes want to go over and dance with the pole, too. I was only being silly, but I started something off. Everybody brings up my pole dancing, but now the pole dancing is quite popular for fitness. Maybe I should have got into promoting it. Ha!

One of the trainers keen on the old pole dancing is my old mate Paddy Busuttin. I rode quite a lot of winners for Paddy and one always overlooked is The Stranger. She only won one race, at Woodville, but it was special because it was Paddy's 700th training success. The Stranger has gone on to be the dam of Crocodile Canyon, a Marton Cup winner.

After all the success Paddy had with such good horses as Castletown, Plume, Coconut Ice and Gallipoli, he decided to try his luck in Singapore and shifted over there to train in 1987. He was the pioneer for the Kiwi trainers going to Singapore. Laurie Laxon, Stephen Gray, Bruce Marsh and Mark Walker followed. He set up at Bukit Timah and got me to go over in 1997. It was just after my 'time out' in Brisbane. I'd got back to reality and I went up there in August for a week or two and actually rode Paddy's first winner in Malaysia. On the same trip I got to ride Ouzo, a Kiwi-bred horse by Oregon who was trained by Malcolm Thwaites; I won the Kelang Silver Bowl at Selangor on Ouzo. Later on he featured in a lot of major races including the Singapore International Cup and the Singapore Derby, and he was the Singapore Horse of the Year twice.

When I came back from Singapore I made history for another trainer, John Sargent. I rode Super Crest to win the Captain Cook Stakes and give Sarge his first Group One win. I also won the Whyte Handicap, Taranaki Cup and Wanganui Stakes on Super Crest. He was a good old horse and really put the Sarge on the map. I've ridden a lot of winners for Sarge over the years and he's one of the best.

The following winter when I went over to Queensland to ride Chatham I met Shannon Melton. She worked for Te Akau Racing Stables in Matamata. We started going out and though it was never going to be a relationship leading to marriage she was good company and we got on well. I ended up leaving Palmerston North and shifting to Matamata in 1999 and we shifted in together. Then later Troy, my son, came up to live with us. Shannon was great for Troy. Shannon and I were together about six years. It was a time in my life when things were starting to fall into place. I'd bought a house, I was happier in my riding and I was getting some big winners.

I was back.

20

'Green — what the hell are you doing?'

I can still remember the look on the late Noel Eales' face that day. It was at Te Rapa and he walked into the jockeys' room after race two to give me the colours for Surface, who I was riding for him in the Group One Waikato Draught Sprint later in the day. He stopped in his tracks and just stood there and stared at my hair. His mouth was open and he looked stunned. When he did speak he asked me what the hell I was doing. I had peroxided my hair blond a few weeks earlier and he'd seen it like that. But now it was green!

I was riding Ana Zeel in the Sir Tristram Fillies' Classic for Patrick Hogan. Being proud of his Irish heritage, he had asked me to dye it green for a bit of Irish luck. But that didn't go down well with Noel. He quickly told me how he hated green. He said it was bad luck for him. I was in a no-win situation. I had to try to please them both and there was only one solution. Surface was in the race straight after Ana Zeel so here I was between races hunched over the hand-basin washing green dye out of my hair. Noel was a great old trainer, but he had his superstitions, just like a lot of us.

I'd won a maiden on Ana Zeel leading up to the Sir Tristram Fillies' Classic but, on the day, the green hair didn't work for her. She finished second-last but, hey, with the green dye washed out I had the luck on

Surface. I settled him last, moved up across the top and he just killed them. He won by a couple of lengths. He ran the 1400 metres in 1:21.4, a quick time, and he did it so easily. He used no petrol to get to them, he went that quickly.

Noel had been unsure whether to run or not. Though he couldn't fault his condition going into the race, he was concerned about lining him up at weight-for-age and having to drop back to 1400 from 1600 a fortnight earlier. I'd won the Anniversary Handicap, a Listed 1600-metre race at Trentham on him, and he'd come out a week later and beaten a good field in the Group One Thorndon Mile — with my peroxided hair! It was excellent lead-up form and the way he won the Waikato Draught showed his class. It was his tenth win from 16 starts and it was all ahead of him.

For me, the win brought back memories of winning the race 10 years earlier on Poetic Prince. I was confident Surface was an ideal horse for the Cox Plate, just like Poetic Prince was when we won it in 1988. He could sit back and sweep round them quickly and that suited the pattern of racing at Moonee Valley. I felt by the time the Cox Plate came around he would be a lot stronger, too. Noel, who also part-owned Surface, was known for being reserved when it came to making big calls like that, but he agreed with me that day. He said he'd seriously consider it, but first Surface had to have a break. That was Noel: a patient trainer who took it one step at a time. The welfare of the horse came before the dream.

When Surface came back he finished third in the Mudgway Stakes at Hastings and two starts later we were in Melbourne for the Toorak Handicap at Caulfield. Things just didn't work out for us that day. He just wasn't the same horse in Australia and he didn't get to the Cox Plate. Instead Noel brought him straight back home, and a few months later he did run an unlucky third in the Thorndon Mile and followed with some useful performances, but won only one more race. That was the Group One Auto Auctions Weight-For-Age at Otaki when we stormed home along the fence. Surface was never really himself after going to Melbourne. It's a shame because he had the potential to win a lot more big races.

Noel Eales didn't travel much to Aussie, but when he did he meant business. He had to be sure the horse was up to it. Like when he won the 1986 Caulfield Cup with (Mr) Lomondy and the 1993 Mackinnon Stakes with The Phantom, two great horses taken over there on the way up. Actually, that reminds me of a story about Bruce Brown, or Rabbit as we all knew him. He worked for Noel for years and Noel told him to get his passport because he was planning to take a team of horses to Aussie. Rabbit didn't believe him, but Noel said, 'No, I'm serious this time.' So Rabbit obtained a passport and he was telling me, 'You wouldn't believe it. Ten years, mate, and there wasn't one stamp in it.' Rabbit's 'overseas' trips were down to the South Island — Nelson or the Blenheim circuit. Over the years Noel did start going, but I think Rabbit had given up by then.

Rabbit was with Noel for years and he was a great asset. Before that he was with Syd Brown. One morning he was galloping a horse and he got past the gap and the horse fell. Rabbit was down and they called the doctor and brought the ambulance up. It was a cold winter morning and they undid Rabbit's raincoat, undid his jersey, and hello, he had his pyjamas on. The doctor said to him, 'So you're all ready for hospital?' He'd just dived out of bed, left his pyjamas on and thrown his work gear over the top. He got a fair bit of stick about that.

Anyway back to the Surface period. That Thorndon Mile–Waikato Draught Sprint double capped off a big couple of months for me. The month before I'd won the Auckland Cup on Irish Chance and that was where my connection with Sir Patrick Hogan really started. Irish Chance was bred by the Dennis brothers in the deep south and 'Jillo', trainer Colin Jillings, had bought him for Patrick, who raced him with Sir Michael Fay. I'd won a couple of minor races on Irish Chance then finished second on him before the Auckland Cup. I gave him a good lightweight chance in the Cup. He was by Sir Tristram and I had no worries about him staying. And the closer the race was the more confident I became. I've told you how I'm superstitious. Here I was riding a horse called Irish Chance. I had been staying in O'Reilly's Motel in Matamata and on the second day of the meeting I'd won on Maybe Irish. And my previous win in an Auckland Cup had been on Castletown, owned by the Irishman Barney McCahill. I had the luck of the Irish on my side.

At the 1000 metres in that Cup it was like riding Castletown in his 1992 win all over again. Irish Chance was at the back of the field and I knew they'd have to feel the pressure up front. It was just like Castletown's year when Melco went hard out in front. With Castletown I knew I could afford to go round the lot, but with Irish Chance I couldn't afford to do that. I hooked in behind them coming round the home turn and waited. When I asked him to go he charged at them and it was all over.

I'd now won two Auckland Cups and three Wellington Cups. All I needed to make a clean sweep of the big Cups was the New Zealand Cup. I'd had seconds on Our Countess, Double Trouble and Manchu and thirds on Waiau Pal and Castletown. I'd been trying for 28 years, ever since I had my first ride on Buza in 1971. And as it turned out I didn't have much longer to wait.

The following November I got my New Zealand Cup win on Wake Forest and it couldn't have happened for a better bloke. Gus Clutterbuck trained Wake Forest and Gus has always said how he should have won the race as a jockey in 1980 on Koiro Trelay. He'd been the regular rider but he cracked his pelvis in a fall at Stratford and Phillip Smith got the ride. Phillip won the New Zealand Cup on him, then the Wellington Cup. Gus was a good rider. He was third to David Peake and Bob Vance in the 1977 Jockeys' Premiership, but he was always having falls. He had five falls in five successive races and that's supposed to be an

Australasian record for a flat jockey.

Wake Forest was down near the minimum in the weights, but Gus thought he'd be hard to beat. One of the part-owners, Paul Walker, flew in from Los Angeles especially for the race and he flew out again the next day. He'd only seen him race once before, when he ran second at New Plymouth. It was a trip he'll never forget. I got a good run just behind the leaders and Wake Forest kicked away to win easily. It was to be his last win, but it didn't matter. We'd won the New Zealand Cup. Gus had finally made up in some way for missing the win on Koiro Trelay and for me it completed 'the Big Three'. Only Grant Cooksley and Chris Johnson, of the riders still going, had done all three at the time and I became one of the group. Sure there were others who'd won the three before us, like Bob Skelton and Midge Didham, but I felt a sense of achievement to have finally done it.

A few months later I ended another drought when I won the Group One Telegraph Handicap on Fritz at Trentham. It was 27 years since I'd won it on Sharif — nearly as long as I'd waited for my first New Zealand Cup win. Fritz was trained down south by Neil Coulbeck and he'd won seven races in the South Island, including four on end the previous season. The Telegraph was my first ride on him, but it didn't take me long to work out how good he was. We got a lovely run behind the leaders and it was a bit tight at one stage, but once he got into the clear he went 'whoosh'. It was Neil's first Group One win and I told him it wouldn't be his last with Fritz.

Another milestone came for me later in the year, on Boxing Day — my first New Zealand Derby. I had been unlucky not to win it on Clear Rose five years earlier and when I finally did win on Hail, it was for a couple of top guys, Bruce Marsh and Ali Cunningham. I always regarded Bruce as one of the best riders of his time. He won the Melbourne Cup on Silver Knight and he's gone on to be a top trainer. I've ridden a lot for Bruce over the years. As I've said, I used to go to Brisbane for the carnivals to ride for Bruce and we had a fair bit of luck, including the Prime Minister's Cup with Shamrock. Bruce owned Hail in partnership with Ali, whom I'd known way back from the days he was racing horses with Baggy Hillis. I used to ride a lot of his horses, the likes of Princess Cecily, who won the Wairarapa Breeders Stakes. Ali is a brilliant guy and he takes the wins with the losses. Boxing Day 2000 was one of the wins — the biggest one, and he'll never forget it.

I knew Bruce had a big opinion of Hail and I soon found out why. He'd already won a couple and run fourth to Tit For Taat in the Bayer Classic when Bruce asked me to ride him for the first time. That was in the Derby Trial, his first run past 1600, and he won it. What impressed me was the way he finished it off. I told Ali and Bruce I thought he'd be a top show in the Derby, provided we didn't have any bad luck. I knew all about that with Clear Rose. And it just about happened again. Coming to the home turn I was confident he could win, but then a few strides later we were gone for all money. We got squeezed up between Sir Clive and Danamite. There was just nowhere to go. But Hail picked himself up and got going again. With any other horse we couldn't have won. Cookie, Grant Cooksley, rode Sir Clive and he was trying to win the Derby for a fourth time. I could see he knew we had him beaten and I yelled to him when we went past — 'Gotcha!'

Ali gave me a $5000 sling for winning the Derby. That's typical of him. And a couple of years later when I finished tenth on Hail in the Caulfield Cup he gave me a percentage of the stake for that, which he didn't have to do. A jockey gets his percentage from the first five placings, but when they pay back to tenth, as they do in the big races in Aussie, you don't usually get anything. It's rare these days to get a sling, even when you win a big race. The surprising thing is sometimes you can win a maiden race and someone with bugger all money will come up and give you, say, $500 as a sling.

I can remember probably my smallest sling. The trainer, who I knew really well, came up to me and gave me an envelope and said, 'The owner's backed it for you.' Well, it turned out his horse was the favourite and he'd put a dollar each way on it and it paid $4 or something. I was going to get about $6 and I said, 'You can stick this up your arse mate.' I gave him the ticket and he couldn't stop laughing. He said, 'No, no, no, the owner is real genuine, this is the first horse he's owned and he doesn't know.' The owner ended up being a great slinger, a lovely bloke. Every time I won for him he'd always give me $300 or $400.

Apart from Ali's sling, Derby Day was a good one all round for me. I won four races, including two of the features. The other big win was on Nikisha, who flew home in the Queen Elizabeth Handicap. On that run she looked a big chance in the Auckland Cup and she did go a good race in it, for third to Our Unicorn. Another of my winners on Derby Day was Shapaz for my brother Peter. Shapaz was just the second starter for Peter and I'd won on him at Hastings to give Peter his first win as a trainer. I remember one of the jockeys saying it should have been 'Harry Christmas' instead of Merry Christmas that year.

Hail went on to win over $1 million for Ali and Bruce. I won the St Leger at Trentham on him and finished third in a Kelt Stakes at Hastings. Greg Childs won the Group One Zabeel Classic at Ellerslie and the Sandown Classic in Melbourne, and he also finished second on him in a Kelt behind Distinctly Secret. Hail had a lot of Group One placings. He'll always be a bit special to me. After all, he gave me my New Zealand Derby win.

21

'You've got to be joking!'

I was on a big-time roll in 1999 and 2000 with six Group Ones and my first New Zealand Cup. But something else happened to me in 1999, something that really rocked me. And the outcome of it all stunned me even more.

It was all to do with the drug testing of jockeys. It was at Wellington in May and I had given a routine sample when I was requested and I thought nothing of it. That was on the Saturday. On the Thursday I rode at Otaki and got back into the weigh-in area after my first ride when the chief stipe Noel McCutcheon came up and the words he said floored me: 'You have returned a positive.' I was totally shocked and I said, 'To what?' He replied, 'Morphine.' I thought back and remembered I'd got a tooth out the previous week and they'd knocked me out with morphine. I told him what had happened and he said, 'No, no, no. Morphine just goes in and out of your system. It has got to be recent.'

I was stood down and retested. They had been deciding whether to let me ride at the Marton meeting on the Saturday or not. I was cleared to ride, then I went to Aussie to ride Believer in Brisbane for Jeff Lynds. I had to wait a week to get the second test back and I found out that it was all clear. I knew it had to be. There had to be a mistake with the first one. Sure enough, the reading from that first test meant I would almost certainly have been dead; I definitely wouldn't have been able to hop on a horse. The lab test result was all stuffed up.

At the time I was pleased the reason I was stood down never went to the newspapers because it could have ruined my career. I was innocent, but if a report came out and said I had been stood down because of an alleged failed drug sample some people would have jumped to conclusions without knowing the facts. *Did he use drugs or didn't he?* And even if the news came out that it had been a lab test stuff-up there would have still been that stigma for the rest of my career. Really, I was more worried about my career than what people thought of me. I decided the best way was to keep it quiet and tell nobody. I just thought it best to take it on the chin and move on.

Later I actually got a letter from New Zealand Thoroughbred Racing (NZTR) and was refunded what I lost out on the day I was stood down. Then I got another letter along with a $1000 goodwill payment. I remember the next time I went to Te Rapa, John McKenzie, the Racecourse Inspector, came up and congratulated me for the way I handled the whole situation. At the time I just accepted the refund and the $1000, but the more I think about the money it was wrong. If I had gone to the press about the mistake in lab results it would have opened a can of worms over other tests. NZTR couldn't afford that to happen so I suppose they thought by giving me the $1000 it would keep me quiet. I never thought of it that way at the time. Thinking back about it now, I should have got legal advice from someone.

The next time I had to do a drug test I was worried something might go wrong. And every time they give me a letter to do a test now my arse puckers. I've been tested well over a dozen times since then and nothing has gone wrong, but I keep thinking about how they stuffed up the lab results before and whether it will happen again. I've been tested only once in Aussie and that was when I went over to ride Princess Coup in the 2007 Melbourne Cup. I was almost 53 years old and they were probably thinking: *How could this guy ride at this age and be so light?*

I'm all in favour of drug testing, but when I was first asked I remember I had John McKenzie worried. He brought the paper to me and he said, 'Mr Harris, we want your sample,' and I refused it. He said, 'You can't refuse. You have signed to get your licence so you have to do a drug test.' I said, 'Nah, nah, I'm not going to do it.' Mr McKenzie's voice got angrier and angrier and he said, 'You know you have signed this. You will not be riding if you don't.' I replied, 'Listen, Mr McKenzie, you can't take the piss out of the Maoris.' I got him a beauty. It was only a joke and, as I said, I have never had any objection to taking a test. As soon as I get a letter I go straight to the toilet and do the test. But what happened with that Wellington test will always worry me.

The winners continued to flow. I ended 1999 with my first New Zealand Cup and I finished off 2000 with my first New Zealand Derby. A week later I was back chasing another Group One on Fritz in the Railway Handicap. He'd won a couple of races since the Telegraph Handicap and he had to carry 58 kilos. You had to go back to Mr Tiz in 1991 to find a horse that had carried more weight to win a Railway. Mr Tiz had 58.5 kg in his third Railway win that year and before that it was Shifnal Chief in 1975 with 59 kg. I thought if Fritz could win with that weight he'd have to be compared with Mr Tiz, and he did win.

It was a huge effort. We were back in midfield and came down the outside. It was my first win in the Railway — and what about Neil Coulbeck? It was his first Ellerslie win and it was a Group One. I'd gone into the carnival having never won a Derby or Railway and I ended up winning both within a week. Five weeks later we tried to get another Group One in the Waikato Draught Sprint. We did our best, but had to settle for second. Fritz was no match for the champion Sunline.

Neil decided to take Fritz to Queensland and asked me to go over. I wasn't about to say no. We struck first up on the trip, in the Carlton Draught Cup, a Group Two race over 1200 metres. We beat a good one in Show A Heart that day, then in the next start we finished fifth to Falvelon, another top sprinter, in the Doomben 10,000. Fritz came straight back after that and Neil gave him a spell and got him ready for Mudgway Partsworld Stakes at Hastings.

Neil is a top trainer and he had Fritz ready for the Mudgway. Mind you, Fritz had to be ready, given what was about to happen. We were back in the field and tracking Hello Dolly, who was ridden by Bootsy (Mark Sweeney). I knew I was tempting fate when I decided to go through on Bootsy's inner. No sooner had I committed myself to the run than the gap started to close and I got two or three beauties from Bootsy's whip. I was lucky Fritz had the acceleration to go through the gap. We actually hit the front too soon, but I had to take the gaps when they came. He got up and beat Cinder Bella, who was a top mare. She ended up winning a couple of Group Ones, a Kelt and a Captain Cook Stakes. I had welt marks on my arm from Bootsy's whip and I remember Bootsy overheard me telling a reporter what happened. With a smile he chimed in with the comment, 'I obviously didn't hit him hard enough.' Fritz won a couple more after that, but I never won another one on him.

A few months before I won the Mudgway I picked up a Group One win for another long-time mate, Chris McNab. It was in the Manawatu Sires' Produce Stakes and we had to fight to win it. I rode San Luis and we came up against Vinaka, who was a smart horse trained by Jim Gibbs. San Luis had run second to Vinaka in the Slipper Trial at Matamata and fourth to him at Trentham. But then I had my first ride on him in the Ford 2YO Classic at New Plymouth and he bolted in — and it wasn't a mug field. Second home was Final Destination, trained by Baggy Hillis' son, Wayne. She also came out the following season and won the One Thousand Guineas and Bayer Classic. After being sold she was a Group Three winner at Santa Anita in California.

In the Sires' Produce I got a good run to the straight on San Luis, but then it all went wrong. Vinaka shifted out and interfered with us twice. San Luis was running at him and if Vinaka had kept straight I would have beaten him anyway. I was called in second, but as I came

Winning the Wellington Stakes on Kingdom Bay, one of my favourite horses. You could take him into the lounge of your home if you wanted.

The 1987 Caulfield Guineas, a race which Poetic Prince should never have lost. The eventual winner Marwong is out of the photo. Robbed is all I can say.

My old mate Castletown carrying me to our third Wellington Cup win in 1994. We had a great association, including an Auckland Cup victory.

Rata Prince (vest) and Paddy Busuttin show their delight as I return to scale on Castletown after his third Wellington Cup success.

Above: Carrying Sir Patrick
Hogan's famous colours, I urge
Irish Chance home in the 1999
Auckland Cup.

Left: The day I shocked Noel
Eales. Saluting after winning the
1999 Waikato Draught Sprint at
Te Rapa on Surface. I'd dyed my
hair green, but Noel hated green
so I washed the dye out.

Above: I'm getting the best out of Hail as we claim Cookie (Grant Cooksley) on Sir Clive in the 2000 NZ Derby at Ellerslie.

Right: 'Put the skullcap back on,' said Neil Connors, despite me just winning the 2003 Auckland Cup for him on Bodie. The Mohawk haircut didn't go down well with Neil.

Who said I can't win from the front? Giving my brother Johnny his biggest training success with an all-the-way win in the 1990 Sydney Cup on King Aussie.

Everswindell gives me my fourth win in the New Zealand Cup, a race I'd actually taken years to win. It was a popular result for a large syndicate of owners.

Coming with the last run to win the country's first $2 million event, the Kelt Capital Stakes, on Princess Coup in 2007. In a mass of legs, Magic Cape, just inside me, was third, with J'adane, the grey, second, and Seachange fourth on the fence.

At home reflecting on a lifetime in racing surrounded by my trophies, photos and invitation colours.

back to scale I gave a victory salute, a cheeky message that I knew we had to get it in the inquiry room. The big thing was Vinaka was never two lengths clear and even Noel McCutcheon, the stipendiary steward, estimated that Vinaka carried San Luis out seven horse-widths before I switched and made my run inside. It had to change and it did. Vinaka was relegated to second and Leith Innes, his rider, copped a five-day suspension for careless riding. That was my second Manawatu Sires' Produce Stakes win, after Ballroom Babe, but it's not the way I like to win races. It's gone the other way for me a lot of times, too. I keep thinking of Poetic Prince losing the Caulfield Guineas.

We tried to win the Sires' Produce Stakes double with San Luis, but he got a rough run in the Ellerslie Sires and finished second to Kapiston. The following November I was third on him in the Group One, Two Thousand Guineas, and that was his last run before he went to stud. I was just happy to get a Group One for Chris.

I ended the 2000–01 season with 59 wins, well short of Michael Walker's premiership-winning tally of 182 or runner-up Lance O'Sullivan's 143, but my mounts had earned over $1.6 million in prize-money. That put me third behind those two for the most stakes won in the season. I was happy with that and so was my bank manager. One of the main contributors was Singalong, a filly raced in partnership by Sir Patrick Hogan and trained by Stephen Autridge. I'd run second on her as a two year old in a stakes race at Avondale. In my first ride on her as a three year old she showed how much she had improved when she won the Hawke's Bay Guineas.

Two starts later Singalong was aimed at the New Zealand Bloodstock Filly of the Year Series races and she started off well with a win in the Desert Gold Stakes. She then ran second in the One Thousand Guineas, stepped out of the series briefly when backing up in the Two Thousand Guineas against the males, and did well for fourth. She then switched back to the series and ran second to Tapildo in the New Zealand Oaks and won the Cambridge Stud Sir Tristram Fillies Classic at Te Rapa.

That meant a lot to Sir Patrick, having sponsored the race, and she went on to be named the Filly of the Year.

Singalong was the sixth Filly of the Year I've ridden during all, or part of, their three-year-old seasons. Tri Belle, trained by Ray Verner, was the first one and I started her on the road to her title. I rode her to win the Lowland Stakes at Tauherenikau then she had a few riders through to becoming the Filly of the Year. I also rode three of Murray Baker's fillies, Kate's Myth, Let's Sgor and Staring, during their runs through to the series win and, of course, there was my mate Gus' good filly, Lady Agnes. Kate's Myth, Let's Sgor and Lady Agnes all shared the title in their respective years.

Lady Agnes was a good filly. I ran second on her in the Eulogy Stakes and won the Sir Tristram's Fillies Classic at Te Rapa. That was a big thrill for Gus, but not as much as when we won the Group Three Adrian Knox Stakes in Sydney. She went on to the AJC Oaks and ran a gutsy race for third to Mahaya. I've been lucky to have ridden a lot of good fillies over the years, right back to the days of New Moon, Porsha, Peg's Pride and company.

Porsha had been my first major winner at Riccarton in the 1976 One Thousand Guineas and I'd won the race again on Clear Rose, then I picked up the Two Thousand Guineas on Kingdom Bay on the course and a New Zealand Cup on Wake Forest. Nine months after the Wake Forest win I won one of Riccarton's winter features, the Winter Cup, for the first time. I won it on Real Vision, trained by John Mason, a hard case character who used to train his horses along the edge of the forestry roads at Whakamaru, a settlement on the north-western access to Lake Taupo. His wife, Andrea, would ride the horses and he'd drive alongside clocking them. I've had a lot of luck for John over the years. I won six races on Real Vision, including the Kiwifruit Cup at Tauranga, before the Winter Cup. Another of John's horses was Danzaman and I won six on him, too, including a Taumarunui Cup.

Other wins I'd had at Riccarton at that stage included three Flying

Stakes (Courier Bay, Kingdom Bay and Mrs Selleck), two Canterbury Gold Cups (March Legend and Red Hawk), the Welcome Stakes (Jongleur), the Churchill Stakes (Ajanta) and the Easter Classic (Aerosmith). I remember in 1988 on the same day at Riccarton I had two dead-heats for first with Atishu (equal with Red Hawk) and Tilbury Docks (who dead-heated with Seve). By the time 2002 was over I'd had another couple of highlights on the track. I'd won both the Two Thousand Guineas and NZ Cup again.

Three months after Real Vision's Winter Cup win I gave Paul Harris (no relation) his first Group One win, with Hustler in the Two Thousand Guineas. It was my first ride on Hustler and we beat a top filly, The Jewel, who had won the One Thousand Guineas on the first day and later went to Brisbane and won the Doomben Roses and was robbed of a win in the Queensland Oaks. After the race Paul, whose father Ray was a successful trainer down south, was in tears and it was the same a few days later after I won the New Zealand Cup for him on Mike. I'd say Paul went through a few handkerchiefs at that carnival. Hustler had picked up three wins and three seconds before the Two Thousand Guineas, but he gave me one of the toughest rides of my life that day. With Mike, I felt I had the race won a long way out.

A funny incident happened at that New Zealand Cup meeting. It's always funny when Jill Bothwell is involved. Jilly, as she's known by everyone, is married to Dick Bothwell, a Taranaki trainer who I've ridden for quite a lot over the years, a top bloke. Jilly is one out of the box. She says it how she sees it. From day one when I met her we got on. She hasn't got a problem telling people where they belong and she loves to enjoy life.

Down at Christchurch that year I'd played golf on the Thursday and we were at the Racecourse Hotel afterwards. There was a karaoke machine going, and I got up there and had a dance with Jilly, who was pretty merry by that stage, and next minute Roy Orbison's song 'Only

The Lonely' came on. She was up on one of the tables singing 'Only the Baloney' at the top of her voice. Baloney was the name of her horse that she had in the New Zealand Cup two days later. I got up on Mike and won the Cup and Baloney ran second. 'You little shit, why couldn't you let us win?' That's Jilly's comment every time that day comes up. I'd have loved to have ridden Baloney for her and Dick, but it wasn't to be.

A couple of years later I ran second on Baloney in a Marton Cup and I did win a race on him, but Jilly still hasn't let up on me about the New Zealand Cup. If you meet Jilly, you'll never forget her. Precious, mate.

22

Harry, the Indian brave

Over the years I've changed my looks a fair bit. The long hair and 70s outfits, the shaven head, the earrings, the peroxided hair, green hair, beard, goatee, and so on. I'm not conventional in the way other people think I should be. I just try to be me, and I don't put up a smoke screen. I don't care what other people think. I like being jovial, being happy and if the jokes are on me I take it in my stride. So when someone suggested I should get a Mohawk haircut to ride Mohican Brave in the New Zealand Derby I went along with it. I was having a few drinks with friends before the Derby when out came the clippers and the job was done. I had my Mohawk.

I'd ridden Mohican Brave for the first time in the Derby Prelude and he flew home for fourth to Woburn. I was impressed and I was even more impressed when he came out and won the Derby Trial. That day he got hit from behind leaving the home straight the first time and we ended up scraping the inside rail. I had to go wide on the home turn to get a crack at them, and I ended up being forced to make my run sooner than I wanted, but he just kept giving. It was a really brave effort, a Mohican Brave effort. He felt like Hail did two years beforehand when he won the Derby. He was so relaxed and I was starting to think maybe I could win another Derby. I arrived at Ellerslie with my Mohawk and it was funny seeing people's reactions. When I walked into the jockeys' room a lot of the boys cracked up laughing and just said, 'Typical Harry.'

The Mohawk haircut didn't help me in the Derby — Mohican Brave finished well back that day. But the Derby was a good result on the day for my mate Chris McNab, who trained the winner, St Reims. Six days later I did have Group One joy with my Mohawk. I won the Auckland Cup on Bodie for Woodville trainer Neil Connors, whom I'd known for years. I've ridden a lot of winners for Neil, but what sticks in my mind most about that Auckland Cup was Neil's reaction to my Mohawk. When we were getting our photos taken at the presentation Neil wanted me to put my skullcap back on to hide the haircut. He was embarrassed by it. The winning jockey in the Auckland Cup got a La-Z-Boy chair and here I was stretched out in the chair on the dais with my Mohawk as the cameras were clicking away. Neil was standing behind me proud of his biggest win, but shaking his head over my Mohawk.

That Auckland Cup win wasn't a surprise for me. I knew Bodie was up to it. In my first ride on him I'd won at Te Rapa then we'd finished an unlucky second in the St Leger Trial at Trentham behind a smart one, Deebee Belle. I'd won a couple more on him, including a Listed race at Ellerslie, but then I missed his win in the Rotorua Cup and Mark Sweeney rode him. I was over in Adelaide to ride Yarradarno for Dick Bothwell and his son, 'Bones' (Chris). I knew Bodie was going to run in the Rotorua Cup and I had to toss up whether to stay in New Zealand or go to Adelaide. I chose to go with Yarradarno because of the Adelaide Cup. I'd won the Taranaki Cup on him and that day he'd beaten two good horses. Victory Smile, who won a Metropolitan Handicap in Sydney, was second and Prized Gem, Murray Baker's top mare who won the Brisbane Cup and Kelt Capital Stakes, was third.

I remember listening to the commentary of the Rotorua Cup on the phone from my motel room in Adelaide then later going out to ride Yarradarno in the lead-up to the Adelaide Cup. Yarradarno finished well back in the race and unfortunately he broke down before the Adelaide Cup and was never to race again. I'd missed the Rotorua Cup on Bodie, but it's a gamble I took at the time and I just had to hope I'd get back on him.

I did get to ride Bodie the following spring in the Counties Cup and he flew home for fourth to Deebee Belle. But then he finished down the track in the Waikato Times Cup and Neil was disappointed, so he changed plans. He was going to go straight into the Auckland Cup, but because of the Te Rapa run he wanted to give him another start to make sure he was all right. He lined him up in the Manawatu Cup and he ran on late for fifth. I was happy enough with the run and told him not to worry about the Waikato Cup.

In the Auckland Cup I just let Bodie find his feet, as I always did, and we were back for most of the way. I moved forward a little at the 1200 and when I asked him to go he finished it off well. I remember it was a close finish with Oarsman and Ebony Honor, but I thought I'd got there right on the line. We won by a nose from Oarsman — who went on to win the Wellington Cup — and Ebony Honor was only a half-head away third.

I'd now won three Auckland Cups within the space of 11 years. Castletown's win in 1992 was special, and it was good to get my second one on Irish Chance. To win the Cup on Bodie meant a lot, too, especially to do it for Neil, who I'd known for so long. In fact years before I'd won races for Neil's uncle, Bernie Connors, on Lone Hand. He was a great old horse trained by Noel Eales. He won 19 races and I won a Masterton Cup on him when he was a 10 year old, and my brother Dessie won a Hawke's Bay Cup and a Manawatu Cup. He was a lovely black horse and he had a big finish in him.

That 2002–03 season had been good for me. I'd won a second New Zealand Cup, the Two Thousand Guineas for a second time and my third Auckland Cup. I'd had 15 wins at Premier meetings and my mounts had earned over $1.2 million. I'd won races for people I'd been associated with for years and that trend continued the following season when I teamed up with the Hillis family for a few big wins. Baggy had been a great supporter when I was starting out, and when he slowed down and eventually retired I starting riding a bit for his son Wayne and his wife, Vanessa.

They had a good filly, Kainui Belle, and I won the Wellington Guineas in my first ride on her then ran second to Taatletail in the One Thousand Guineas. Kainui Belle backed up a few days later and finished third to King's Chapel in the Two Thousand Guineas before winning another stakes race, the Eulogy Stakes. She then came out and won the Group Two Eight Carat Classic at Ellerslie and was stiff not to make it three on end in the Royal Stakes. She finished second in the Royal Stakes after getting checked near the finish. I rode her in all those races. She was a tough filly and was so strong she was like a colt.

Later that January I picked up the ride on King's Chapel in the Group One Telegraph Handicap at Trentham. King's Chapel had been a top two year old the previous season and had won the Two Thousand Guineas and run third to Russian Pearl in the Bayer Classic with Opie Bosson in the saddle. Mark Walker, his trainer, had decided to go fresh up into the Telegraph Handicap, but he had only 52 kg which put Opie out of contention, so Mark offered me the ride. I snapped it up and he won like a really good horse that day. He repeated what O'Reilly had done seven years beforehand and won the Bayer Classic–Telegraph Handicap double as a three year old. I got to ride him only once more. That was in his next start when we finished fourth to Sedecrem in the Waikato Draught Sprint. He won another Group One and has gone on to become a successful sire.

A few months after my third Telegraph Handicap win, I won the Hawke's Bay Cup. I'd already won it three times, with Glengowan, Shamrock and Stylish Dude, but what made it special in 2004 was that I won it for my brother Peter on Royal Secret. It was just the way things worked out, but that Hawke's Bay Cup was the only time I rode Royal Secret. She had won five of her first 10 starts and her performance in the Hawke's Bay Cup was a huge one. We'd got back and I managed to sneak her through along the fence and she got up to beat Regal Krona, who won a couple of Avondale Cups.

It was Peter's biggest training success. He never had more than a few horses in work at a time and when you're dealing with small numbers it's hard to get a lot of winners. It was great for him and the way she won that day had us thinking that maybe she could be just the horse to win a Melbourne Cup for the family. But it wasn't to be. Royal Secret broke down after the Hawke's Bay Cup, but a couple of years later she did make a comeback. Her owners had decided to send her up to John Sargent. I know losing her really knocked Peter and he gave up training after that. Royal Secret had one start for Sarge then broke a leg on the training track.

I won a Sydney Cup for my oldest brother, Johnny, and the Hawke's Bay Cup for Peter and I could have won an Avondale Cup for my other brother, Dessie. I had been riding Makorby for Dessie and won five races on him, including three in a row. But he had only 50.5 kg in the Waikato Times Cup which was too light for me and I talked Jimmy Cassidy into riding him. I said, 'Get on this mate. He wins.' Makorby didn't win at Te Rapa, but he came out the next start and won the 1982 Avondale Cup. Dessie had ridden many great horses as a jockey — La Mer was the best — and the Avondale Cup was his biggest win as a trainer. He did have some other handy ones, too, like Saunter.

Two months after I won the Hawke's Bay Cup for Peter there was an even bigger family highlight for me: my son Troy had his first race-day ride. It was up at Ruakaka and I'd never been to the course. I'd ridden at the old Whangarei track at Kensington Park. I remember the day I won the Whangarei Cup on Happy William. It was a false start and it was quicker to keep going around than pull the horse up and come back to the barrier.

Troy had a large support crew for his first day's riding. I went up and so did his mum. Jock even made the trip up from Palmerston North and some of my aunties were there, too. Troy was apprenticed to Mark Walker, and Mark had bided his time with him, making sure he had plenty of trials experience and was fully prepared before he had his first ride. Mark put him on the stable runner Southern Storm, a horse who was a big chance. Southern Storm had five seconds in seven starts and Troy couldn't have had a better opportunity. Whereas I had to wait 21 rides for my first win, on Phar Lace, Troy started off brilliantly. He won on Southern Storm that day and it couldn't have worked out better, especially with Jock there to see it happen.

I've always believed Troy has that X-factor and not just because he's my boy. It was like that in any sport he played. He was in the Under 11s Rep team for soccer and he played league when he was only young. And when he came up to live with me in Matamata he wanted to play rugby and made it into the Roller Mills team and played for Waikato. But when he went to college he was just too light so he gave his rugby away.

I never pushed Troy into being a jockey. He had nothing to do with horses for six or seven years then, one day when he was living with me, he said he wanted to be a jockey. He needed to make the decision himself. I was pleased to see him become the third-generation jockey in the family, and there was nobody more proud than me at Ruakaka on 23 June 2004, the day he rode his first winner. My son was on his way and I couldn't have been happier. It was an emotional day with the family there, but little did we know at the time Troy's promising run as an apprentice was going to come to a screaming halt eight months later.

23

A father's nightmare

One minute you're riding the crest of the wave, the next you've crashed to the ground. You never know what's just around the corner in the racing game. I'll never forget that sickening feeling when Troy had his terrible fall at Wairoa. It was 13 February 2005. I'd been invited to a party at Jim Gibbs' place and I was at home getting ready to go out. Troy had ridden 20 winners since the beginning of the new season and he had become a sought-after 3 kg-claiming apprentice.

He was riding a horse called Blarney Star and I was watching the race on TV, but couldn't pick him up. Then suddenly with about 1000 metres to run a horse went down and another crashed over the top of it. I had this gut feeling it was Troy. I wasn't sure, but a cold feeling went through me. It was then announced that it was him, and a few minutes later Robbie Hannam, one of my jockey mates from Palmerston North, rang me to say Troy had broken a leg. I thought: *Oh well, that's not too bad. It could have been worse.* Then about a minute and a half later Robbie rang back to say he'd broken both legs and had been taken to Hawke's Bay Hospital.

I jumped in the car and headed off to Hastings; when I got there the whole story unfolded. Blarney Star had collapsed of a suspected heart attack and Troy was flung into the piping upright supporting the running rail. What made it worse, the uprights had been held in place by concrete slabs and that's what caused the damage. Thomas

Russell, who had gone down to Wairoa with Troy, was on the horse that crashed over the top of Blarney Star and he saw Troy wrapped around the upright and the concrete slab. Apparently, the impact moved the upright, with the concrete slab attached, a metre and a half down the track. Troy had hit the concrete slab with full force and he had broken the femurs (thigh bones) in both legs.

It was a long, slow recovery for Troy. When he was lying in the hospital bed in Hastings he said he wouldn't ride again, but then a few weeks later after he saw me riding winners he changed his mind. I admire him for coming back from that fall. After those sorts of injuries a lot of jockeys wouldn't have come back. But he was only 16 and he had youth on his side. You tend to bounce back better when you're young. It took about eight months for him to fully recover, and he rode 33 winners the next season, one less than me. But I had to remind him I rode six Group or Listed winners that season and he had still to ride one.

Troy did go on to pick up a couple of stakes wins the following season and he was so thrilled when he won the Group Two City of Auckland Cup at Ellerslie on New Year's Day on Highflying. I don't blame him for getting excited. It was special for me, too, because Highflying was trained by Dick and 'Bones' Bothwell. It wasn't only Troy's biggest win at that stage; it was also the biggest for Bones. I'd won a race on Highflying earlier at Trentham.

Troy went on to be the champion apprentice that season. He was the fourth member of our family to do it and it made Jock and me proud. Johnny had been top apprentice three years in a row, Dessie one year and I was the top apprentice twice. Troy rode 61 winners, one more than me, but it was still a good season for me. I won seven stakes races and my mounts earned over $1.6 million.

The day before Troy had his fall, I had won the Group Two Sir Tristram Fillies Classic at Te Rapa on Murray Baker's filly, Tusker, and I went on to win a Group Three race on her, too. Around that time I had been riding Pulcinella for Don Sellwood. I won the Group Three Eclipse Stakes at Ellerslie and finished second to Mi Jubilee in the Group Two Matamata Breeders Stakes. But the thought of what had happened to Troy at Wairoa was always on my mind, and I made a stand the following month at Avondale.

I had complained about the fixed wooden rail at Avondale two years beforehand and the Jockeys' Association had also expressed its concern, but nothing had been done. That day I went up to Avondale races for four rides and when I got there on course and found Avondale's collapsible aluminium running rail was not in use, I told the stipes I wouldn't be riding.

I wasn't picking on Avondale, but if I had ridden that day I would have gone against everything I believe in. I had to make a stand. Ironically, just hours after I made my call Melbourne jockeys were standing in silence to honour Adrian Ledger and apprentice Gavin Lisk, two jockeys who had been killed in race falls during the week.

Racing has claimed the lives of many jockeys over the years. It's one of the dangers of the profession. You're riding 500-plus kilo animals at speed and if something goes wrong it can mean disaster. As well as the ones who have been killed, there are jockeys who have ended up in wheelchairs. It only takes a split second and sometimes the fall doesn't look a nasty one. It can be just the way you hit the turf. But if you're in front or among the field and come down, the odds of being injured are high.

One of the most recent jockey deaths in New Zealand racing was the apprentice rider Sam McRae, who was dragged by his mount and died. That was in a race at Riverton in March 2005 and he was only 16. Earlier on, Jo McGartland was killed in a race fall at Rangiora in February 2002, and Ray Hewinson died the following July at Ashburton. I knew Hewie quite well. About 18 years earlier his nephew Hunter Thomas died in a race fall, also at Ashburton. Hewie gave up for about 14 years because of Hunter's death, but made a comeback.

I've mentioned how Dad's brother Desmond, or Dodo as everyone knew him, was killed in a fall at Marton. My brother Dessie was named after him, and I often heard the story of what happened to Dodo. In those days the skull caps were like papier-mâché and in coming off a horse in a race and hitting his head on a concrete post at speed, he had no chance. He was 18 at the time and a promising rider. It was scary to think a concrete slab could have also claimed the life of my son Troy if he'd hit it with his head rather than his legs.

Dodo's death isn't the only racing fatality we've had in the Harris household. One of our young stablehands, Stephen O'Neill, was also killed. It was during the late 1970s and I was riding in Singapore, but I heard all about it. Stephen had come from Upper Hutt and he wanted to be a jockey. He was living at the stables and going to Tararua College. I think he was about 15 and his parents let him come up to see if he was cut out to be a jockey. Jock and Johnny had a few kids working part-time for them at the time.

Stephen used to go to the track in the morning, hose down the horses and head back to the stable with one of the first horses worked. He'd then jump in the shower and go off to school. There would usually be two of the boys together and they were supposed to lead the horses back, but as kids do, they decided to jump on their backs and ride them bareback. They were only small so they'd lead them over to the fence to climb on. Jock and Johnny didn't know any of this was going on. They only found out later.

This particular morning they jumped on two horses and apparently one set off before the other. Stephen slipped off the side of his horse and the horse bolted. His boot got caught in the reins and he was dragged along the tarseal road. Of course he didn't have a skull cap on because he wasn't supposed to be riding and his head was exposed. Moss Robinson, Lance's father, was the first on the scene. He lived up the road and he saw the horse coming with Stephen being dragged.

The poor kid was dead when Moss got to him. It was a tragedy and obviously it shook everyone up.

It's one of those things that shouldn't have happened, but kids being kids there was no fear and they just jumped on the horses bareback. It was a quick way to get them home. We've all done things like it and usually if you're on bareback and fall off you just hit the ground and get a few bruises and scratches. It was a freak accident the way his gumboot got caught in the reins and, sadly, he paid the ultimate price.

I remember earlier Syd Brown's horses going up through town in Woodville on the way to the track. We'd be mucking out in the mornings and you could hear the horses coming up the road. You would see sparks coming off the horses' shoes as they trotted along. It's just amazing to think you could ride one and lead two horses through the main street in Woodville and along main roads. In those days it was common to do that and it used to happen everywhere, all over the country. It was a way of getting three to the track at once. And it was a regular sight to see a loose horse or more. Mind you, the roads weren't as busy in those days. You just didn't worry about the dangers.

Whenever you are handling animals you have always got to be careful, and with horses it's not just the riders that can be injured. You've got to respect the horse and be aware of the dangers and other horses around you. I learnt my lesson early on when I copped a kick in the chin from a colt that day I tied him up just through the fence from New Moon.

One of the most recent tragic cases occurred at the Hastings races in October 2010 when Blair Busby, a Matamata stablehand, was killed after being kicked by the top filly Katie Lee. He was just going about his business with his horse down near the hosing bay and Katie Lee lashed out and caused what ended up a fatal blow. Blair was taken to hospital, but died from his injuries. He was no inexperienced novice. He was 37 and he'd been around horses most of his life. It just goes to show it can happen to anyone.

As for injuries on the racetrack, I've told you all about the most injury-prone jockey I know, my mate Gus Clutterbuck. He even fell twice from the same horse. While Gus has broken just about every bone in his body, except his neck, I've been lucky. I'd had a few minor injuries, a few pulled muscles, but no broken bones in 36 years. However, that changed at Tauranga 13 months after Troy broke his legs. I was riding Buena Ventura for Graeme Rogerson and had just finished third. I was going past the winning post and was pulling up when he spotted the Clerk of the Course on his horse coming towards us. He shied and I came off. It was really minor. I fell off the side and I thought I'd escaped any injury, but then he stood on me.

I broke three ribs and punctured my lung. My safety vest saved me. If it hadn't been for the vest I don't know where I'd be. I was off for five weeks and it could have been seven weeks. The doctor had told me not to come back before seven, but I had a horse called Captain Kurt going to Australia. He was worth riding so I decided to come back early. I'd run second on him as a two year old and third in the Hawke's Bay Guineas and second to Darci Brahma in the Two Thousand Guineas. I got my clearance, then found out they were going to use an Aussie rider, so I could have had two more weeks out. He ended up running third in the Gold Coast Guineas and that was it for him.

One fall I had at Wanganui many years ago could have been nasty. I was trailing and five of us came down. I know there were Peter Ayres, Jimmy Walker, Kim Clapperton and me, but I can't think of the other rider. Kim was the only one to get up and walk away. The rest of us all went to hospital. I had concussion. I can just remember the horse going down and the next thing I remember was in the back of the ambulance asking what the next race was.

I was all right and allowed to go home from hospital. Jimmy was out in the corridor on a stretcher. The X-ray machine had broken down and they said Jimmy could go home, too, and to take him to his local doctor the next morning. Jimmy's wife, Bev, drove him home and he had to put the seat right back. When he got back to Hawera the doctor took one look at him and got him in an ambulance. He was rushed to New Plymouth Hospital. He had smashed or crushed hips. There was no way he should have been allowed to go home in the first place.

Over the years some jockeys have decided to call it quits after having a fall. They take it as a sign to finish before they get seriously hurt. It's a high-risk business to be in and some jockeys just lose their nerve. I've seen it time and time again. If you're not focused, accidents can happen.

24

Bizarre jigger claim

Lisa Cropp has had more than her share of headlines, both for good reasons and bad. She's a top rider and she's proved that here and in Australia. I'd never had a problem with her until 3 March 2007, and to this day I still can't believe what she did.

It was one of the most bizarre events in New Zealand racing and created headlines worldwide. It certainly stunned as many Aussies as it did Kiwis. It all centred on the return to the birdcage after the New Zealand Derby. Vinnie Colgan, one of my best mates, won the race on the Sydney visitor Redoute's Dancer, Lisa was second on Mettre En Jeu and I finished third on Uberalles.

As we were heading back to the birdcage I gave Vinnie a high five, congratulating him on his win. Vinnie was excited and he had every reason to be. It was his fourth New Zealand Derby win. As I think back, it was quite funny the look Lisa was giving us when we did the high five. It was strange, and she was muttering something to herself.

I never thought much of it at the time then when we got back into the jockeys' room I saw people heading into the inquiry room. They called us in and we didn't know what was going on. Vinnie thought I'd protested or there had been a protest against him. I looked at Vinnie and said, 'No, no, you're meant to have a jigger.' Well, Vinnie's eyes said it all. He couldn't believe it. Lisa had told the owners of Mettre En Jeu that as we did the high five she had seen Vinnie pass to me a 'silver device', which she believed to be a jigger — an electronic device used to shock a horse. They all went to the stipes and she repeated the claim.

All the riders were kicked out of the jockeys' room, except Vinnie and me, as the racecourse detective and some stewards checked our bags and lockers. They then inspected the area of the track where Lisa said it happened. It was ridiculous. While all this was going on the presentation was stopped and Tim Martin, the trainer of Redoute's Dancer, and the owners gathered outside the inquiry room wondering what the hell was going on. Finally, they were told and they were as stunned by such a bizarre claim as we all were.

It was totally unbelievable, ludicrous, to think we would even consider doing something like that. I'd been riding more than 35 years and needed only about 60 winners to get my 2000. I told the stipes, 'Why would I jeopardise my career for the sake of this?' Vinnie explained: 'Lisa knows Harry is like a koro or a dad, to me. We were only celebrating and she put a big spoiler on it.'

The stipes got the Trackside TV video footage and it clearly showed Vinnie had an empty hand both before and after the contact. I don't know what Lisa was dreaming about that day, but whatever it was, we didn't want to be a part of it. And what made matters worse was later on when the races were all over I saw the connections of Mettre En Jeu walking down the straight looking for this alleged 'silver device'. It was so stupid. The track had already been checked; there was nothing there. It was only in Lisa's imagination. But what annoyed me was that someone could have gone down to the shops and bought a silver battery device and dropped it on the track. We'd have got blamed for it.

Vinnie is still angry about what Lisa did, but I've let it lie. I got over it, but Lisa never apologised for making a mistake. That's what really annoys us. She made a huge mistake and hasn't had the guts to admit it. I've never even seen a jigger. I'd heard a lot about the Aussies and how they'd have one in the leadbags and put little batteries in their whips, but that's just what I've heard. Ivan Allan had something like a pig prodder tied to bamboo and he used it to make horses jump out of the barriers. That's the closest thing to a jigger I've seen.

Later on I had a silver lighter and when I went out of the jockeys' room for a smoke I'd have it down the side of my riding boots. A few times I'd be cheeky when the Racecourse Inspector John McKenzie came past and I'd say, 'Is this what you're looking for?' as I lit my cigarette. Another day at Hawera, Lisa was in the tea hut and I stood behind her and put the silver lighter beside her coffee. She didn't acknowledge me. She just grabbed the coffee and off she went. She knew who it was behind her and why I did it. Vinnie will never forgive her for what she did.

I've known Vinnie for years and I can still remember the first time we met. He was apprenticed to Roger James at Matamata and was riding at Hastings. I was sitting in the jockeys' room and Vinnie walked through the door and stood on my toe. He said, 'Sorry,' but kept walking. I walked up behind him and grabbed him on the shoulder and said, 'When you say sorry, you say it as though you mean it.' Vinnie went white. We laugh about it now, but Vinnie said at the time he just about shat himself.

A few months after the Derby I landed a dream result for Cambridge trainer Ross McCarroll when I won the Taumarunui Cup on Figure Of Speech. Ross said he had wanted to win the race since he was a kid and he was calling me a genius for the winning ride. I'd won the Kiwifruit Cup a couple of starts beforehand on Figure Of Speech, and in the Taumarunui Cup I had got him across from a wide draw to be one off the fence and he got up late. I read in one of the newspapers Ross said that I'd keep riding until one day I'd drop dead and fall out of the saddle. It was his way of saying he couldn't believe how I could keep going for so long and still be riding winners.

Less than three months after the Taumarunui Cup win I proved to everyone I was still up to winning the big ones. I picked up my biggest win in New Zealand, the $2 million Group One Kelt Capital Stakes at Hastings on Princess Coup. Seachange was all the rage after she'd won the first two legs of the Hawke's Bay Triple Crown, but I felt Princess Coup would be hard to beat. I'd ridden her in the previous start when she'd flashed home late for third to Seachange and the extra distance was always going to suit her better.

I'm not normally a religious person, but that day around at the start before the Kelt I looked up towards the man up top and thought: *God, if you let me win this one it doesn't matter if I don't win another race.* You don't have to go to church to believe in God. I believe in a certain God, that someone looks after you, like having a little bird on your shoulder, as Bill Skelton always said. I don't know if it was God or that little bird, but someone was looking after me that day. But don't tell Darren Beadman. He'll think he's converted me.

Princess Coup put up a huge finish that day and got up right on the line to beat J'Adane by a half-head. It was a blanket finish, with Magic Cape a nose away third, and another nose to Seachange, who tried so hard for Gavin McKeon. Mark Walker, Princess Coup's trainer, didn't want to shake hands with anyone until the judge's call was confirmed. He had seen me salute the judge, but he remembered I'd done the same a couple of years earlier when I thought I'd won another Group One, the Bayer Classic, on Shikoba for him. That day we were beaten a nose by Wahid.

Yeah, I got it wrong in the Bayer, but this time I knew for sure, though only on the line. I had a feeling we'd just got there. Then a bit of doubt crept in when I saw Mark Du Plessis going up with a salute. He was convinced he'd won on J'Adane and I thought to myself, *Oh no, not another Shikoba.* But I shouldn't have worried. Princess Coup got there. It was history. I'd won the richest race in New Zealand at the time — a couple of years later they made the New Zealand Derby $2.2 million. Winning the Cox Plate was phenomenal and winning the Kelt that year was exceptional, too. It was my third win in the race. I won it in 1997 on Secret Seal when it was the Ormond Memorial Gold Cup and I won the first running of the Kelt Capital Stakes in 1991 on my old mate 'Mac' — Castletown.

Mark then took Princess Coup to Melbourne: Glen Boss finished third on her in the Caulfield Cup and Kerrin McEvoy was second on her in the Mackinnon Stakes. I picked up the ride in the Melbourne Cup. She only had 51 kilos and I had to waste, but she was a form horse and it was another opportunity to win the Melbourne Cup. It was my eleventh ride in the Cup, but it wasn't lucky 11. Princess Coup finished down the track, while Michael Rodd won the race on Efficient.

A month later I was in Christchurch attempting to win another New Zealand Cup. I had won my third New Zealand Cup 12 months earlier on Pentathon for John Wheeler, who had got me over to Brisbane the previous year to ride him in the Queensland Derby. Pentathon ran fifth in the Derby and wasn't far away, and my first ride back on him was a winning one in the lead-up to the New Zealand Cup on the first day at Riccarton. I knew he'd be a top ride in the Cup and on the day he was just too strong for Cluden Creek, who had won the Wellington Cup a couple of years earlier.

Everswindell was my ride in the 2007 New Zealand Cup for John Sargent. I'd won the Wellington Cup Trial on her then she'd run a good race for third to Willy Smith in the Wellington Cup, so I had no worries about the 3200 metres at Riccarton. The plan was to ride her midfield one off the fence, but things got really tight early on and I got knocked back and down on the fence. Then in the straight I thought for a moment we might not get a run, but the gap appeared and she went so quickly into it she knocked a couple of others out of the way. I don't often let excitement overtake me at the finish of a race, but that day it happened. I waved my whip in the air before the post and copped a $400 fine for it. But it didn't matter. I'd won another New Zealand Cup. To think I had tried for so long to win one, then within nine years I won four.

Everswindell gave me my tenth 3200-metre Cup win in New Zealand and that equalled the record held by one of the legends, Bob Skelton. As well as the four New Zealand Cups (Wake Forest, Mike, Pentathon and Everswindell), I've won three Wellington Cups on Castletown and three Auckland Cups (Castletown, Irish Chance and Bodie). Bob won three New Zealand Cups (Oreka, Princess Mellay and Heidsieck), five Wellington Cups (a hat-trick on Great Sensation, plus Ark Royal and City Court) and two Auckland Cups (Rose Mellay and Royal Cadenza).

Bob has it over me as he's won a Melbourne Cup on Van Der Hum and two Perth Cups on Magistrate. Even though he retired in 1987, I haven't got much hope of beating his tally of 20 wins at 3200 metres. That's eight more than me. I've won a Sydney Cup on King Aussie and a 3210-metre race at New Plymouth on News to go with my Auckland, Wellington and New Zealand Cups.

The big thing with 3200-metre races is getting your mount to relax and riding a patient race. Jock always told me to talk to my horses to help them relax and it's something I've done to help them settle before a race. It also helps during a race. You get in sync with them.

The New Zealand Cup on Everswindell was the second Cup I won for Sarge within 12 months. The previous December I picked up the Avondale Cup on Sharvasti and, like my ride on Everswindell, I didn't have all the luck in the running. Leith Innes had learned a few tricks riding in Japan. Jeez did he have me tight on the home bend. I was going nowhere. Leith was on Upstaged and on the bend I was yelling at him and he wasn't listening — not that I blame him. I'd have done the same. I was so desperate to get out I nearly went up inside Leith's horse, but I didn't want to do that. Instead I waited until Leith went forward then I followed and switched to the outside. The gap was narrow and I had to wait for a bit before I went on her. When I did she got up to beat Upstaged, who dead-heated for second.

Naturally, Sarge was thrilled to get the Group One win with Sharvasti and he was unlucky not to get another one. She ran second in both the

Zabeel Classic and Whakanui Stud International Stakes at Te Rapa. I rode her in each of her four wins.

I won another Group One for Sarge, the Manawatu Sires' Produce Stakes on Il Quello Veloce. That was four months after the New Zealand Cup and, like Everswindell, she was raced by a large syndicate of owners. I was on Il Quello Veloce in her first win and she deserved to win the Manawatu Sires. She had been runner-up to Te Akau Coup in the Matamata Breeders Stakes and third to Fully Fledged in the Group One Ford Diamond Stakes at Ellerslie.

A month earlier I was back in Murray Baker's stable colours riding his good three year old Nom du Jeu. I'd won my first ride on him a couple of starts beforehand and we'd finished sixth in the Wellington Stakes. Murray had a big opinion of him and not just because he was a son of Prized Gem, his Brisbane Cup and Kelt Stakes winner. He was a good horse. I remember in the Waikato Guineas he was back and I rode for luck, got the gaps and he went to the line full of running. He was more relaxed that day than he had been, and he showed his class. I knew that's what you needed in a Derby horse. I felt he might have been six months away in maturity, but he might still just have been talented enough to win the Derby.

Nom du Jeu had one more start before the New Zealand Derby and was desperately unlucky. That was in the Championship Stakes at Ellerslie when he was held up for most of the run home. He never got to stretch out that day. In the Derby we struck a slow track and Dummy Myers won it that year with C'est La Guerre, who went on to be a top horse in Aussie. Nom du Jeu still went a good race, running on late for fourth.

I then ran second on Nom du Jeu in the Manawatu Classic and Murray took him over for the Group One AJC Derby. Jeff Lloyd, a former top South African rider, got the ride in the Derby and won it, beating Sarge's horse, Red Ruler. Sure I missed out on the AJC Derby ride, but at least my judgement was on the mark. I'd said he could be up to winning a Derby.

Jeff Lloyd picked up a Group One second on Nom du Jeu after that, and I was back on when the horse started up again in New Zealand. We won first up at Te Rapa, but he later lost the race through a swab. That was to be the last time Nom du Jeu was first past the winning post. We chased Princess Coup and Opie Bosson home when second in the Stoney Bridge Stakes and third in the Kelt Capital Stakes. Murray took him back to Aussie and Jeff Lloyd finished second on him in the Caulfield Cup and eighth in the Melbourne Cup.

When I think back over my time with Nom du Jeu, I remember I had to make a tough choice between him and Red Ruler as a three year old. I had won a three-year-old 1600 at Ellerslie on Red Ruler and Sarge had offered me the New Zealand Derby ride. I had to make the call whether to ride Nom du Jeu for Murray or Red Ruler for Sarge. I'd ridden a lot for both trainers over the years and had a lot of success for them. It was a tough choice.

I summed up the loyalty and the horses. It took a lot of cogitation, but in the end I stuck with Nom du Jeu. I knew there was a chance I was going to be disappointed either way. I had all these scenarios and I worked out Nom du Jeu would probably be the better horse. It was a fine line and as it turned out I was right, though both horses went on to be Group One winners. Vinnie Colgan picked up the ride on Red Ruler, and when they won the Championship Stakes I was an unlucky tenth on Nom du Jeu. I was wondering whether I'd made the right decision, but we turned the tables in the New Zealand Derby when Red Ruler ran eighth.

People say I must have been pissed off when Murray didn't take me to Aussie for the AJC Derby and instead put Jeff Lloyd on. But Murray had come to me and told me he was going to use an Aussie-based rider. I appreciated his honesty. And he was true to his word that when Nom du Jeu came back to New Zealand he'd put me on again. The New

Zealand trainers have been using Aussie riders more and more and I copped it. But I could have gone the other way, but then that would have cost me a lot of money. I did well out of Nom du Jeu.

I've learnt over the years it pays to take it on the chin and not make a big fuss. A lot of times it will come back and work in your favour in the long run. But if you blow up, you've burnt your bridges — and in this game you have to be open to as many rides as you can get.

You never know who is going to have the next great horse.

25

New focus in my life

The main focus on me as I started 2008 was how close I was getting to my 2000th winner in New Zealand. It kept cropping up on the radio and television and in the newspapers every time I rode another winner. But to me there was an even more important focus — my marriage to Kylie Hyland.

I'd been on my own for a year and a half, just cruising along, when I met Kylie at, of all places, a funeral. It was the funeral for Jim Gillies, an old former jumps jockey and trainer. The Gillies family has been in racing for many years and old Jim had a good send-off. You could say as one chapter in life was finishing for Jim, another was starting for me. I got talking to Kylie. When I meet someone I either like them or don't. I hit it off well with Kylie and it wasn't long before we started going out together. I had heard of her father, Dick Hyland, through racing. He was an ex-amateur rider who had trained for a time.

Kylie knew a bit about racing, even though she wasn't directly involved. She and her sister, Nicky, were into the pony club and hunting scene. Before long Kylie had shifted from Rotorua to live with me in Matamata, and I soon found out she's an on-to-it lady and very motivating. She has taught me a lot about how to handle different and difficult situations. And that's something I needed with what was ahead.

On Wellington Cup day in 2008 we announced our engagement, and to celebrate I kicked home a couple of winners. We decided to get married in Fiji the following June and rather than send out invitations we put the word out to all our friends and family. Whoever wanted to come was welcome. It was quite surprising to end up with over 80 guests. We were blown away by the number of friends and family who turned up.

All our guests treated the week as a holiday and that's the way we wanted it. We stayed at the Sofitel in Denarau and most of the guests were at the Radisson Resort next door. About 20 of our guests were on the same flight over as we were, and really the holiday started there and then for all of us. We wanted it to be laidback. It was more than a wedding; it was also a reunion in a way because we hadn't caught up with some of the guests for a long time. It was great.

My Aunty Billie, Jock's sister, is a Justice of the Peace. She conducted the marriage service in a quaint little church. It was a perfect setting and everyone was having a ball. You can imagine how some of the guests were feeling after drinking champagne for a couple of hours in 32-degree heat. And Mickey Coleman, one of my jockey mates, got the show going with his impersonation of Borat, the crude Kazakstani reporter. Kylie says she can still hear that squeaky voice he put on and how he had us all in laughter. Everyone had a ball.

But it wasn't all plain sailing. In fact you could say I felt like a seasick sailor with a bad case of diarrhoea for most of the week. It had nothing to do with marrying Kylie. I had looked forward to that and I couldn't be happier. But a day before the wedding Aunty Billie broke the news that Darrell, my ex-wife, could be turning up in Fiji. I tell you I started to cringe and I thought, *Hell, here we go. This wedding mightn't go through.* It was like a nightmare with all these thoughts rushing through my head. *This can't be happening to me*, I kept thinking.

We had been talking to Darrell a week or two before we went over and she wished us good luck. Then she turned up at the time of our wedding. Shit, if anyone says good luck to me now I start to wonder what bad thing is going to happen next. If she said then she could be over on the island at around the same time it wouldn't have been such a shock. But just to front up like that. Later on when I confronted her about it, she just said they normally go at that time of the year and she had gone over to support the kids because Troy and Cushla were there.

Truly, it was like something you see in the movies, the ex appearing on your wedding day. Even though Darrell didn't turn up at the actual wedding, I was on tenterhooks the whole time and, true, I did have diarrhoea for a week. I ended up about 49 kilos stripped. Talk about a quick way to lose some weight. It put a dampener on our big day.

After the wedding we came back to Matamata for one night then hopped on the plane and honeymooned in Singapore for a week. It was good to finally be able to relax. It was hard enough for me, but for a bride it's an even bigger day in her life. I felt so sorry for Kylie, but she handled it well. We laugh about it now, but at the time it was shocking.

Among the guests at our wedding were Bill and Suzi Pomare. I've known Bill for many years and ridden several of the horses he's trained and owned. I was sitting on 1999 wins when we got married and I had hoped to have ridden my 2000th before we went to Fiji. It brought back memories of chasing my 1000th win, having to sit one short for what seemed like ages. At the wedding Bill said he'd give me my 2000th and I thought it would be great, but things don't usually turn out like that.

We got back to New Zealand and Bill gave me the ride on Beau Casual on Taumarunui Cup day at Te Rapa. It was a meeting that had treated me well in past years and she looked an OK ride. It started raining and you couldn't say, *This is going to be it*. But Beau Casual put it all together that day. She hit the front about 300 metres out and it was a real grind to the finish. I kept thinking, *Her legs are going to fall off any minute*. But she kept going to beat Jacowils, who turned out to be a good sprinter. He went on to win the Railway Handicap the following New Year's Day at more than 100/1.

It was a relief to finally get my 2000th and I was rapt to do it on Bill's horse. The pressure was off and for good measure I came out and won the next race, too, on Chatterbox for John Sargent. Yeah, it was like the day of my 1000th win all over again. To think both Bill and Sarge had made the trip to Fiji for our wedding. Bill had been saving a 70-year-old bottle of scotch until he trained a Group One winner, but he said giving me my 2000th win was like a Group One win to him. He actually drove to Rotorua to grab the scotch and came back to Matamata to celebrate.

It was great to get into the 2000 club. I'd joked to a couple of ex-jockeys, PD (Peter Johnson) and JC (Jim Collett), that there were too many in the 1000 club so I wanted to get in the 2000 club. There were only Lance O'Sullivan (2357), Bill Skelton (2156) and David Peake (2093) at the time, but David Walsh beat me into it.

When I got to 1000 wins I thought it was an achievement so to get to 2000 is something special. I never thought I'd get there because of the weight problems I'd had. But since the move north to Matamata things had really happened for me. I never ring for rides, except to confirm the ones that I know I'll be on, and I've been lucky that I haven't really had to call. I'd got on some good horses and won my share of races. And a month later it happened to me again.

Brian Hibberd had been suspended and he recommended me for the ride on Fritzy Boy in the Mudgway Partsworld Stakes at Hastings. 'Hibby' had won the South Island three-year-old triple crown — the Gore, Dunedin and Southland Guineas — on Fritzy Boy who had gone on to run third in C'est La Guerre's New Zealand Derby, one placing in front of me on Nom du Jeu. I knew Fritzy Boy was a good horse and Hibby rang me on the Friday night to discuss tactics. He told me he couldn't bear to watch the race. I just said, 'Okay Hibby. I'll look after your horse and you just read about it in the paper on Sunday.'

I've known Hibby since he was apprenticed to Jock, and when I was trying to win my first New Zealand Cup I was envious of him as he had already won it a few times. He made it five wins in the race when he won it on Waltermitty for Wheels, so he's still one in front of me.

Thanks to Hibby and Fritzy Boy's trainer, Alby MacGregor, I got to add another Mudgway win to my Group One tally. I'd won the race on Volare for Malcolm Smith back in 1982 when it was the Hawke's Bay Challenge Stakes, a Listed race, and as the Mudgway I'd previously won it twice (on Poetic Prince and Fritz). As I said, I was filling in for Hibby and he was back on next time when he ran third in the Stoney Bridge Stakes, but then he lost the ride for the Kelt. I did get back on Fritzy Boy, but he wasn't the same horse as he was in the Mudgway.

Over the next couple of months more attention was on my son Troy than me. He got his first Group One win on the old-timer Dezigna in the Captain Cook Stakes at Trentham. He was trained by Wayne and Vanessa Hillis, so it was the old Harris–Hillis association. I rode Dezigna a few times and ran second on him to Gee I Jane in the 2006 Telegraph Handicap and third earlier in the Concorde at Avondale.

Troy didn't have to wait long for his second Group One and that's one I wish he hadn't won. It was the Two Thousand Guineas at Riccarton and he rode Tell A Tale and just beat me on Il Quello Veloce. We had been in six tight finishes before then and it had been six–nil to me, but he had beaten me when it came to the $1 million race. There had to be a catch to it, didn't there? Good on him and I was proud that we picked up the quinella in such a big race, a classic.

New Year's Day 2009 and I was back in familiar colours and winning another Group race. It was at Ellerslie, the race was the Group Two City of Auckland Cup, and I was wearing the Busuttin stable colours. My mount was Six O'Clock News and his win that day brought back memories of the old stable star, Castletown. It was the same race I had won on Castletown in 1990, just a new name for the race and different part of the carnival. The following year Castletown finished second in it then won the Auckland Cup. Six O'Clock News was never going to be a Castletown, but he did go on to win the Wellington Cup (Castletown's claim to fame) for Paddy Busuttin's son, Trent, and was third in the

2012 Auckland Cup to Shez Sinsational.

A month later I won the St Leger Trial at Otaki on Six O'Clock News and that capped a very special day for me. The Otaki Maori Racing Club had organised a Harris Family Reunion race day, in recognition of the success of Jock and the family. Johnny, my oldest brother, came over from Aussie for the meeting and my aunties and uncles all got together. Most of us were there. The weather wasn't good, but the occasion was great. We really appreciated the gesture by the club and it meant a lot to Jock. He deserved it. He put a lot into racing, and it had been his working life.

There was more celebration the following day when Troy won the Matamata Breeders' Stakes on Te Akau Rose. But what happened afterwards sent us crashing back down to earth. It was a wake-up call of what is going on in this world.

Troy did a drug test that day and it came back positive for cannabis; he was disqualified from riding for three months. I was so disappointed and I felt for Jock. I was worried what he would think of it all. It was the Harris reputation Troy had affected. But when I did talk to Jock about it he just said, 'He'll find his way.' Jock was right. Everyone makes mistakes and as long as they learn from them and move on it has been a worthwhile lesson.

Troy did his 'time' and fortunately he was accepted back into the scene by most of the trainers, including some of the bigger ones. He was soon winning races again and the future looked bright for him. But the next autumn it all crashed down around him once more and he had only himself to blame.

It was at a Matamata meeting in March 2010 and he was just stupid. First of all, he attempted to use someone else's urine sample as his own and when that failed, he left the course without giving a sample. I was at the Te Rapa hearing when he was put out for 21 months, one of the longest disqualifications handed out in modern times. The Judicial

Control Authority panel was sceptical that Troy had gone to such lengths to avoid detection for taking diuretics, which he had been on to help him lose weight. He gave a voluntary sample at Te Rapa racecourse three days later and it was clear of any banned drug.

What was highlighted at the hearing was Troy's dishonesty, and that resulted in such a lengthy disqualification. I always said to him, 'In my house, you don't lie.' I hate lies. Sure, there are little white fibs, but his were blatant lies. Troy has also come along in this era where some of them think they can beat the system, but they can't. When he got put out the first time for cannabis I hoped he'd learnt a lesson. It's like telling a kid not to touch the fire and the first thing they do is put their finger in it.

Troy obviously didn't learn from the first mistake and he was disqualified a second time. I hope there won't be a third. It's up to him; he's got to work it out himself. I was disappointed with him for letting so many people down, the ones who had given him opportunities again after he was put out the first time. In racing you only get so many strikes before you're out for good. If you continually let people down they will eventually get sick of that happening. Troy is my son and I will help him if I can, but he's in his mid-twenties now and he's got to stand up for himself.

There have been some top jockeys here and in Australia who have been done for drugs and they've come back. Racing has given them another chance and their past has been virtually forgotten. Some jockeys have taken drugs to help lose weight. I know of jockeys who were using Kronic to give them a buzz — it's a synthetic cannabis product that was banned in New Zealand in 2010.

In my early days of riding, one jockey I knew would have had a joint by the time we got to the races and he would come out and ride three winners — and you wouldn't have known he'd smoked one. If I had a joint, mate, I would be sitting there laughing and I wouldn't be able to hop on a horse.

I did have a puff of marijuana when I was an apprentice, but I never tried any of the heavy shit. In those times you'd go to parties and there would be a lot of druggies around. I had a couple of puffs, but thought nothing of it. I would rather stick to my booze. I've been like that ever since. I even said to Troy when he was living with me, 'If I catch any drugs around here mate I will kick your arse.'

Racing isn't the only sport affected by drugs. What about all these international cycling riders caught for steroids and suchlike? It has been going on for years. It's the same old thing with money. Whenever it's to do with money, you will get cheats, corruption. They will cross that line and when they're caught they will try to find some other way to beat the system.

Racing in New Zealand makes the headlines when there are drugs involved, like the Lisa Cropp case. The mainstream media seems to be more focused on the negative side of racing than reporting the positive side. And there are plenty of good things that happen in racing. The good side completely outweighs the bad.

Getting away from all this heavy stuff, I remember a funny episode with Barry O'Reilly, an old racing scribe from Wellington. Barry had glasses as thick as the bottom of a Coke bottle. A few times I asked him if I could look through them and when I did I couldn't believe he could see anything. I would have been better looking through the bottom of a bottle!

Barry was a likeable bloke and gave me such great coverage in the papers when I started riding. I always remember one of the stories he told me. He was heading towards Foxton in his little Volkswagen on the way to Wanganui races and he had picked up a hitchhiker, a young guy. They had travelled on a few miles and the guy asked if Barry smoked. Barry said yes, so the guy rolled him up a smoke and handed it to him. 'Christ, I am puffing away on it,' Barry told me, 'and I'm halfway over the Foxton bridge and I look in the rear vision mirror and there are about 100 cars behind me. Noel, I actually thought I was speeding and I look down at the speedo and I am only doing 40 miles an hour. It wasn't until I was a bit further on that I realised what I was smoking.'

Barry used to smoke 'rollies' and he hadn't realised the guy had given him a joint. I always laugh when I think of him telling me that story. He was one of the straightest guys you would ever get and here he was fooled into having a joint!

26

Not too old for a Group One

Ten days after I celebrated by fifty-fifth birthday I proved a point to the New Zealand racing industry: I wasn't too old to win a Group One race. Even though I'd won 31 races, including three Group or Listed races, and over $1.5 million in stakes the previous season, I had my critics. People were saying I was getting too old and I had better step aside for the young ones coming through. Well, I might be getting older, but I don't feel I'm slowing down and I'm confident I'm as competitive as ever. I just needed the right horse to prove my point and it all came together at Trentham on 23 January 2010.

Tim Carter, a former Maori All Black who had been a friend for a long time, and his wife, Margaret, had got me on Vonusti the previous season. I won on my first ride on him at Ellerslie then won again the following month. I went on to win five races and run second in the Pegasus Stakes at Riccarton before it was confirmed he would run in the Group One Telegraph Handicap. I had won the race three times (on Sharif, Fritz and King's Chapel) and I was quietly confident I had the horse who could make it four. I just needed the breaks.

I knew he'd get back and he was in the last couple in the early stages, but once I wound him up in the straight I knew I was on the winner. He let down brilliantly and we flew down the outside to win by two lengths. I let my emotion show as I looked across to the stands, cocked my whip and smiled to the crowd. I may be the elder statesman of the jockeys' room, but I had shown them that, given the right horse, the job is done. I beat two of the young guns: Craig Grylls, on runner-up Tootsie, and Kelly Myers on third-placed Stupendous.

It was the first Group One win for Tim and Margaret, so it was celebrations all round. But straight away the big question came out: 'When are you going to retire?' Hadn't they seen my ride? I was still winning big races and enjoying it. Why should I retire now? I just told the reporters I had a beach house to pay off and would have to keep going for a few more years. It was true. Kylie and I had bought a beach bach at Mt Maunganui. It's our little haven away from the hustle and bustle of racing.

By the end of the 2009–10 season I had won almost $1 million in stake-money and lying ahead were a few other highlights to celebrate the following season. The first was winning the Group Three Taranaki Breeders Stakes at Hawera on Dancing Jess for long-time supporters Dick and Bones Bothwell. I had been runner-up on her in the Group Two Cal Isuzu Stakes at Te Rapa and the Bothwells, as loyal as ever, had kept me on when possible. I won a Te Rapa race on Dancing Jess before the big one at Hawera and there were more in store.

Later that season I finished an unlucky fourth on Dancing Jess in the Group One New Zealand Thoroughbred Breeders' Stakes at Te Aroha and was second on her in the Group Two Travis Stakes, placings which boosted her value as a broodmare even more. Then came another boost, a win in the Listed James Bull Rangitikei Gold Cup at Awapuni. It was a special win for me because I'd won the race as an apprentice on Glengowan in 1972 and also won it twice on Magnitude and also on Phareef.

A couple of months later Kylie and I went over to Singapore–Malaysia. It was a break for Kylie and a working holiday for me. I got a buzz riding four winners at Ipoh. I'd had a lot of success on the track during the late 1970s as a young guy riding for Ivan Allan and other trainers. On this trip I had been unlucky in Kuala Lumpur and Penang, but my luck changed big time at Ipoh. And just a fortnight later I kicked home my third stakes-winner for the season and it was for one of my mates, ARA, alias Alexander Fieldes.

ARA has been one of my most loyal fans and we go a long way back. He keeps reminding me I rode his first winner, Early Bird, at Hastings on New Year's Day, 1990, and he still raves on about it being the best ride he'd seen and that I got Early Bird up to beat one of Noel Eales' horses by a head. I have ridden other horses for ARA over the years, including Lankruza, and he'd given me the call-up to ride Capecover in the 2009 Melbourne Cup, my twelfth ride in the race, but again a Melbourne Cup win eluded me and we finished down the track. It was still a big thrill for ARA to saddle up a runner in the Melbourne Cup. He'll never forget that day and he also won't forget the thrill he got from me winning the Taumarunui Gold Cup on Marea Alta.

When ARA rang me about the ride, I knew the horse was promising, but I had to lose three kilos to make the weight. I made the correct weight and Marea Alta did the job. And as I returned to scale I looked at ARA and he still had his handkerchief in his hand. He told reporters how he'd had to stop when coming down the stairs to wipe away a few tears. I had never seen him so emotional, especially without a drink in his hand!

There is also another long-time link with Marea Alta. She was bred and is part-owned by Awapuni trainer Mark Oulaghan, I've known Mark since his days training at Woodville and I won the 1983 Owens Trophy for him on Bridge Player, his first good horse.

I almost gave ARA another tear-jerker at Ellerslie five months later when I rode Marea Alta in the Group Two City of Auckland Cup. Remember how I asked for some divine help when I won the Kelt on Princess Coup in 2007 and I didn't care if I didn't win another big race? Well, I did the same again with Marea Alta on New Year's Day. I looked up and said, *OK, I'd like to cop this one, too*. But it wasn't to happen. She tried hard, but had to settle for second to Single Minded. Maybe God was saving my wish for my birthday a few weeks later because I rode a winner, Galaxy Star, for trainer Lisa Latta, at Awapuni on my fifty-seventh birthday.

Galaxy Star shaped as a very promising type and I went on to win on him at Matamata the same day I won on another up-and-comer, O'Fille, for Wayne Marshment. Wayne and I go way back, too. I rode Starska, a very smart mare, for him back in 1981. She bolted in by five and a half lengths in the North Island Challenge Stakes at Trentham. Then, I was second on her behind Noel Eales' top mare Orchidra in the Breeders' Stakes at Te Aroha and third in a weight-for-age at Ellerslie.

I suppose when you've been riding as long as I have — over 40 years — you do go around in circles and ride winners again for some of the people who helped your career along the way. It's really satisfying and it's a great feeling. But you do realise you are getting old when you're winning races on the granddaughters or grandsons of horses you've ridden. And in some cases they're even a further generation back.

To think I began in racing at the end of the pounds, shillings and pence era, and started race-riding after decimal currency was introduced in 1967. I paid $3500 for a new car and I think for value for money, you got more at that time than you do now. Every two years I'd get a brand new car. I think it cost me $9000 to buy the little house in Woodville. Fish and chips were cheap. It was cheap to go to the movies. As a trainer, Dad could virtually employ one staff member per horse. Every day one of the staff could take out two horses for a pick, or take them for walks around the blocks. You couldn't afford that now staff-wise. Oh, no. Years ago, the good trainers put more time into training their horses. As the years passed I could see some trainers cutting corners. Costs and wages haven't made it possible to do what the old trainers once did.

Another big change has been the judicial system in racing. When I started you virtually got a doctor, a farmer, a butcher and they used to sit on the judicial panels. They were sitting there taking my livelihood away from me, yet most of them had never ridden a horse. Most of the time the stipendiary stewards would advise them what they should do and that was it. You had no comeback.

I think the more professional panel these days is a big improvement. I believe it is on the right track, yet the more you deal with it, the more circumstances that crop up. It's the inconsistency in New Zealand that annoys me. I know in Australia they are like judge and jury and the stewards will charge you. And if they charge you, you know you are virtually gone and you will get a minimum of three weeks. You know the consequences. But here in New Zealand one jockey will get a week, another jockey might get three weeks and they're both on the same charge. It's wrong. The system has to be more consistent.

I've had very few run-ins with the stipes and judicial panels. Sure I've copped fines and suspensions along the way, but 83 offences in New Zealand over 40 years — I'd say that's not too bad. The biggest fine I've copped is $600 and the longest suspension was probably the three weeks back in 1973 which cost me the outright Jockeys' Premiership. A lot of those offences were minor ones, like the day I left my lead vest off.

It was in a welter and I was riding quite light at that time. I had heaps of lead in the lead-bag, but it still wasn't enough so I borrowed a lead vest. But instead of putting it on, I just put it over my saddle. When I came back after the race and hopped on the scales I just couldn't fathom why I was too light. It wasn't until I got back to my locker and found the lead vest. I had forgotten to put it on and so I was fined.

I've ridden on all types of tracks and in all sorts of ground. But I'll never forget one day at Trentham back in the early 1970s when I was an apprentice. When people talk about heavy tracks I just recall riding Te Whero that day at Trentham. That was the ultimate heavy track. Two-minute miles. I was just trotting past the winning post. I had won the race and Te Whero fell over in exhaustion just past the post. I've got a photo of it. Wet tracks in Wellington and you get two-minute miles and now when I explain that to jockeys, they look at me as if my head's in the wrong place. There's no way they would hold a meeting now if the track was as bad as it was the day I rode Te Whero. And he was a good winter galloper!

There was also the day they did call Trentham off because of the cold. Our hands were numb. I had one ride and I was flat out getting my fingers off the reins. They were stuck. What annoyed me that day were the comments of Nigel Tiley, a former jockey turned trainer. He called us weak, but he should have known better. I'd like to have seen him go out there and ride. In fact I told him, 'The club is going to have a nude trainers' race after this and you're riding.'

I've ridden on every racecourse in the North Island with the exception of Ruakaka and Dargaville, the two most northern tracks. Maybe I'll do that before I retire. Gus Clutterbuck and I went up to Dargaville and we rode work on the beach. That's the closest to riding on the track we got.

I rate Trentham as the best track I've ridden on, even allowing for the Te Whero day. To me, it's the ultimate track because it gives every horse a chance. It's been great to me and I hold the record for the most wins there. I like Palmy (Awapuni), Hastings, Te Rapa and Riccarton, too.

Ellerslie is a tricky track and it suits certain horses. You can get a horse like Kingdom Bay. He was placed at Ellerslie, but he wasn't at his best there. He won at Waipa, right-handed, but he just didn't feel good at Ellerslie. I've ridden a lot of horses up there that don't really handle it. I remember Etoile Du Nord, who won the Marton Cup. She was placed there, but she just didn't like it either.

If I ranked my favourite tracks in order they would be Trentham, Palmy, Riccarton, Hastings and Te Rapa. It might be a surprise to many people that Ellerslie isn't in my top five, even though I've won so many big races there.

As for races, I still love winning the staying races most of all. A staying race is brilliant — it's a true character of patience and when to take off and when not to. It gives you great satisfaction, especially the two miles (3200 metres). I've won three Auckland Cups, three Wellington Cups, four New Zealand Cups and a Sydney Cup. To me, it's the ultimate. Not many jockeys can win a two-mile race.

Over the years I've adopted little habits and one of them is being in my special spot around at the start. I've seen horses that the closer to the barrier, the quieter they become. It's probably like talking to a horse. The more you talk to them, the quieter they are, and I've always found the further away you got from the barrier, the further the horse wanted to get away. So early on in my career I'd just go straight up to the gates and make them stand around there or walk in a little circle.

I remember one day 'Lofty' (Paul) Taylor came over and wanted to walk in the same corner. I said, 'Lofty, I don't mind that you keep going in the same circle, just don't go the opposite way round!' But it has worked. I just feel the closer you are to the barrier, the quieter the horse. I know some horses are just rogues and you have a lot of problems with them. I think the further away from the barrier you go just lets them think, *If I can sneak away a bit more, I won't have to line up.*

The worst thing when a horse won't go in is staying on them. Jump off a horse and they'll usually walk in. I've seen jockeys who've been riding for years who still haven't quite worked it out. But Jock always said, 'Get off them and nine out of ten times they'll go in.'

I've heard all types of remedies for problems with horses and one of the funniest was in Jock's time and concerned one of his mates, Billy Aitken. Jock told me the story about Billy waiting to go out to get on his mount and one of the stipes came up to him and asked why he wasn't on his horse. Billy replied, 'I am just deciding.' The stipe said, 'Deciding what?' Billy said, 'Deciding whether to take a whip or a tennis racquet.' The stipe was dumbfounded, so Billy told him to have a look under the horse's arse. The trainer had a half-cut tennis ball inserted so the horse wouldn't windsuck up the rear end. They used to do that in the old days. A tennis racquet or a whip? What a beautiful answer.

That reminds me of a story that has been told a million times, but it's still a good one. The boss says to the apprentice, 'Why didn't you take that gap when it came?' The kid replied, 'Because it was like this boss, that gap was going quicker than my horse.' The funny thing is, every jockey can relate to that.

I had Murray Baker on one day about one of his horses I rode. I called out, 'Murray, this horse has got a heart as big as a peanut that has been poked up his arse with a short stick.' Murray turned around and said, 'Well, what does that mean?' I said, 'Murray he has got a small heart and it is in the wrong place.'

Some trainers are known for their quick wit and one of them was the late Tommy Smith. He was in at the Melbourne Cup Carnival. All the trainers used to congregate in the middle, Bart Cummings and the like, and all the horses and foremen would come up to the trainers before they worked. They would trot around the middle, warming them up. Tommy Smith was standing there and a horse came trotting along and stopped; it actually stopped to have a dump. Tommy turned around and said, 'Son, just go twice round and the last half mile just sprint it up the straight.' The boy on the horse turned around and said, 'Mr Smith, this is not your horse.' With that, Tommy replied, 'Well, I can't be training everyone else's horses.'

27

Changing of the guard

Over the years I've seen so many trainers and owners come and go and training centres switch from being busy, lively tracks to almost ghost towns. I was fortunate to start off when there were so many great old trainers still in action. Taranaki, Hawke's Bay and Awapuni were strong Central Districts training centres and the others like Woodville were doing well, too. There was so much support from all the studs around the areas and the farmers. That's why Hawke's Bay and Palmerston North, in particular, were thriving.

But when the sales moved from Wellington to Karaka that killed a lot of the studs. Many of them either closed down or shifted north. So much was happening and it was sad to see Wellington lose the sales. Trentham used to be the Mecca for racing and breeding people. They would stay a whole week down there in caravans, at Burnham Lodge, Totara Lodge, all around. It was one big party. Everybody had a good time and one and all seemed to make money.

Jock had a lot of owners who were farmers, true stockmen, and they always seemed to have a horse or two in work. Because they understood animals, it was easier to describe what was going on with one of their horses. Nowadays you're getting people in the game who don't know a hell of a lot about horses and racing and it can be difficult to explain things to them. An owner often thinks that if the horse is beaten it's automatically the jockey's fault, and they will want a different jockey on. It makes it hard on the trainers.

It's often said the easiest part of training is training the horse. The hardest part is training the owners, because you can have the best horse in your stable, but it might be a nightmare to train for the owner because they want to do this or that. If you don't do what they want, they'll move on to another stable. Years ago a horse would have so many races and then it would be out for a spell for a couple of months before coming back into your stable. These days, if you do that, there's a good chance they'll end up in a different stable, so the trainers have got to be careful. I can understand in a way why some of these trainers keep horses going. They just don't want to back off a horse because tomorrow they mightn't have that horse.

Sure, there have been owners like that around for years — ones that will listen to advice from so-called experts, rather than the professionals doing the job for them. All trainers have experienced it. But back when Jock was training he was lucky to have so many loyal owners, like John Galvin, Millie Pivac and Graham Lambert. John and his son David came from the Wairarapa and they were great owners for Jock. They'd always have a horse in work with him. They'd leave it up to Jock to tell them when to come over and look at the horse. Millie had a fish and chip shop in Feilding for 50 years and once a month he'd bring over what seemed half the fish and chip shop for the staff. We just thought he was Christmas. He raced Sharif and Shaheen with Graham.

Mainly because of the state of the economy and racing in general, there are more and more syndicates racing horses. It was something unheard of when I was young. Racing needs owners and being in a syndicate is a way to be involved without having to foot all the bills yourself. I've had a lot of success riding for syndicates, but sometimes it can be a bit testing. You can run into about 100 different people in different syndicates and it gets to the stage where you don't know who you should be talking to or what you should be saying, because no doubt they've got managers and you're supposed to go through them.

Sometimes you end up repeating the same thing over and over to different owners of the same horse. But there are other syndicates that leave it to the syndicate manager to deal with the jockey and the trainer. That's a more professional approach and it's better for everyone. It's far different from when the old farmer could race three or four horses and wouldn't come and see them.

I find that trainers in general are different people today. What's made it so different is big money for two year olds. In my era Jock wasn't keen on two year olds unless they were natural. Noel Eales raced very few of them and Eric Ropiha had the odd one or two, but it was more the three year olds and older horses they concentrated on. *Let the horse develop* was their thinking. In those days you could do that, but now you're paying big money for a horse and the owners usually want a quick return. When you hop on a young horse you know straight away whether he or she is going to be a natural two year old. Yet some owners and trainers do more harm by pushing the horse to get to a certain race, then realise too late that the horse is not ready and, by that stage, they've often ruined his chances as a three year old, too.

As I said, I've seen trainers come and go and often I reflect on the good ones I've dealt with over the years — right back to when I was starting out and there were so many top horsemen spread throughout the country.

In Taranaki you had the likes of Brian Deacon and Wally McEwan, who had huge stables, Don Couchman and Herb Bergerson. And Malcolm Smith was going strong up there, too, before he shifted to the Palmerston North area. In Hastings there were Don Sellwood and Keith Couper training in partnership, and Bob Quinlivan was doing well. Later on Bruce Marsh set up training there before he shifted to Woodville, and Patrick Campbell also started at Hastings. The travelling was not a problem, and staff wasn't a problem. It was probably the 1980s that saw a lot of those trainers move out or retire.

I didn't ride a lot for Bob Quinlivan. He was winding down at that stage, but he had a lot of top horses and probably the best was Game. He had Bruce Marsh riding a lot for him. Keith Couper was fantastic. He had a lot of top horses, but he was just winding down, too. Davey Jones was also training and he had only a smallish team and did well. I rated all of those older trainers. They had the knack. They put the finishing touches on and they were real horsemen. Don Sellwood was just a young trainer when I got to know him. I've ridden quite a bit for him over the years. He's a bit like the old school; he likes to give his horses time.

I rode a bit for Smithy, Malcolm Smith, but Dessie did more of his riding. When Dessie retired, I took over for a while and rode a lot of winners for Smithy. I got on Volare, who was a good horse, but he got really colty in the end. He savaged the strapper, Marshall Ngaia, when they were on the float. He reached through the float cubbyhole where you can let their heads out and actually grabbed Marshall and tried to pull him through into the stall on the horse float.

One day at Wellington I thought Volare was unbeatable. But I should have known better. He would have won the race, but when he jumped out he hit the bar. They were the old blue stalls, all barred starting gates with a bar down the bottom. He hit the bar and did a somersault and stood on my back, down by my arse. I'd done a flip and I didn't know where I was. I was into next week. I thought Volare would measure up to anything.

Noel Eales was a great trainer, a real horseman. He treated his horses like they were human beings. He'd rug them up three times a day. If the wind got up he'd get another rug on. When the sun came out the rug would come off. He'd worry sick over a horse if it wasn't right. He'd just know something was wrong and he wouldn't relax until he knew he had got it better. I would go to the track and everything was either 'the big fella' or 'the little girl'. He would say to me, 'Noel, just go and hop on the big fella.' He would have about 50 horses there: 'Which one is the big fella?' He also had nicknames for them and when he'd talk to you about them, he'd think you knew the horses' nicknames.

Noel could get a horse to win five races to open company when it wasn't an open company horse. I rode a lot of winners for Noel and two of the best I rode were Surface and Commissionaire. I was on Commissionaire in the latter part of his career and I won the Taranaki Cup on him and beat Kiwi. I had six rides on him, all in 1984, for the win, a second, three thirds and a ninth. Noel was always one of those guys who would love to keep you on a horse if you won on it. Horses for jockeys; jockeys for horses. He believed in a jockey suiting a horse. After those placings on Commissionaire I remember Noel saying, 'I think Jimmy [Commissionaire's nickname] is getting too used to you and I'd like to try someone else.' He replaced me and later on he came back and said, 'I apologise Noel. I shouldn't have taken you off. I think he's just had enough.' He didn't need to say that, but he was a gentleman. Commissionaire won only one more after I rode him.

I remember when Noel had Lomondy, who won the Caulfield Cup, Gus Clutterbuck was the only one who rode him in work early on. He was a bit of a rogue. Gus would sing and he and the horse got along so well.

One day Chris McNab and I were sitting at the races at Awapuni and I asked Noel why his good sprinter wasn't in at Christchurch. He replied, 'When I was doing my nominations I looked out the window and saw it was raining. This horse doesn't like a wet track.' This was looking out a window in Palmerston North on a Tuesday and the races were at Riccarton on a Saturday. He soon realised what he'd said and we all laughed about it.

Tempo, Eric Temperton, was another great old trainer at Awapuni. He'd sit there in the hut at the crossing with a cup of tea. Tempo was in charge of the pot. Every morning he'd come up with a story. He was so full of wisdom and advice, a lovely gentleman. He had a big team, jumpers and everything, and he had a good record. I remember the likes of Young Ida, Magnifique and Charger. I did some riding for him. There was also Garth Ivil at Awapuni. I'll always remember him being a champion trainer of horses by the sire Pakistan II for the Fells, who stood him at their Fairdale Stud. He used to have a stable full of Pakistans and I was able to ride a lot for Garth.

I had a lot of success for Margaret Bull, too. Being a woman training during those years it was tough for her at times, and in racing there is always gossip going around. When any of it got back to her she'd take it hard as she was very sensitive. She was a very good horsewoman and had a lot of top horses. Magnitude was one out of the box.

Woodville was going strong with not only Jock training there, but also Syd Brown, Eric Ropiha and others. I caught the tail end of Syd Brown's time in Woodville. He had a huge stable and had so many great horses, Daryl's Joy, Classic Mission, Weenell, Triton, Wood Court Inn. I was an apprentice at the time and I rode a few for him, but not the better ones. He moved over to Australia and he made it in Sydney against the big boys. Guys like that will never be replaced.

Eric Ropiha, like Garth Ivil, had a lot of horses from the great Pakistan family. It's amazing what you learnt from Eric. He was hard, but a great horseman. He was also into the pony club and his horses would be out working there in the running reins and he'd break horses in the back of a cart. When I was young, I picked up so many things from him. After he dropped out of racing, he became more involved in the equestrian scene. I ran into him a couple of years ago and he's still the same dapper gentleman.

Ian Bradbury was a lovely old chap and a good trainer, too. I got a lot of rides from 'Brad'. We would go with him to Wairoa and he'd come up with the stories. He used to tell us about the days when they used to catch the train to the races or walk their horses to the races.

Dessie and I were breaking in yearlings for Brad and getting good money. He taught us a lot. He brought in a lot of yearlings and cut down on his gallopers. He concentrated on 20 to 30 yearlings and would do most of the Woodville breaking in for other trainers. When he was breaking them in, he wouldn't put shoes on them. He'd work them up on a stone road so they'd be feeling their feet. The last thing you want them to do was buck. He had have a sawdust pit and it came up to their knees so we'd put them in there if they started bucking. They soon got very tired.

Brad had a filly by Sovereign Edition that I think he was breaking in for Syd Brown. She was a real bitch of a thing and she used to pee all the time. I remember when Dessie was riding her and Brad was leading her around the two-year-old track. He had a pigskin whip that he used to flick her on the bum, and every time he touched her, she would pee. When he got back in, he said to us, 'I think I'll give this horse to the Woodville Fire Brigade the amount of pissing she's done.'

Old Brad was still going at 91. He used to have a few turns in the stalls and you'd think, *Oh no, that'll be the end of him.* Come the next morning, though, he'd be back at the track. He'd think nothing of it. Fall down and get up and carry on with his work. He used to get up at three o'clock every morning. Old-time trainers . . .

Among the other trainers at Woodville during my younger days were Morrie Murphy, Percy Burgess and Kay Bowman. Percy used to go to the pub on his pony and on his way home he'd have a couple of flagons tied over the saddle as he rode the horse home. And back in Jock's time John Carter was training. He won the 1964 Melbourne Cup with Polo Prince and I remember his rider Ron Taylor telling me there was a four-leaf clover stitched in the covers. I grew up with the Carter kids and John ended up being the caretaker at the Woodville racecourse.

Jock and John Carter used to have a lot of jumpers. I remember the Gaisford Steeplechase at Woodville when about 12 runners started and only two finished, but a couple were remounted. They had painted all the fences, I think it was yellow or some crazy colour. It was unbelievable how many horses fell.

All the surrounding areas — Levin, Otaki and Foxton — had plenty of trainers. Clem Bowry was a good trainer in Otaki. Dessie rode a lot for him and he had a lot of top horses like Black Rod, Sharda and Topsy. Dessie has always said Black Rod was one of the best horses he rode. If he wasn't so unsound, he could have been a champion. Mick Preston was also doing well as a trainer and down at Masterton there was Tup Jennings. Tup was a top trainer at setting a horse up. Merv Andrews was a good trainer, too. Dessie did more riding for him than I did.

Over the years I've also had a bit of success for the South Island trainers. I rode for Rex Cochrane, Ted Winsloe, Ned Thistoll and Barry Taggart, all now either well settled into retirement or passed away. And I've had a lot of winners for Neil Coulbeck, John and Karen Parsons and Peter and Dawn Williams, and I've picked up some good ones for Paul Harris. I won the 1995 Dunedin Gold Cup on Good Greef for Ted Winsloe, and I got to ride his top filly Tartan Tights a few times. I filled in for Chris Johnson and won a race at Washdyke before Chris won the New Zealand Oaks on her. She went on to win her next two races, too, and I rode her both times. The last of those wins was in the Group Two Championship Stakes at Ellerslie and she beat Love Dance, who went on to win a couple of Group One races.

Rex Cochrane is a good friend of Dad's and I went down to stay there as an apprentice for a week. I never rode race day while I was at Gore, but it was an excellent eye-opener. It was really Gary Lee who got me going down south when he was training at Riccarton before he shifted to Australia. He would also bring his horses up north and I'd ride them.

That reminds me of a funny story about Gary and a jockey, Maurice Thornley. At the time, Maurice was an apprentice down in Christchurch and I remember Gary saying he was a good rider but had a lazy attitude. Maurice was wasting and said he was going for a run around the Riccarton racecourse. He had taken off and Gary gave me a nudge and said, 'Come with me for a walk. This Maurice, he thinks I'm stupid. That bugger has gone over there with his sweaters on and he'll be lying under a hurdle having a sleep.' So, we went over and, sure enough, there was Maurice sitting behind the hurdle. Gary had taken the stock whip over and he started chasing Maurice; they went twice around the track. 'It nearly killed me mate,' said Gary, 'but I just thought I wasn't going to give up.' Gary just wanted to get a bit of dedication into Maurice. You would never see trainers doing things like that these days.

Of the northern trainers, Trevor McKee, Bill Winder and Jack Winder used to give me a lot of rides when I was an apprentice, and another northern trainer who supported me was Joe Bromby, who was near the end of his career. I rode a good little filly, Touch 'N Go, for him. And I used to ride a horse called Polperro for Stuey Dromgool. The northern trainers usually stuck to their northern jockeys a lot, but when they took horses south I got offered rides.

Ever since I returned from Singapore in 1980 I have been a freelance rider, although I've been offered 'stable rider' positions at times. I have been the main jockey for certain stables, but never on a binding contract. When I moved up to Matamata in 1999, Te Akau Racing Stables offered me a contract, but I turned it down. I have learnt through a lot of other trainers that some horses are going to suit certain jockeys and vice versa and I felt being attached to one stable has got its rewards, but it has downfalls, too. Imagine if I was with Te Akau and Sunline came along and I was made to ride Te Akau's runner, even though Sunline was a better ride. Sunline goes and wins 13 Group One races and almost $14 million in stakes. I didn't want to be put in that position.

I say to a lot of trainers who have helped me that it's only common sense to be loyal. But loyalty has to work both ways. I have seen too many jockeys lose so many contacts, so many good horses, through not being loyal.

I've had a lot of success riding for Paddy Busuttin over the years and he was loyal to me with Castletown. Paddy is known as much as a practical joker as a trainer. When I went to ride for Laurie Laxon in Singapore in 2004, I was booked to go home on the Monday and Paddy invited me to lunch. We had lunch and before long I had to collect my gear and get to the airport. I gave the taxi driver Laurie Laxon's address, where I had been staying, but I never made it. Paddy had set me up with this taxi driver and told me the words to use. Well, this taxi driver even stopped at the cop station; he was taking me all over the show. Here I was abusing the taxi driver and I kept thinking, *You bastard Paddy. You've done this.* I flew out the next morning and I made sure I got my own taxi driver.

John Wheeler is another hard case trainer. Wheels is quick-witted and loves a joke, too. I remember one year in Brisbane when what Bart Cummings was saying was making the headlines. The Aussie media love Bart and whatever he says gets into the papers the next morning. Wheels used to work for Bart in the early days and he jumped in on the act and said he didn't agree with Bart. Next morning the headline was: 'Wheels disputes Cummings'. This went on most of the week. I used to say to Wheels, 'You're a Philadelphian lawyer, mate, with the words you've come up with.' The public loved it. Wheels has had so much success up there he is virtually an honorary citizen of Brisbane. He's also something of a legend at Oakbank in South Australia.

28

Wasting — a way of life

Wasting, dieting, fasting or straight out starving yourself. Call it what you like, but it's the biggest pain in a jockey's life. Some are lucky. They are small enough not to worry about it, but that's only a minority, a very small minority. Most have it as a daily problem. I've had jockeys say to me, 'You're lucky, you don't have to waste so hard.' But then I tell them I went through 20 years of wasting hard. It got to the stage where I could've given up riding altogether. Your health is more important. True, I've been luckier than a lot of the jockeys, especially the taller and bigger-built ones. I feel sorry for those that have to do it every time they ride. They deserve a medal, how they keep going. But, as I say, I've experienced it all.

It's part and parcel of a jockey's life. I was probably exposed to the laxative tablets and 'pee pills' when I was a stablehand. Some of the jockeys were taking them to keep their weight down. I saw it all the time when I was growing up. I was probably five and a half stone (35 kg) when I started as an apprentice and I used to have a stone (weight) saddle when I first began riding, and in the flaps I'd have big bits of lead up to the tree. I'd have a bag full of lead and sometimes I had to get someone to carry my saddle, it was that heavy. But by the time I was 18 I was eight and a half stone (54 kg). I put on a stone a year. It got to the stage I was taking laxatives and pee pills. When you're constipated you would normally take one laxative, but instead of taking one or even two, you'd take half a dozen. They can be hard on you. It was a quick clean-out. But you made sure you never coughed!

The pills were a lazy way of taking the weight off. It got so that if I took three pounds off, I'd put four pounds back on and I'd be doing it again the next week. I'd be increasing the number of laxatives, then I couldn't get the piss pills down. I started taking them with milk to make it work quicker, but I'm shocking with milk; I can't handle it. The next best thing was in an ice cream. I just couldn't swallow them. Every time I thought about taking them I'd want to dry-retch, but I was relying on the pills to get my weight down to ride.

The piss pills probably took an hour or so to work, but they were quite harsh on you. I started taking half a pill the morning of the races, then the next time it wouldn't work so well so I'd increase it and take one before the races. That would be all right for a while then I'd have to start taking two pills. To this day every time I think about them I almost retch.

I was taking the piss pills for about eight to 10 years. I went up to Singapore in 1977 and up there I think I took one or two, but the heat just knocked the stuffing out of me. It was hard to do. I started weaning myself off them but later got back on them. Then in the 1980s I got to the stage where I was trying to take them occasionally — going from the heat up in Singapore to the start of winter here — but I thought if I've got to keep taking these I'm going to give up riding.

Most of the jockeys were taking them, even at the races if they had to lose more for a ride later in the day. It was legal, but that's been changed. The worst thing was that I'd go into the sauna and I had been sweating all week and dehydrating then I'd take the piss pills and there was nothing left in your system to take out.

I wasn't dieting. I'd eat and drink normally, but then I'd use the pills. I got lazy and just took more and more of them. I realised if I kept taking them it would probably kill me so I decided to concentrate on the sauna instead. I did run for a while, but Jock always said, 'You start running, you start building muscle up and it's hard to take off.' Jock was a muscly jockey and I can see why he always told me not to build up too much muscle. He also warned me not to do a lot of hard physical work as far as building up the body. Some jockeys can't sweat and they can't sauna. Maurice Campbell is an example. He used to run for miles. Each jockey is different.

Dessie, my brother, was different from me. He'd go and have a little bit of a sauna, but then he'd come out and eat and drink afterwards. He didn't have to take a lot of weight off and I thought he'd never get big, but when he gave up riding he piled on the weight. Garry Phillips was different again. I always remember he used to take half a pill the morning of the races and he never really had to do it. He probably just did it to clean himself out. It was a mental thing. Garry wasn't a robust jockey. He was always quite light, but jockeys get funny habits and they feel good about them.

Over the years I've seen how it has affected jockeys. I saw a lot of jockeys who were wasting and taking Duromine, an appetite suppressant. Their stomachs went to fat and they actually got cellulite around their tummy. It's a shocking look. You get a lot of rugby league players that bulk up when they finish. And take my older brother, Johnny. He wasted hard every week when he was riding and the weight he's put on now is mainly the result of that hard wasting. Some jockeys get fat when they give up and others stay slim; some are even lighter than when they were riding. You've only to look at guys like Warwick Robinson and, going further back, Trevor McKee. I reckon Trevor could sit on the scales at 49 kilos with a pair of binoculars in his hand.

I got off the piss pills at a time when, if I'd kept going, I would have finished riding a lot earlier, probably 20 to 25 years earlier. I had to discipline myself to get off them; there was no other way. I went up to ride Shamrock in Brisbane in 1980, and I had wasted my guts out for a week to make the weight. I had Bruce Marsh coming to the sauna every night, rubbing me down. I had to take off nearly a stone, probably about six kilos. I was on top of it and I went to the races and I was about a quarter of a kilo over. The stewards dragged me off. The worst thing is that over there you had to weigh out with the number cloth, which I forgot about and I didn't allow for it. That would have made the difference. Shamrock was ridden by Gary Palmer and came out and won. It was such a disappointment. I remember taking half a dozen piss pills and they didn't work. That pissed me right off.

Over the years jockeys have been made more aware of the dangers of constantly taking piss pills and laxatives, and it has become more of a health and safety issue. I haven't heard of any jockeys dying from them, but in saying that there are a lot of stories out there you don't hear about.

I think in the long run it is good they have been made illegal. Jockeys nowadays are a lot taller and they look washed out. I know how they feel. There's nothing worse when you've got six or seven rides and you might be fit, but these piss pills make you so weak. I've seen jockeys just faint after the race and they can't continue. Before I gave up taking the pills, I got to the stage of taking them the night before the races, so I had a good sleep. I woke up and I felt a lot better just having that sleep. I felt if I took one the morning of the races then went and rode, halfway through the day I wanted to pull the pin and give up for the day.

I do believe taking the pills affects both your riding and your mental attitude. When I was taking them I knew that next week I'd have to go through the same thing again. And, as I said, it got to the stage my body was rejecting them and I'd have to eat ice creams to get them down. It was telling me and I didn't want to listen.

Now, without the pills, jockeys have to find other ways to lose weight. I've see a lot of these jockeys who will start eating and drinking then they'll put their fingers down their throat in the toilets and throw up. You can't keep doing that and carry on. Something has got to give. And I've seen other jockeys like Opie Bosson, one of New Zealand's best riders, and what he's gone through. He'd be pulling up after a race and be dry-retching off the side of the horse. He'd just want to throw up. Even though I've been there as far as wasting goes, I've never got to the stage where I've dry-retched when I'm riding. And there are other jockeys who head to the toilet between races and vomit or splash water over themselves and take gulps, just trying to get that composure back to go out and ride in the next race.

It's hard for these younger ones because that's when they're growing up, 15 to 21 normally. When my son, Troy, started to have trouble with his weight, I tried to give him advice to go on a diet. But here I am saying that when I couldn't diet myself. I was either eating and drinking or starving myself completely. My advice to the young ones is to go light and watch what you eat. Sounds simple, but it's also actually your mental attitude. I got to the stage where I'd hop on the scales every day and the more I worried about my weight, the worse it was. I try not to stress too much about it. I know it's hard to do when you're a jockey and it's your livelihood. When I feel happier in myself that's when my weight is more under control.

It's not the lack of food that makes it hard for me, it's the lack of liquid. I can hop out of the sauna or steam bath and be watching TV and they've got Coke or lemonade ads on. It's as though they're taunting me. Nothing is worse than feeling dehydrated. I find if you can keep yourself busy, it's easier to handle, and you're not thinking about eating or drinking. That's the problem with a lot of apprentices. Rather than sitting watching videos or playing video games they're better off keeping active. I know it's tough for that time of life when your body is growing and it seems everyone around you is eating and you've got to go without food. And it's hard to explain to a person that doesn't have to do it. A lot of people try diets and they don't work for them, but you'll find some diets will suit one person and not another. But with these kids, well, some you're not going to help — they're going to get bigger and it's only a matter of time.

With my weight, the worst thing for me is coming through winter, not that I put a lot of weight on. But getting down to the 53 kg that I've had to do in winter at times does make it hard. In summer I would do it a lot easier. Your blood thins out in summer, but in winter it thickens up. And with the cold your body needs more insulation, body fat. But jockeys can't afford the luxury of putting on a bit more body fat to counter the cold, wet winter months. The more you put on, the harder it is to get off.

These days if I've got to take a lot of weight off I know how to do it — not so much easily, but in a way that I can handle it. Maybe being a little older you lose a bit of muscle tone, but at the same time you still have to be fit. If I have to waste I don't like taking too many rides. I try to look after myself. It was like when I had to lose three kilos from the Thursday to ride Marea Alta in the 2011 Taumarunui Cup on the Saturday. When I was young I could have done that the night before the races, but being a bit wiser now I spread it out over a few days. And I know from my weight when I'm stripped what weight I'll be for the ride. I've got it down to a tee over the years. If I am stripped I can add two kilos on for all my gear, the saddle, girth, colours, silks and boots, and that is the weight I will ride. There's also the safety vest, but you get a kilo allowance for that when you weigh out. So if you're riding at, say, 55 kg then you weigh out at 56 kg.

The lightest I've had to get down to in the last 10 years was 48.5 kg for Falkirk in the 2004 Stradbroke Handicap. Paul O'Sullivan, the trainer, had permission for me to ride half a kilo over, but I ended up getting fined for the half kilo. Falkirk didn't go any good, so I lost out all round.

I got down to 51 kg to ride Princess Coup in the 2007 Melbourne Cup and she ran down the track, too. I also got down to 51 kg for an Auckland Cup. Another disappointment was when I was booked to ride Silky Red Boxer in the Doncaster Handicap in Sydney. He was on the ballot and I wasted all week. There was talk there could be a scratching and he'd get a run. On the morning of the races I got a call saying he didn't make the field. I jumped out of bed, felt like a feather, and the rest of the day I was in the pub.

29

What makes a top jockey?

Jock has always said, 'Riding horses is probably the easiest part of being a good jockey. It's dealing with the owners, trainers, other jockeys and people in life who you've got to see through that determines how long you ride for.' It's something I quickly realised and I've heeded Jock's advice. I'm sure it has helped me get through all these years riding.

When I was growing up I had so many good riders to look up to. Bruce Marsh and Herbie Rauhihi were my idols, and I followed the career of my older brothers Johnny and Dessie closely. And there were the Skelton brothers, Bill and Bob, too. They could measure up anywhere in the world. Herbie won some good races in Aussie and Bruce won a Melbourne Cup on Silver Knight.

I remember when Bob Skelton and the other Kiwi jockeys like Brian Andrews and Gary Willetts tried to break into the Aussie scene. They got slated, but they proved themselves. They'd had the grounding here that stood them in good stead. And over the years we've had so many of them go to Aussie and make it. Brent Thomson, Jimmy and Larry Cassidy, Shane Dye, Grant Cooksley, Brian York, Bruce Compton, Nigel Tiley, Greg Childs . . . the list goes on and on. Brent won just about every major race in Australia when he was the number one stable rider for Colin Hayes for eight years, and he went on to be a world-class jockey in England and Europe, then later in Hong Kong. He won over 3000 races and 53 Group Ones.

It should be no surprise that Kiwi jockeys can measure up anywhere. It happened years and years before my time with the likes of Hector Gray, Maurice McCarten, Roy Reed and Keith Voitre. Gray won races in England, France and Belgium, McCarten went over to be a top rider in Australia then a successful trainer, and Reed and Voitre both won Melbourne Cups, Reed in 1929 on Nightmarch and Voitre six years later on Marabou. Tragically, both Reed and Voitre were killed in race falls.

When I went to Australia I never had any trouble with the Aussie riders. I wasn't a threat to them because I wasn't going to settle there. I kept them guessing and I just fitted in. As I said earlier in the book, when I stuck up for Roy Higgins after he hit Glengowan over the nose with the stick, I was accepted. They respected me because I respected them. But not all the Kiwis have had it so well.

Jimmy Cassidy had a problem with Kevin Moses, one of the top Sydney jockeys. Jimmy Cassidy was a very cocky rider and went over with the *Hi, I'm Jimmy Cassidy. I'm here and I'm going to take over your scene* attitude. The problem was Jimmy didn't know Kevin Moses was golden gloves boxing champion. One day Jimmy came back from a race and wasn't happy. He fronted up to Moses and Moses put him in his place. There was hell to pay with the stewards and all that, but they soon sorted it out.

Aussies and Kiwis are different. Aussies love winning. I think at the time with the Kiwi riders, nine out of ten would go over there and be humble. Jimmy Cassidy wasn't one of those guys. He was like a Shane Dye. He was brash and he wanted to be heard. Then there was Gary Willetts. They used to call him the ferret because he used to steal rides.

When I was an apprentice I used to go up and stay at Matamata with Gary. He took me to the hot pools, my first experience of them. I was swimming around and next minute I was out to it. I didn't realise you just went there to sweat. We went out to dinner with his wife, Raewyn, and I remember ordering dessert and the waitress said, 'You better ask your mum and dad.' From that day onwards Gary used to call me 'Son'.

Gary wasn't a supremely confident type like Jimmy or Shane. But one jockey who is a bit like them is Michael Walker. He's also got that *I'm going to show them how to ride* attitude. Michael has always been cocky and it's got him into trouble at times. It's all right being cocky, but you've got to know when to harness it. He'll work it out.

I remember when I won the 2001 Trentham Stakes on Smiling Like. I thought *Wow, this horse is going to be hard to beat in the Wellington Cup*. I was offered the ride, but I'd already taken the mount on Grant Searle's horse Kaapeon, whom I had ridden to win the Marton Cup. Being loyal, I stuck with my commitment, even though I thought Smiling Like would win. Michael picked up the Smiling Like ride. He'd won the New Zealand Cup on her a couple of months earlier.

Once I got to the start of the Cup I knew Kaapeon couldn't win. He was going all right across the top, then within a couple of strides he'd gone. But seeing Michael Walker, the way he was travelling, I yelled out to him, 'Go now bro, go now,' and so Michael was off and ended up winning the Cup. Michael thanked me afterwards for giving him the signal when to go. Even though I didn't ride the winner, I knew I'd helped him.

I also gave Michael the tip when he won the 2010 New Zealand Derby on Military Move. I rode the horse in the lead-up, the Championship Stakes, and he went a huge race for fifth. Michael had picked up the Derby ride and I gave him some advice on how to ride Military Move and told him I thought he could win. Sometimes it's not a good move to give another jockey advice. But if they treat me right, I'll treat them right. It's like horses that can be quite hard to ride in a race and with certain jockeys you don't mind going and telling them the horses' little quirks. There are other jockeys who don't treat you well, so you don't say a word and let them work it out.

I've always believed in loyalty. It goes a long way. It's hard not to get angry and express your feelings. If you do, it gets to the stage where you do yourself more damage and harm. The biggest thing is being humble. In this day and age it's all *Stuff you*. I've always been brought up to be humble.

I've got more of a laid-back attitude. And it's not about getting nasty; I just let things ride. For some jockeys nowadays nastiness can ruin a friendship. I class myself as a lucky rider. People think I'm talented, but I'm lucky with the way I've dealt with a lot of owners because I haven't got nasty. They have come back. I could say *Fuck you*, and I know sometimes I probably should've said it after being dragged. But, no, their money is as good as anybody else's money.

When someone says to me no one else would have won on that horse, well who's to know? You just get an affinity with a horse and there are some jockeys who can do things with a horse that others can't. Lester Piggot and Tony Cruz were both like that and in New Zealand the same went for Bruce Marsh and Herbie Rauhihi.

One of the riders I can relate to is Grant Cooksley. Cookie and I are on the same wavelength. With a lot of jockeys there's a lot of competition, but you admire them. They haven't got a lot to say afterwards and we don't sit down after a race and talk about it. Well, we do for about five seconds, then we move on. It just sticks with you. It's like jockeys nowadays when you're in trouble — if it's a big race and you're on the favourite, you ask for a bit of a help. Nah. Nothing there. You'll say to the local jockeys: 'Bit of room, bit of room!' Nah. You explain to them later, 'Next time you're on a big race winner and you need help, you're not going to get it.' Whereas with me and Cookie, if he knew I was talking to him, he'd know where I was coming from. That's the difference.

Cookie's a lovely guy. Always had a battle with his weight, but he's very talented. To think he was resigned to riding over fences when he was young because he was getting too heavy for the flat. He ended up winning a Great Northern Steeplechase on Ballycastle. I admire the guy so much because he got his weight down, went over to Aussie and the rest is history. He's well renowned in Australia as 'The Iceman' and he did well in Singapore, too. Cookie's in the twilight of his career, like me, and we've been talking about where we go from here. It's been enlightening.

The big thing with jockeys is the camaraderie. When you go into the inquiry room and if there is interference you try to look after each other without getting yourself into trouble. But there are quite a few jockeys who will go in there and only look after themselves and dob you in. They don't have a second thought about it, so those are the ones you will remember. It works both ways.

I've had instances where other jockeys have pinched my rides. I might say something at the time to let them realise I know what happened, then I just let it go. But there was one instance that really upset me. It was when I was riding Kiwi after Jimmy Cassidy had gone over to Aussie. I just took it for granted that I was going to ride him and I rang up Snowy Lupton to confirm that all was well. Snowy said, 'Oh, I have engaged David Walsh. He told me you were riding Bidston Hill.' That was news to me, and I told Snowy that it was far from the truth. I was so wild I rang up David and said, 'I don't mind you ringing owners or trainers for my rides, but you never ever tell them I have got a ride in a race unless it is gospel.' I've always got on well with Walshy, but every now and then I'll remind him of that incident.

I know it's happened a few times with other jockeys behind my back. I'd rather they were straight up and confronted me than do it sneakily. Snowy felt so bad that he actually scratched the horse. That just showed you what a gentleman he was. He just didn't want to upset anyone. Some jockeys are known for what we call 'necking' — getting under your neck, and you need to be wary of them.

Things have changed so much in racing since I started. In my younger days you would get 12 jockeys and maybe only two apprentices in a race. Now it's the other way around, with 12 apprentices and two

Above: Natasha, Whitney, Troy and Cushla. My kids back in the day when it was all fun.

Left: A hongi with Jock. We're descendants of the Te Atiawa tribe in Taranaki.

It was a great night as we celebrated Jock's seventieth, although Johnny (at back) was suffering from the flu. Next to me are Peter, Jenny, Jock, Karen and Dessie.

A proud dad, even though Troy had just beaten me in the Group I 2000 Guineas on Tell A Tale.

Kylie and me enjoying time out. Kylie is not only my wife, she's my soul mate.

Kylie and me with my Singapore friends, PK Leong and his wife, Rina, and their son, Kelvin.

Bill Pomare told me at my wedding he'd give me my 2000th winner and he was right. Beau Casual did the job for us in July 2008.

They call me the veteran, but at 55 I was still up to winning a Group One race as I proved on Vonusti in the Telegraph Handicap at Trentham in 2010. And I'm excited about it!

jockeys. It's quite sad, actually, because I feel that apprentices can't learn from apprentices. We learnt from the senior riders and that's the way it should be. But now you're lucky to find enough senior riders to follow in a race, with all the apprentices riding.

The apprentices nowadays have also got so much pressure on them from the trainers. For example, out of, say, six apprentices, they'll be told to ride a horse handy, up amongst the first three or four. They'll all be trying to get there and if they can't they won't be put back on next time, so it's not doing them any favours. In my time, most trainers would let you go out there and ride your own race and the apprentices around used to follow the best jockeys and learn from them. You get top apprentices who are quick learners, and I'm sure they learn from the better jockeys. But a lot of apprentices just can't relate to that.

Apprentices have a lot more opportunities now. Just look at the likes of Daniel Stackhouse, Rosie Myers, Jason Collett and James McDonald, and the opportunities they get in Australia. In the past, there was no distinction between city and country wins in New Zealand. When I was 18 and had been apprenticed three years, I received an offer from a top Sydney stable, but they declined me because I couldn't claim an allowance as all my wins were regarded in Australia as city wins. Nowadays, they are classed city and country. So that stopped me from going to Australia and opening a new career.

I think the licences are granted too freely nowadays and I see a lot of apprentices out there who aren't ready to be centre stage. When I question it, the stewards say to me, 'That's the best they can do.' Well, if that's the best they can do, they shouldn't be out there until they're ready.

In Australia you get the best of the best and it's always tight riding. You can only put a matchstick between each horse, but it's safe. Here in New Zealand, I've not only got to ride my race, but sometimes I've got to ride the apprentice's race as well. I've got to think what they are thinking and what they are going to do. It makes it very hard, that unpredictability.

The more often you ride against someone, you learn their riding styles and what they're likely to do in a race — the ones, for instance, that panic and go around. Some jockeys are pattern riders, like Lance O'Sullivan. He would be in the first four. Nine out of ten times he trailed on the pace. To me that's pattern riding. Mind you, Lance had the horsepower to do it.

I admire Lance. He was a champion jockey and he worked hard to make it, especially early in his career. However, he was fortunate to have a powerful stable behind him and the ammunition to do it. His father Dave and brother Paul had some great horses to put him on and the results are there for all to see. He loved to be on the pace because the odds of winning are in your favour.

I remember Lance saying to me that it was easy to ride a horse from the back and I was a bit gobsmacked. I think it's hard to ride a horse from last because you have so many horses to get past and the timing of the run has to be spot on. Because I've ridden so many winners from the rear, I'm regarded as a back rider. I'll get a phone call: 'Oh you're good on back runners so you will suit this horse.' It has stuck with me for years. In saying that, in that position I can see a lot of things that are happening up front. A jockey who more often than not rides from the front doesn't know what's going on behind. It's hard to explain unless you're out there every week doing what I do. To me, it just comes naturally.

If you're back you can see horses and riders making mistakes, clipping heels or whatever and you try to keep out of their way. But in saying that, I've seen the top riders doing the best they can and still come down. There are no rules to it. You can just clip a horse's heel and in a final clip you can go for a decent flip. Then you get jockeys that are riding up someone's arse, a young apprentice, he'll be clipping and nothing happens. It's not until they have a fall that they learn. When you have that fall, the next time you're aware of it, and the next fall you have you're more aware of it. And too many falls can knock the confidence. That's the decider whether to get out or stay riding.

Sure, I'm known for winning on back runners, but I'm just as good on front runners. I won the Sydney Cup on King Aussie from the front and had Ballroom Babe in front all the way when she won the Sires' Produce Stakes at Awapuni by 14 lengths. As I keep saying to everyone, it all depends on the horse.

I've ridden against a lot of top jockeys over the years, international ones, too, like Willy Carson, Yves St Martin, Walter Swinburn, but I'd have to say Lester Piggott is the best I've seen. He was a magician on a horse. As I've said so many times, he could get a horse to do things nobody else could. I also rated Roy Higgins, Harry White and Peter Cook right up there and I was always a fan of Herbie Rauhihi and Bruce Marsh of the Kiwi jockeys.

Of the modern-day Kiwi riders I believe Opie Bosson is the best. He's got that X-factor. He's a lucky rider, but very gifted with it, a kind rider. If I had a horse and it was running in a million-dollar race, he'd probably be the first jockey I'd ask.

Vinnie Colgan is a top rider, too, and I'm not just saying that because he's a mate. He's a big-race rider and he can handle the pressure, and that's something that some jockeys can't do. I've seen it many times where a jockey falls to pieces on the big occasion and does things in a race he or she would never usually do.

Michael Walker and James McDonald have come along since Opie and like him they've won premierships. They've been the new whiz kids. Michael is a good rider and he knows it. He's got that spunk in him which you need. If you haven't got it you aren't going anywhere.

James is playing a different game because so far he hasn't shown as much cockiness as Michael, but it's starting to come. I have heard him say, 'If I don't ride a winner, I sulk.' He's got to change that attitude. I've always believed that to be a good winner, you've got to be a good loser. Time will tell and he'll learn. You can't win all the time. Sure, he's had a dream run, but any top jockey will tell you it won't always be like that. You've got to take the good with the bad.

To succeed you've got to have the skill, but also a bit of luck. You can put a bad jockey on a good horse and get beaten and even good jockeys get beaten when a wrong decision is made. But a good jockey always rectifies that. They have just got the X-factor that they can get that little extra out, and a horse will want to run for them.

It's easier getting to the top than it is to stay there. Any top sportsperson or successful businessperson will tell you that. Racing is no different. As they say, you're only as good as your last big winner.

I've seen it happen so many times where a jockey is king one minute and on the scrapheap the next. It's the same when a jockey finally calls it quits. Some do end up still in the public eye through media work or such, but most are left to just slip into the background. They've gone from hero to zero. I've seen so many good jockeys retire and nobody wants to talk about them any more. But when they were riding winners everyone wanted to be with them. It has probably happened more in Australia than New Zealand. The Aussies love winners and when one star has finished they go to the next.

Not everyone can be top of the list. I do admire those jockeys who aren't there but who keep trying. They'll never win a premiership and won't win many Group One races, usually because they don't get offered the horsepower. But they go out there week after week doing their best. And if they do break through for a big win, it's always well-deserved.

30

Praise and criticism

Roy Higgins, one of the true greats of the Australian jockeys, says he always thinks of me when he recalls some words of wisdom from the legendary trainer J.B. Cummings.

Bart Cummings is a household name in Australia, and in racing Down Under you just don't get any bigger. He has been inducted into the Racing Hall of Fame both in Australia and New Zealand and he is the most successful Melbourne Cup trainer ever. He's won the Melbourne Cup 12 times more than I have and he's a marvel when it comes to preparing stayers.

So when Bart talks about stayers, people listen. And in this case it was Roy who was on the receiving end of the advice. I've read Roy's comments and I'm flattered by what he says.

'Bart told me one of the major keys to winning staying races was to train them to settle, teach them to settle and have a rider who can get them to settle,' said Roy. 'As a jockey, Noel had been doing that before Bart even gave me that bit of advice.

'Noel has got this unique ability to settle horses and get them to sleep for the first half or three-quarters of a race and that's why he's been such a great rider of stayers.

'Bart always said it's no use riding them on the speed if they don't relax and breathe properly. They can't finish it off. That's why Noel has won so many staying races. He puts them to sleep and they're able to conserve so much energy then flash home with a tank full of petrol.'

I was a bit stunned when I saw what Roy thought of me. I couldn't ask for higher praise. Roy really is a legend in Aussie. He was inducted into the Australian Sporting Hall of Fame in 1983 and he rode Bart's first and third Melbourne Cup winners. He won the Cup in 1965 on the New Zealand-bred mare Light Fingers and two years later he was successful on Red Handed. Roy also made the following comments about me:

'Noel is unique in that he was one of the first riders down this way to ride so very short. He'd be high up in the saddle and I'd look at him and shake my head. But now it's a style adopted by so many. Noel was a forerunner.'

Roy still clearly remembers when I got beaten on Glengowan in the 1973 Melbourne Cup and all the criticism I copped. And to this day I'll always be grateful to him for the way he stood up for me. Reflecting on it now, Roy made the following remarks and I laughed when I read the last bit.

'Noel was an 18-year-old kid on the favourite and they blamed the loss on his inexperience, but it certainly wasn't his fault. In fact I couldn't fault his ride. Unfortunately, there are still people who blame him, as there are people who remember Shane Dye's ride on Veandercross or a certain Roy Higgins for dropping his hands in the 1978 Moonee Valley Cup on Hyperno. In time people may forget. At least that's what I've always hoped. I still cop it for the Hyperno ride, so I know how Noel feels.'

Roy gave up race-riding at 45 and is amazed I'm still kicking home winners well into my late fifties. 'You should be sitting back in retirement you silly bugger,' Roy told me. He's one person I love to catch up with when I get to Aussie, but it doesn't happen often. Even in this busy day and age, you've just got to make time. I'll catch up soon Roy.

You encounter a lot as a jockey and the biggest hurdle to deal with is criticism. Every jockey knows he's got to cop a mouthful from a trainer or owner at some stage. It goes part and parcel with the profession. You're on the horse so they usually feel it's your fault if you don't win.

I'm pretty relaxed with criticism. A lot of times I'll come out and say, 'I didn't have a lot of luck,' or 'I made a mistake.' Most people handle that pretty well. But I remember one occasion with the top Aussie trainer George Hanlon in Melbourne. Two horses fell in front of me and my horse ended up jumping them.

It put me back last and the horse ended up running second or third. George could've strangled me. He flew off the handle and I just stood there and copped it. Half an hour later George actually apologised to Jock for the way he talked to me. Knowing George as a punter, he probably lost a fair bit. Once he cooled down he apologised and I admire him for that.

Earlier this year I had an apprentice come up to me and say how he had been barrelled by a trainer because he got caught wide. I just said, 'Listen, there are trainers out there who are like that and you can't change them. You're better off being humble and copping it and they'll be right with it. If you come back at them they won't put you on again.' I know it's hard, because you feel like saying: *Maybe it's your training.*

It's easy for trainers to put the blame on to the jockey. It happens more so now. The old-time trainers were quite understanding, and they knew things could happen in a race. I haven't been dragged off many horses over my time.

I remember Jillo, Colin Jillings, with Seascay in the New Zealand Derby. I'd won the Wellington Guineas on the horse and run second in the Avondale Guineas. I was talking to Richard Yuill in the birdcage and there were no instructions. I knew the horse. Next minute Jillo came roaring over: 'I want you in the first half dozen, you can't win the Derby from last.' What do I do? I was in the first four in the running and I finished third. The winner was Popsy and she came from last and won. I felt like saying to Jillo afterwards, *You so and so. You stuffed it up.* I could probably say it to him now, but not while he was training and I was riding. As far as Jillo was concerned, he would have been right and I would have been wrong.

I've struggled a fair bit with being given the wrong instructions since I've been up north. I've had more success from horses getting back and hitting the line hard. Since I've been up here a lot of trainers would suggest it might be better ridden handier and, especially over the last few years, I've been trying to please them.

It has cost me wins. I remember Murray Baker saying one day, 'Don't get too far back.' Due to circumstances, I was back last and I got up and won. When I was getting off the horse I said to him, 'Was that handy enough for you Murray?' It's probably a bit to do with owners who can't understand why a horse is running at the back of the field. They sometimes think it's not giving the horse a show.

Away from the racetrack, my profession as a jockey has brought some entertaining sidelines. When you're in the spotlight in any sport you get asked to do all types of promotions and charity work. I'm always the first to give it a go and it's been a lot of fun over the years, like being on the TV show *Sale of the Century*.

One of the funniest promotions was for the rugby final between the All Blacks and the Springboks. It was taped for the racing channel and at the time the South African winger James Small was to face Jonah Lomu, who was a sensation. Paul Kingi, the New Zealand Iron Man, looked a bit like Jonah from behind so they used him and they got me to dress up as James Small. I had to run towards Paul and try to tackle him. I kept bouncing off him. They wanted to do more takes and a couple of times I got a bit winded, but it looked hilarious.

Yeah, I've experienced and seen a lot in my riding days. Racing has opened my eyes to a lot right from my young days, not the least of all, the 'silk chasers', as they're called.

Basically, they are jockeys' groupies. Girls who would hang over the birdcage fence and chase after jockeys. And there have been cases of female stalkers of jockeys, not that I've had any of them.

Many years ago I had a letter saying I was the father of this woman's child. Most of the other apprentices got the same sort of letter. These women were infatuated with jockeys or any sportsperson who was successful. I knew it was a lie and I didn't have a problem. But you can't afford to have these rumours going around. When you're successful you're always expecting someone to put the acid on, some way or another.

There's also the other side of success, the one I really appreciate: the supporters who are there with you through the good times and bad. There are many who are fans when you're going well, but the ones who mean the most to me are those who are always there for you, no matter if you're not riding big-race winners.

I'd say one of my most loyal fans is Ted McLachlan, who is now a committeeman of Racing Te Aroha. I rode for Ted's father, the late Ted senior, and remember winning on Delarenne for him.

I've known Ted for many years and he's been passionate about my career. He's followed me all the way through and even kept a tally of my last 100 winners as I got close to my 2000th win on Beau Casual.

I've had my share of fan mail over the years and some of the letters are from people I don't even know. There is one lovely lady down in Dunedin who sends me a Christmas card and a birthday card each year and wishes me well. She never forgets. I've never met her.

I've also received letters from people wanting me to sign birthday cards for their father, grandmother or the like. I always do it. If I can make someone happy, that's great. There have been cards and letters from owners I've ridden for and members of the general public wishing me good luck. I've also had letters from young kids who want to be jockeys or are fans. I've kept most of the cards and letters. They're precious. A couple of them were from kids whom I've gone on to deal with in racing. One is now a former jockey and the other a *Trackside* presenter. Here are a couple of the letters — spelling mistakes and all:

Dear Noel, I hope that you don't mind if I write to you because I am your no. 1 fan. I don't no if you remember me, but you met me at the Hawera races about a year ago and I follow what you ride in the papers, not that you do so good sometimes (just kidding). I still would like to be a jockey. I am now 8 years old and weigh 23 kg (51 pounds). Paddy Payne's sister, Bernadette, was staying here last week and she is going to ask her dad if I can go over to Ballarat for a month when I am 10 to learn about horses. We are going to the Hawera races on Saturday so I hope you are riding there so I can watch you. . . . Hoping to meet you again some day soon.

From Ben Ropiha.

30th Aug, 1988

Dear Noel, Your are a good rider, I have seen you at the shop you were talking to my dad and you gave a winner to my dad it didn't win. I have seen you at the Hawkes Bay. I told you to win and you did win, do you remember what race it was. I do. It was race 8, did you know that? I remember you beat Bonecrusher and he was the favourite. I didn't know you were riding and you were number 8 and you won. From Brendan.

(P.S.) Brendan is six years old and a big fan of yours. He's seen you riding and has told his father to back the horse because you were riding it. He will no doubt see you at Hastings again when his father takes him next. Thank you for indulging a little boy's wish. Annette Popplewell.

And another letter from a young Brendan Popplewell, long before his *Trackside* days began.

234

Praise and criticism

To Noel Harris, Do you know what my dad's name is. It is Don. We use to live in the shop. When you were talking to my dad did you see a boy next to dad. I am the one. I am the one writing to you. I've been backing you lots of times so has my dad. Do you remember getting beaten by Misty Pink at Hastings. I backed you in every race but not race 1 because it was a jumps race. You rode 3 wins at Hastings and I got some money then I went down. I was putting $1 pl on you. You are a good rider. Do you like Hastings racecourse? Poetic Prince last race is on Wednesday then go to Australia and win races. You did a good race on ice court. In race 2 you just beat David Walsh, but he came 2nd, but that's good too. You have been 2nd lots of times, I'll say you have. I do hope to see you at Hastings. From Brendan.

31

Reflections and the future

I'm 57 now and I'm at another crossroads in my life. Will I be riding when this book comes out? I'd like to think so, but I'm a bit tired of the game at the moment. Racing has changed a lot and not all for the better. I've been through the good times, the memorable 1970s and 1980s, and I'd like to see New Zealand racing bounce back to its glory days. But I won't be riding when that happens.

I've had my time in the spotlight. I've put pressure on myself to win a Group race or at least a Listed race every year. It has happened for me most years, 99 percent of the time. But now I'm looking towards the day I actually finish riding. It's going to be quite scary and I'm hoping something just clicks in for me. They say one door closes and other one opens. It's wanting to do something that makes me happy. Racing is all I've known and I've been happy riding.

The wind-down for me has been going on for the last couple of years. The opportunities to get on good horses, on a regular basis, are not there. I'm only getting a few rides a meeting up here, but when I go down the line I can get half a dozen easy. I know that a lot of people think I'm retiring or I'm semi-retired and I don't ride mid-week. They've already made their mind up about my retirement, even before I have.

What I've seen happen in the last few years with apprentices getting more and more rides and the increase in jockeys' managers has made me think. If that had come in 10 years ago I'd have given it away back then. You've got to be able to talk and ride and sell yourself. With more syndicates racing horses, the ability to sell yourself has become increasingly important.

I'm fortunate to be doing something I enjoy. Sure there are times I might get a bit sick of it, but that's like any job. Racing is a hard game. It's never-ending and has a lot of pressure and, like any job, you can get tired of it at times. And if you have to waste continually, thinking all week you've got to lose weight, it's quite sickening. Over the last 12 years I've ridden a lot of Group winners and that makes you hang in there.

The biggest call I made was before I won my first New Zealand Cup in 1999. I had never won the race, no matter how I tried, and I had it up to my eyebrows with riding. Then I won it that year on Wake Forest and it all changed for me. I've since won it three more times.

I've had a lot of jockeys come up to me and ask what they're doing wrong. They'd been having a good run then it all dried up. I just tell them the harder they try the worse it can get. You start panicking and making poor decisions. I just ride through those rough patches and come out the other side. I don't change anything. It worked before and it's just the way it goes in racing.

Some people had me retired a couple of years ago. When asked about retirement in a television interview a few years ago I said, 'Why would I retire? I'm still earning good money.' But in saying that, I am actually mentally winding down and preparing for it. It's a case of working at something that I will be happy doing when I retire. I'd like to put something back into racing. But if nothing comes up, I'm the type of person who will turn around and get out of racing altogether. Disappear.

I've got friends and they're always going to be there if I want them, but I've seen jockeys and trainers finish and it's hard to get out of racing. It's like a magnet. Then I've seen jockeys and trainers who have gone on and have said to me, 'I should've got out years ago.'

I always ask myself, *If I didn't ride, what would I like to do?* I don't know. For a start, when I was in school, it was going to be rugby and gymnastics, but it was never really going to happen because my life was mapped out because of my old man being in racing. My brothers, sisters, we've all been in racing. I loved riding. I often reminisce and wonder whether I could have done this or I could've done that. Everybody says, 'You're successful, you've made money,' and I say, 'Yeah, and I've spent money, too.' If I'd done something else I might've made more money, you never know.

But not everything is about money. To me, it's a happy medium. I see people who get a million and they want two million. You see all these finance companies fall over. How much money do you need? Can't you be happy with one million?

Looking back, I wouldn't have changed anything. I've had my ups and downs, probably more ups than downs, but it's character building. I'd be driving to the races and thinking, *What am I doing? Things aren't clicking for me.* If you start trying too hard, things don't happen. Then, all of a sudden things change and you think: *What was I worrying about?* It can happen again and again. You get cycles. You're up and down. That's life with anybody. You could be not wanting for anything in the world, but moaning away, then you lose somebody in your family and it puts everything into perspective.

When I get to the races I like to just get on and get my job done. It's like going to the office now. I pull up in the carpark and people want to come up and talk and talk. Sometimes I get that feeling that I just want them to go away. As Jock said, 'Racing can be quite lonely.' It is at times. I'm focused on riding the horses and a lot of people want to talk to you. I try not to be rude, but I'm deep in thought and I can't relax talking to people. As soon as that horse goes past the post after the last ride, it's such a relief. My job is done and I'm ready to unwind.

Many people see me for so many years and they don't really know me. I can look happy, but deep down I'm lost in thought. Some people come up and have got advice on how to run my life and it can get me quite upset because a lot of them can't run their own lives. I get on with most people and I'll tolerate a lot. I put my word in, but I hate to offend people, although sometimes it's unavoidable.

Even though people think they know me, they will never know me. I think I'm a very deep person. Even my wife Kylie said to me that I'm very hard to read. She's got to know how deep I am now and she can see why I can react to certain things. Family can pinprick, but it's constant with my riding and being successful. Sometimes I just feel like screaming down their throat and putting them in their place. My nature doesn't let me do that until I've taken too much.

People keep asking me how I've kept going so long as a jockey — over 40 years riding thoroughbreds in a profession which requires fitness, strength and, most of all, focus. One trainer, Murray Baker, even suggested that when I die I should donate my body to science. He and a lot of others can't believe the pressures I have put on my body with the wasting and hard living at times. They say there would be very few sportsmen still successful in their profession and going into their late fifties.

Well, the answer is easy for me. It's something I love. Being a jockey is all I've ever wanted to do in my life. Looking back I can't imagine myself doing anything else. Racing has been kind to me. People say that I've been kind to racing. I look at these jockeys that have battled for 30 years and how they kept going. They've been kind to racing.

It's an exciting life being a jockey, but you've got to keep a happy medium, a good balance with yourself and your riding. I couldn't wish for anything more out of racing. I've been lucky to get a good horse every carnival; there are a lot of jockeys out there who haven't been as lucky.

As for unfinished business, it's got to be the Melbourne Cup. I realise that it's not going to happen. I've often had the dream that I'm in front on the favourite in a Melbourne Cup and I never get to the winning post. There have been nights I wake up in a lather of sweat thinking I was never going to get to the winning post. It still happens. The other fear is not actually arriving at the races, getting caught up in traffic. It did happen, especially when I started riding, because there were huge crowds at the races and the traffic jams would mean you'd be banked up for an hour and a half.

Sure, I haven't won a Melbourne Cup, but I've won the next best one, the Cox Plate. And I've won other major Cups and Derbies. There's not actually a race now that worries me if I don't win it. I'm quite content with what I've won. Some races I've won several times, like the Taranaki Cup, I've won seven of them, and the big two-year-old race at Taranaki, I've won five of them. That's just the way it goes.

What do I put my longevity in the saddle down to? Well, it's probably not riding trackwork every day and an overkill of race meetings. I had half a cartilage out of one knee and if I'd pushed myself I would have been finished by now. You see jockeys riding here, there and everywhere. I've been selective in where I've been riding. I don't go all over the country chasing wins. There's got to be a burnout at the end of all that. I've seen it happen to others.

I never set myself a time when I'd give up. You'd like to be thinking it'd be at 35 to 40 years of age as you see entrepreneurs making money, but it's your situation. I was separated at 40 and it was like going back through my apprenticeship again. It's plan B. When anyone ends a marriage, 50/50 is gone isn't it? I don't know if my life's been mapped out by the good Lord, but everything fell back into place and it has kept me busy and focused. Kylie's probably the best thing that's happened to me. She understands my nonsense and she's my soul mate. I just love being with her.

I've had a second chance. It's not often that you run into someone that you're going to be happy with. You have your ups and downs in marriages. I remember Jock always saying, 'You could live with someone for 30 to 40 years and it still might not be the right person.' But I'm confident I've found the right person now. We have our moments, like everyone does, but we can sit down and talk. It's the communication. Kylie has got a different perspective on life and so do I, but when it comes to the crunch I can be sitting there and I'll come out with something and she says, 'I was just thinking about that.' We're on the same wavelength.

Kylie has been brilliant for me. I was at a crossroads in my life when I met her, being on my own and wondering how much longer that situation would persist. She's kept me going, whereas before I'd met her I was at a stage where I could've thrown it in no problem. It gives you that sense of something to work for. It's no use having money if you've got no one to share it with. She's been good for me with her basic outlook on life. It's not all about racing; she has opened up another world for me.

Kylie is a people person. Whether it's me or anybody, she goes out of her way to talk to people and she's very interested in different people. In racing and with my job, you can get quite reserved and you talk when you're spoken to. You're in your own little world, the racing world. Before I met Kylie I would go down to the TRAC Bar in Matamata Thursdays and Saturday nights and be hanging around the racing people. The racing scene can get quite monotonous. Same people, same stories, all expected to lob up and entertain. Now I'm very happy to keep out of that zone. Kylie and I go away for weekends and it's great to meet up with all her friends.

Kylie's parents, Dick and Ann, are great, too. They made me feel part of the family right from the start. Dick often comes to the races with me. He loves catching up with his old mates and Ann is a neat lady. I've also got to know Kylie's sister, Nicky, a lot better. I've always had a family and now I've got two families. I love it.

I've got four grandchildren. Cushla has twins and lives in Melbourne and Natasha has two kids, too, and she lives in Auckland. When holidays come Natasha's two children might come and stay a few days. As much as I'd like to spend more time with them, my job still takes up most of my time. But they know I'm always here for them and the same goes for all my kids, Natasha, Cushla, Whitney and Troy.

Kylie is actually discussing different jobs with me. She's giving me rundowns on certain jobs and what to do and what not to do. As I've said, all I know is racing. But I'm a hands-on person. Gardening, labouring jobs, I love that. It's not good money, but it's physical. I prefer that sort of work instead of mental pressure.

I love my garden; I've always loved gardening. Jock used to grow potatoes in his lawn. I wouldn't go that far to dig my lawn up to put potatoes in front and back, like he did. But I've changed my garden around 100 times. I've made little themes. It's therapeutic for me, a world away from racing.

Down at Longburn, there was always something to do on the 10 acres, fencing, planting trees and so on. I wasn't so much into gardening until I shifted to my house in Matamata. I took all the lawn out. I had said to Troy, 'You can start doing them,' but they ended up like hay paddocks so I dug the lawn out. I threw it all over into the next door neighbour's paddock and told him, 'I'm being a typical Maori; when I want that land back I'll come and grab it.' I put down stone chip, then Kylie moved in and, bless her, she put the lawn back in.

It's a home now. Before it used to be like the railway station and all the jocks used to come around and get on the piss. I was single and I didn't mind. Kylie's been brilliant. We've renovated the house and the next step was investing in the beach house at Mount Maunganui. It's a typical 1950s bach. We took it back to the rimu floors it had and it looks so cute. The first thing I did when we looked at it was get up on the roof to see if I could see any sea . . . and there it was. Bang, you've got a sale! Every time we drive past it, we wish we were in there. I can see us ending up living there one day.

When I do finally give up riding, Kylie and I can move on in our life together. I'd love to see more of the world. It would be nice to say, *Right, let's go and be a tourist*. I can see it now. No pressure and no stress, just chilling out with not a worry in the brain. Just relaxing with a few drinks and listening to my favourite singer, the late, great Barry White.

I've experienced it all in racing — corruption, suicide, death threats and even seen death itself. I've also been very fortunate to have enjoyed the other side of it all — the success, the thrills and the good people I've met and great places I've been. Racing has given all of that to me and when you put it all together I've no regrets at the career path I've taken.

Every week I buy a $14 Lotto ticket, but then I look at my trophy cabinet and realise this is my Lotto. They may only be trophies, but I've earned them, I've achieved something in my career. And there are all the great memories to go with it. Nobody can ever take those away from me.

Thank you, racing.

Noel Harris — The Highlights

Year	Race	Winner
1972	George Adams Tatt's Hcp (Gr I)	Egmont Park
1973	Telegraph Handicap (Gr II)	Sharif
1973	Wellington Derby (Gr II)	Peg's Pride
1973	Feehan Stakes(Gr II)	Audaciter
1973	Caulfield Stakes(Gr I)	Glengowan
1974	VATC Chirnside Stakes (Gr II)	Grey Way
1976	NZ 1000 Guineas (Gr I)	Porsha
1976	MVRC Governor's Stakes (Gr III)	Shaitan
1978	*Singapore Gold Cup	Saas Fee
1978	*Perak TC Sultan's Gold Vase	Star Prince
1979	*Singapore Lion City Cup	Butterfly Boy
1980	Wellington Derby (Gr II)	Lovelace Watkins
1980	Avondale Cup (Gr I)	Shamrock
1981	Ellerslie Sires Produce Stks (Gr I)	Loughanure
1981	GCTC Prime Minister's Cup (Gr III)	Shamrock
1982	QTC P.J. O'Shea Stakes (Gr II)	Shamrock
1983	VRC Queen Elizabeth Stks (Gr II)	Fountaincourt
1984	NZ 2000 Guineas (Gr I)	Kingdom Bay
1985	NZ St Leger (Gr I)	Sir Vigilant
1985	BATC Black Douglas Stks (Listed)	Kingdom Bay
1985	VRC Oaks (Gr I)	(My) Tristram's Belle
1987	STC Carringbush Cup (Gr II)	(Our) Palliser
1988	TVNZ Stakes (Gr I)	Horlicks

1988	MVRC W.S. Cox Plate (Gr I)	Poetic Prince
1989	Lion Brown Sprint (Gr I)	Poetic Prince
1989	STC Tancred Stakes (Gr I)	Poetic Prince
1989	Queen Elizabeth Randwick Stks (Gr I)	Poetic Prince
1990	Sydney Cup (Gr I)	King Aussie
1990	STC Shannon Handicap (Gr III)	Go Bush
1990	Bayer Classic (Gr I)	Eagle Eye
1991	Wellington Cup (Gr I)	Castletown
1992	Auckland Cup (Gr I)	Castletown
1992	NZ Oaks (Gr I)	Staring
1992	Wellington Cup (Gr I)	Castletown
1992	Caulfield Stakes (Gr I)	Castletown
1993	Bluebird Foods Classic (Gr I)	Staring
1994	Wellington Cup (Gr I)	Castletown
1995	Manawatu Sires' Produce Stks (Gr I)	Ballroom Babe
1995	VRC St Leger (Gr III)	Count Chivas
1995	South Australian Derby (Gr I)	Count Chivas
1995	NZ 1000 Guineas (Gr I)	Clear Rose
1997	Captain Cook Stakes (Gr I)	Super Crest
1999	Auckland Cup (Gr I)	Irish Chance
1999	Thorndon Mile (Gr I)	Surface
1999	Waikato Draught Sprint (Gr I)	Surface
1999	NZ Cup (Gr II)	Wake Forest
2000	Telegraph Handicap (Gr I)	Fritz
2000	Auto Auctions WFA (Gr I)	Surface
2000	NZ Derby (Gr I)	Hail
2001	McDonogh Railway Stakes (Gr I)	Fritz
2001	Manawatu Sires Produce Stks (Gr I)	San Luis
2002	NZ 2000 Guineas (Gr I)	Hustler
2002	NZ Cup (Gr II)	Mike
2003	Auckland Cup (Gr I)	Bodie
2004	Telegraph Handicap (Gr I)	King's Chapel

2006	NZ Cup (Gr II)	Pentathon
2006	Avondale Cup (Gr I)	Sharvasti
2007	Kelt Capital Stakes (Gr I)	Princess Coup
2007	NZ Cup (Gr II)	Everswindell
2008	Manawatu Sires Produce Stks (Gr I)	Il Quello Veloce
2008	Mudgway Partsworld Stakes (Gr I)	Fritzy Boy
2010	Telegraph Handicap (Gr I)	Vonusti

* Denotes international rating